Chinese As

2021

Year of the Metal Ox

Donna Stellhorn

Published by
ETC Publishing
Carlsbad, California
WWW.ETCPUBLISHING.COM

First Edition, First Publication 2020

ISBN: 978-1-944622-43-5

Cover design by Gary Dunham and Donna Stellhorn

Concepts presented in this book derive from traditional Chinese,
European, and American metaphysical and folk lore. They are not
to be understood as directions, recommendations or prescriptions
of any kind. Nor does the author or publisher make any claim
to do more than provide information and report this lore.

Contents

Introduction

2021 is the Year of the Metal Ox. The Rat energy of 2020 and the Ox energy of 2021 couldn't be more dissimilar. In 2020, the energy was represented by a tiny mouse hiding in the safety of his home, scurrying out to grab food, and then running back to his hole in the wall. Ox energy is very different. The Ox, a mature male cow, is a draft animal. On the farm, he has a job to do. He works very hard throughout the year, occasionally resting between tasks. The Ox understands what needs to be done and does it. There's no hesitation, procrastination, or fear. The Ox is traditional, patient, and achieves prosperity and success through hard work.

In 2021, there will be times where you feel a substantial burden, as if you're wearing a yoke, and pulling the plow. But there is great purpose in what you're doing. You're planting seeds for the future harvest to support you, your family, and the community.

Change is difficult during a Metal Ox year. Metal is inflexible, and the Ox keeps working on the same task until the job is done. It will take effort to change course this year. That said, it's valuable to make changes But if you've been plowing the same row for a long time and the rut is deep, it will take effort to move on to something new.

Things don't happen quickly in a Metal Ox year. While the focus for 2021 is on rebuilding, the process is painstakingly slow. The land must be cleared from the past growing season. Then comes the plowing, harrowing to break up the soil, and leveling. The soil is enriched by adding in organic matter. Only then does the planting begin. One seed is planted and then another and another. Still, there's nothing to eat until the seeds grow and are finally harvested. In a Metal Ox year, you know all the steps to take because this is rebuilding. You're confident as you move forward. But steps cannot be skipped, and steps can't be rushed. We are more pragmatic in the Metal Ox year. There's work to do, leaving less time to be emotional. What has happened before is in the past, and the only thing we can change is what we do right now. There is a sense of acceptance. In a Metal Ox year, you can gather and use resources effectively to build what you want. If you want to make bread and you have no flour, you'll look for substitutes like oats or rice. In Metal Ox years, you have the determination to continue even though you are making do with substitutes.

In Ox years, we can work alone, but we prefer to work in teams. You will receive encouragement from many, and you will probably give support to others. Encouragement and support help the Ox move forward. This comes in many forms. Employees are motivated by being paid, treated fairly, and given interesting things to do and succeed at. Coworkers are encouraged when you give them your support and what they need to succeed. In a Metal Ox year, people do this for each other and for their community.

In Ox years, we are stronger. A team of two oxen can pull a pallet of bricks weighing up to 11,000 pounds. This is a reminder that you can do more than you think possible. There's synergy this year, where the whole is greater than the sum of the parts. You can't push an Ox, but you can guide one. When working with others this year, recognize you can't push people into doing things they don't want to do. But you can guide them through your own actions. Be gentle as you direct your team. Use subtle hints and lead by example. By the same token, you can't push yourself. To change your life, you need an environment that supports your goals. You can use Feng Shui to help by setting up your personal space to encourage and guide you towards the good behaviors you want.

In Ox years, we enjoy problem-solving. When you're in the very practical Ox energy, you recognize what's outside your control. Creative solutions to obstacles occur to you, and your confidence increases with each problem solved. Problems are easier to solve in a Metal Ox year as you have access to more resources. This will be the second Metal year as the elements always come in pairs. Metal is about organizing resources, knowing what you have, using what you have, and storing just enough for the future.

Metal Ox years can be more peaceful as we take life one day at a time. We can connect more deeply with family and friends as we support and encourage each other. We achieve success as we rebuild one row at a time, one seed at a time, tirelessly, until the job is done.

In This Book

In this installment of my annual Chinese Astrology series, I have expanded the predictions for each month of the year. There are several Feng Shui cures suggested for each Chinese Zodiac sign to help you focus and bring in positive energy. At the end of this book, you'll find sections on Feng Shui principles, the upcoming eclipses, Mercury retrograde, and the Flying Star. There is also a large section on compatibility.

In the predictions section, you'll find Your High-Energy Days. On these days, plan to take significant actions, make vital phone calls, and send emails. These are days when energy and luck come together for you. On these days, you may find the most significant happenings of the month will occur. The more positive action you take on these days, the better your overall results and satisfaction will be.

For more information on Chinese Astrology, check out my YouTube channel at https://www.youtube.com/c/DonnaStellhorn

If you would like a reading, please email me at DonnaStellhorn@ gmail.com and I'll send you the details and prices.

I hope you enjoy this book and find it useful. Please take a moment and review it so more people can find this book.

I wish you joy and prosperity in 2021.

Donna Stellhorn

Celebrating Chinese New Year

The biggest holiday of the year in China is Lunar New Year. Based on the lunar calendar, Lunar New Year falls on a different day each year—most often on the second New Moon after the Winter Solstice which occurs in January or February. The 2021 Lunar New Year is on February 12, 2021.

Occasionally, the Lunar New Year will fall on the third New Moon after the Winter Solstice. We can next expect to experience this in the year 2033. In historical China, emperors were in charge of keeping time and telling the people when important dates would happen. Emperors marked these important dates with festivals. Lunar New Year is one such festival.

There's a legend in China, the tale of a "Nian," a fearsome creature with the head of a lion and the body of a bull. Every winter, the Nian would grow very hungry and finding nothing to eat, he would come down into the villages to snack on the villagers. But over time, the villagers learned that the Nian was afraid of loud noises, fire, and the color red.

One night, the Nian was spotted coming down from the mountains, so the villagers lit fires, waved red flags, and made lots of noise by banging gongs and setting off firecrackers. Their village was spared, and to this day, New Year's is celebrated with lots of firecrackers and red banners.

Before New Year, there is much to do. The house must be thoroughly cleaned to sweep away any of the remaining bad luck from last year. Lots of special foods are prepared. The night before New Year, it is considered "lucky" to stay up past midnight—to symbolize enjoying a long life. At midnight the firecrackers start popping.

On the first day of the New Year, everyone wears their best clothes, and everyone says only positive things to one another to secure good luck for everyone. Red envelopes are filled with money and given to children.

This begins a multi-day holiday. At Chinese New Year there is the dance of the Golden Dragon (sometimes called the Lion Dance). This dragon is decorated with representations of the five elements, lights, silver, and fur. It can take as many as a hundred people to carry the Golden Dragon through the streets. At the end of the route, the dragon is met with fire-crackers and cheers from the crowds.

On the second day of the New Year, there is a vegetarian feast, after which people go and visit relatives, bringing them oranges to wish them a prosperous new year. People eat long noodles, the longer, the better, to symbolize a long life. They indulge in Nian Gao—which is a cake made of rice flour, brown sugar, and oil—to bring prosperity.

I offer a series of videos on the subject of what to do before and during the New Year's Celebrations to bring luck.

Here's the link: *https://www.youtube.com/c/DonnaStellhorn*

Find Your Chinese Zodiac Sign

The annual Chinese Zodiac sign changes each year in January or February. If you were born in January or February of any year, check the date carefully to make sure you find your correct animal sign. Below you'll find listed the element and Yin or Yang quality for the year. If you have any difficulty determining your sign, element, and Yin or Yang quality, please email me at DONNASTELLHORN@GMAIL.COM with your birth date, and I will help you find your sign.

02/20/1920 to 02/07/1921 Yang Metal Monkey
02/08/1921 to 01/27/1922 Yin Metal Rooster (or Cock)
01/28/1922 to 2/15/1923 Yang Water Dog
02/16/1923 to 2/4/1924 Yin Water Pig (or Boar)
02/5/1924 to 1/24/1925 Yang Wood Rat
01/25/1925 to 2/12/1926 Yin Wood Ox
02/13/1926 to 2/1/1927 Yang Fire Tiger
02/2/1927 to 1/22/1928 Yin Fire Rabbit (or Hare)
01/23/1928 to 2/9/1929 Yang Earth Dragon
02/10/1929 to 1/29/1930 Yin Earth Snake
01/30/1930 to 2/16/1931 Yang Metal Horse
02/17/1931 to 2/5/1932 Yin Metal Sheep (or Goat or Ram)
02/6/1932 to 1/25/1933 Yang Water Monkey
01/26/1933 to 2/13/1934 Yin Water Rooster (or Cock)
02/14/1934 to 2/3/1935 Yang Wood Dog
02/4/1935 to 1/23/1936 Yin Wood Pig (or Boar)
01/24/1936 to 2/10/1937 Yang Fire Rat
02/11/1937 to 1/30/1938 Yin Fire Ox
01/31/1938 to 2/18/1939 Yang Earth Tiger
02/19/1939 to 2/7/1940 Yin Earth Rabbit (or Hare)
02/8/1940 to 1/26/1941 Yang Metal Dragon
01/27/1941 to 2/14/1942 Yin Metal Snake
02/15/1942 to 2/4/1943 Yang Water Horse
02/5/1943 to 1/24/1944 Yin Water Sheep (or Goat or Ram)
01/25/1944 to 2/12/1945 Yang Wood Monkey
02/13/1945 to 2/1/1946 Yin Wood Rooster (or Cock)
02/2/1946 to 1/21/1947 Yang Fire Dog
01/22/1947 to 2/9/1948 Yin Fire Pig (or Boar)

02/10/1948 to 1/28/1949 Yang Earth Rat
01/29/1949 to 2/16/1950 Yin Earth Ox
02/17/1950 to 2/5/1951 Yang Metal Tiger
02/6/1951 to 1/26/1952 Yin Metal Rabbit (or Hare)
01/27/1952 to 2/13/1953 Yang Water Dragon
02/14/1953 to 2/2/1954 Yin Water Snake
02/3/1954 to 1/23/1955 Yang Wood Horse
01/24/1955 to 2/11/1956 Yin Wood Sheep (or Goat or Ram)
02/12/1956 to 1/30/1957 Yang Fire Monkey
01/31/1957 to 2/17/1958 Yin Fire Rooster (or Cock)
02/18/1958 to 2/7/1959 Yang Earth Dog
02/8/1959 to 1/27/1960 Yin Earth Pig (or Boar)
01/28/1960 to 2/14/1961 Yang Metal Rat
02/15/1961 to 2/4/1962 Yin Metal Ox
02/5/1962 to 1/24/1963 Yang Water Tiger
01/25/1963 to 2/12/1964 Yin Water Rabbit (or Hare)
02/13/1964 to 2/1/1965 Yang Wood Dragon
02/2/1965 to 1/20/1966 Yin Wood Snake
01/21/1966 to 2/8/1967 Yang Fire Horse
02/9/1967 to 1/29/1968 Yin Fire Sheep (or Goat or Ram)
01/30/1968 to 2/16/1969 Yang Earth Monkey
02/17/1969 to 2/5/1970 Yin Earth Rooster (or Cock)
02/6/1970 to 1/26/1971 Yang Metal Dog
01/27/1971 to 2/14/1972 Yin Metal Pig (or Boar)
02/15/1972 to 2/2/1973 Yang Water Rat
02/3/1973 to 1/22/1974 Yin Water Ox
01/23/1974 to 2/10/1975 Yang Wood Tiger
02/11/1975 to 1/30/1976 Yin Wood Rabbit (or Hare)
01/31/1976 to 2/17/1977 Yang Fire Dragon
02/18/1977 to 2/6/1978 Yin Fire Snake
02/7/1978 to 1/27/1979 Yang Earth Horse
01/28/1979 to 2/15/1980 Yin Earth Sheep (or Goat or Ram)
02/16/1980 to 2/4/1981 Yang Metal Monkey
02/5/1981 to 1/24/1982 Yin Metal Rooster (or Cock)
01/25/1982 to 2/12/1983 Yang Water Dog
02/13/1983 to 2/1/1984 Yin Water Pig (or Boar)
02/2/1984 to 2/19/1985 Yang Wood Rat
02/20/1985 to 2/8/1986 Yin Wood Ox
02/9/1986 to 1/28/1987 Yang Fire Tiger

01/29/1987 to 2/16/1988 Yin Fire Rabbit (or Hare)
02/17/1988 to 2/5/1989 Yang Earth Dragon
02/6/1989 to 1/26/1990 Yang Earth Snake
01/27/1990 to 2/14/1991 Yang Metal Horse
02/15/1991 to 2/3/1992 Yin Metal Sheep (or Goat or Ram)
02/4/1992 to 1/22/1993 Yang Water Monkey
01/23/1993 to 2/9/1994 Yin Water Rooster (or Cock)
02/10/1994 to 1/30/1995 Yang Wood Dog
01/31/1995 to 2/18/1996 Yin Wood Pig (or Boar)
02/19/1996 to 2/6/1997 Yang Fire Rat
2/7/1997 to 1/27/1998 Yin Fire Ox
1/28/1998 to 2/15/1999 Yang Earth Tiger
2/16/1999 to 2/4/2000 Yin Earth Rabbit (or Hare)
2/5/2000 to 1/23/2001 Yang Metal Dragon
1/24/2001 to 2/11/2002 Yin Metal Snake
2/12/2002 to 1/31/2003 Yang Water Horse
2/1/2003 to 1/21/2004 Yin Water Sheep (or Goat or Ram)
1/22/2004 to 2/8/2005 Yang Wood Monkey
2/9/2005 to 1/28/2006 Yin Wood Rooster (or Cock)
1/29/2006 to 2/17/2007 Yang Fire Dog
2/18/2007 to 2/6/2008 Yin Fire Pig (or Boar)
2/7/2008 to 1/25/2009 Yang Earth Rat
1/26/2009 to 2/13/2010 Yin Earth Ox
2/14/2010 to 2/2/2011 Yang Metal Tiger
2/3/2011 to 1/22/2012 Yin Metal Rabbit (or Hare)
1/23/2012 to 2/09/2013 Yang Water Dragon
2/10/2013 to 1/30/2014 Yin Water Snake
1/31/2014 to 2/18/2015 Yang Wood Horse
2/19/2015 to 2/7/2016 Yin Wood Sheep (or Goat or Ram)
2/8/2016 to 1/27/2017 Yang Fire Monkey
1/28/2017 to 2/15/2018 Yin Fire Rooster (or Cock)
2/16/2018 to 2/4/2019 Yang Earth Dog
2/5/2019 to 1/24/2020 Yin Earth Pig (or Boar)
01/25/2020 to 2/11/2021 Yang Metal Rat
2/12/2021 to 1/31/2022 Yin Metal Ox
2/1/2022 to 1/21/2023 Yang Water Tiger
1/22/2023 to 2/9/2024 Yin Water Rabbit
2/10/2024 to 1/28/2025 Yang Wood Dragon
1/29/2025 to 2/16/2026 Yin Wood Snake

02/17/2026 to 02/05/2027 Yang Fire Horse
02/06/2027 to 01/25/2028 Yin Fire Sheep (or Goat or Ram)
01/26/2028 to 02/12/2029 Yang Earth Monkey
02/13/2029 to 02/02/2030 Yin Earth Rooster

Where Are You in the 12-year cycle?

In 2021, as the Year of the Metal Ox begins, we are in the second sign of the universal 12-year cycle of the Chinese Zodiac. However, your personal 12-year cycle is based on your individual Chinese zodiac sign. Here's where your sign falls in the 12-year cycle.

First, let's define the cycle itself. We can liken the 12-year cycle of the Chinese Zodiac to a single year on a farm in the following manner: three months of the year equals three years of the 12-year cycle.

Therefore, the first three years of the Chinese Zodiac represent the three months of spring, bringing the farmer the opportunity to plant seeds. The next three-year segment brings a similar energy as the three months of summer when the farmer is busy tending the growing plants, weeding the garden, and protecting his fields.

This period is followed by the three-year segment representing the three months of autumn and harvest time. This period is marked by significant achievements, but also hard work. The cycle ends with a three-year segment representing the three months of winter, a time when the farmer finishes up tasks he didn't have time to complete during the other busy months of the year, as he plans for the future. He eats from his storehouse of food and waits for the next spring planting season to begin.

If you are born in the Year of the Ox, this year marks the beginning of your personal springtime, which will last for the coming three years. During this period you will want to plant lots of seeds by trying new things, meeting new people and going to new places. Anything new you do can sprout into real opportunities during these three years and the three following years.

For Tiger, you are in your last year of winter. You have been through some busy years. It's time to think about what needs catching up, what to release, or let go. Think of what plans you need to put in place to make it easier for you to plant new seeds and start new things this year.

Rabbit natives are in your second year of winter, and it's time to take stock of what you have accomplished over the past ten years. Where are the investments of your time and energy still paying off? Think of letting go of what isn't working, and how you can accumulate more with less effort.

Dragon natives are in the first year of winter. Your storehouse and pantry are as full as they will get. To gather more, you can use the skills you've developed over the last few years. Now you're clever in identifying and gathering opportunities others have missed. This is the year you begin your time of rest and recuperation. You need to take care of yourself and your body.

Snake is in its last year of autumn, and the harvest is underway. Take everything you have learned so far and let the world know about your skills and what you have to offer. Demand to be paid what you are worth. This is a time when you can accumulate more.

Horse natives, you are in your second year of autumn, and the harvest is in full swing. Opportunities abound, but require you to be out in the world to gather them up. Think big, connect with people who can help you gather even more.

Sheep (or Goat or Ram), your autumn is beginning, and you must adjust to the new workload. That said, now is the period when you can gather what you want and need. Don't be shy. You can accumulate much with just a little effort.

Monkey, you are in the final year of your three-year summer. It's time to focus on the aspects of your life working the way you expect! Don't put effort into things in your life that are not bringing results. You also want to take steps to gather as many people around you as you can this year—people who will help you with your harvest in the coming three-year period.

Rooster natives, you are in the middle of your summer. You see the results of the effort you've made over the past few years.

There's still time to make decisions and point your life in a more fruitful direction. It's good to identify and find ways to protect what's yours and weed out anything less desirable.

Dog natives, you are at the beginning of your summer. There are sprouts taking root everywhere. Many things you have tried now start yielding results. This is the year you need to be discerning and try not to be everything to everyone, nor should you attempt to take on every project alone. A good manager knows when to delegate.

Pig native, you are in your last year of spring. You have planted many new seeds over the past couple of years. Look at what is sprouting and determine if you're happy with it. You still have time to try new things, reinvent yourself, and make progress on your goals.

Rat natives, you are entering your second year of spring. You are creating new options for yourself, but may not yet see impressive results. Now is an excellent time to study and improve your skills. Follow your heart and plant seeds for what you want to do with your life. The sprouts are coming soon.

Rat

January 31, 1900–February 18, 1901: Yang Metal Rat
February 18, 1912–February 5, 1913: Yang Water Rat
February 5, 1924–January 24, 1925: Yang Wood Rat
January 24, 1936–February 10, 1937: Yang Fire Rat
February 10, 1948–January 28, 1949: Yang Earth Rat
January 28, 1960–February 14, 1961: Yang Metal Rat
February 15, 1972–February 2, 1973: Yang Water Rat
February 2, 1984–February 19, 1985: Yang Wood Rat
February 19, 1996–February 6, 1997: Yang Fire Rat
February 7, 2008–January 25, 2009: Yang Earth Rat
January 25, 2020–February 11, 2021: Yang Metal Rat

Rat Personality

I am a Rat. It's hard to admit. I really wanted to be one of the cute animals. But after exploring so much about the 12 different Chinese Zodiac signs, I have come to love and appreciate being a Rat.

Rats are hardworking, ambitious, and thrifty. The Rat individual is very focused on getting ahead. Rats want to achieve success in life and aspire to reach the top first. They have a frugal reputation but are generous with loved ones. They are drawn to a bargain and are skilled at making and saving money.

In the traditional stories about the animals who make up the Chinese Zodiac, little Rat ran ahead of the other animals to be named the first of the Chinese Zodiac. This drive to move quickly is indicative of people born under this sign, and they desire to arrive first and to be noticed.

Rat natives want positive recognition for their work and to be awarded honors for their achievements. That said, they also love a challenge—but once the award is won, it's easily tossed aside as Rat focuses on taking the next step up the ladder.

Even though Rat may not be the cutest of the Chinese Zodiac menagerie, they are well-liked. Initially acting reserved, they become more social as they get comfortable with their surroundings (it's perfectly understandable to be cautious when you're a little mouse…). You'll find Rat to be more talkative when topics relating to business and money are involved.

Rat makes a loyal friend. They may not have many close friends, but those who make it to Rat's inner circle will be looked out for and supported. Those born in Rat year will gravitate to other successful people. They have trouble tolerating lazy people, and can't be bothered with anyone who wants a free ride.

Reading a Rat's feelings is easy. When upset (and they are easily irritated), they can be critical. They also tend to compare and contrast everything. This helps them identify and locate the best of everything—from bargains to close friends. Rats are adept at writing and communication. They possess excellent memories and are always asking questions.

Rats like to accumulate, although it varies from Rat to Rat what they are collecting. Some Rats accumulate money, others material things, and still others gather social or business contacts. Rat is adaptable and has acute intuition, so they can quickly determine the benefit in a situation.

Because Rat is the smallest of the animals of the Chinese Zodiac, safety and self-preservation are considered paramount. They can sense danger, but Rat finds it hard to heed the warnings if they simultaneously smell opportunity and potential success. Rat needs only to follow their gut and finish what they start, to end up the wealthiest of all the signs.

Rat: Predictions for 2021

How to use your High-Energy Days: On these days, plan to take action for your most important goals, make vital phone calls, send important emails. Your high-energy days are when your energy and luck are the strongest for the month.

January 2021: *Uranus goes direct on January 14. Mercury goes retrograde from January 30 to February 20. Your High-Energy Days are 1, 7, 13, 19, 25, and 31.*

Your seed-planting year comes to a close. It has been an eventful year, and you have planted many seeds by trying new things and making lots of changes. You will see many of these seeds sprout. As you get results, see them as signs to put more energy into the projects and possibilities they represent. Specifically for business, put energy into the products and services, bringing profits. Put time and effort into the relationships which bring you happiness.

Children or younger relatives want more of your attention now than usual. Changes may be happening in their lives, and they are reaching out to you for support. You may have to ask them to make changes, even though they have made it clear to you they don't want to change. Once the process starts, things will go better for all involved. Be open to discussion, knowing that excellent results are on their way.

In the middle of the month, the energy shifts as Uranus moves forward again, clearing the way for new technology in the home or at your job. You may be asked to learn a new computer system, or perhaps you bought a new game console for you and the kids. Get purchases and installations done before the end of the month. Mercury will go retrograde soon.

Mercury goes retrograde on January 30, and you may have to spend some extra time in the office. A team member may not be doing their fair share, or perhaps one or more people are on holiday. Either way, your desk is piled high. This is par for the course during a Metal Rat year, and Rat natives have no trouble blazing through the list of things to do.

February 2021: *Lunar New Year begins on February 12. Happy Year of the Metal Ox! February 20 has Mercury going direct. February 27 is the full moon. Your High-Energy Days are 6, 12, 18, and 24.*

The first two weeks of February mark the last two weeks of the Metal Rat year, your year, and you may feel focused on getting your finances in order. A new money opportunity could present itself. However, it is slightly outside your comfort zone. You will move forward, though, because Rat natives love a challenge.

The new moon is on February 12 and welcomes the beginning of the Year of the Metal Ox. For Rat natives, it may feel like someone has put the brakes on, as energy suddenly shifts to a slower pace. The Metal Rat year may have been about survival and making things work through quick actions; now the Metal Ox year is about rebuilding and taking the time to prepare the soil for planting the seeds.

After the new moon, the focus for the next two weeks will be on friendships and associations. Expand your tribe by connecting with like-minded others. Join some Facebook groups or check out Meetup.com for people who have the same interests as you do. Others may invite you to join their organizations, perhaps even take a leadership role. If you're already involved in a nonprofit or professional organization, expect more duties coming your way.

On February 20, the planet Mercury stops, turns, and moves forward. Now things like contracts and agreements you've been expecting come through. You're able to connect with the right person to consult about a problem. Issues with devices such as laptops and cell phones may mysteriously clear up.

The full moon comes in on February 27, emphasizing your sphere of daily routines. You feel an extra boost of energy as you get back on track with an exercise program or a healthy eating plan. You may also look at your schedule and identifying times when you are more likely to procrastinate. Now is your opportunity to set up the Feng Shui of your personal space to support your goals. This could mean arranging a dedicated space in the house for exercising, cleaning out the pantry and tossing out junk food, or posting supportive affirmations on your bathroom mirror.

March 2021: *March 13 brings the new moon, March 20 marks the first day of Spring, March 28 is the full moon. Your High-Energy Days are 2, 8, 14, 20, and 26.*

While during the last part of February, you felt as though things were moving along, as March begins, you feel you are walking through mud. The energy of the Metal Ox is now settling in. Over the past few months, you have put out a lot of energy, and now you need a break. This could be something scheduled like a mini-vacation, or you may just need to spend some quality time on the sofa.

This month there is a spiritual connection between you and your finances. Do a little money magic—dust off your Feng Shui cures, especially those around the front door. You can add stacks of coins to your windowsill in the kitchen to attract additional sources of revenue. Also, do affirmations in the morning as you're getting ready for work.

Regarding love relationships, you may have a secret admirer. Sometimes you focus so intently on the road ahead you don't notice someone is noticing you. Rat natives looking for love could find serendipitous romance. If you're happily single, you may be staying home to watch romantic comedies, or indulging in a steamy romance novel or two.

March 13 brings the new moon and a focus for the next couple of weeks on spirituality and intuition. You may have vivid dreams during this time. You may sense who's calling before the phone rings. You picture someone in your mind, and they text you. This is a great time to practice your psychic skills.

On March 28, the full moon lights up your area of relationships and partnerships. If you've been seeking a connection with an influencer or mentor, you have good energy for the next two weeks. As you reach out, you are more likely to get a response than previously. The more people you connect with, the better your odds. This is also good energy for love relationships. For Rat natives who are dating, now might be the perfect opportunity to talk about living together, or even getting engaged.

April 2021: *April 12 brings the new moon. April 27 is the full moon and Pluto goes retrograde. Pluto moving backward can cause you to review underlying assumptions about your life and to eliminate what is unnecessary. This brings you back to what is essential. Pluto will be retrograde until October. Your High-Energy Days are 1, 7, 13, 19, and 25.*

April brings an increased period of communication and decision-making for Rat natives. You may have reports due for work, large projects for school, or you may put together a business plan to present to a bank or angel investors. You could find yourself at a crossroads in some area of your life, needing to make some decisions. There will be lots of support for you for finding the information you need to make those decisions and for getting necessary advice.

Additionally, there is a strong emphasis on transportation; you may consider getting a new car, or your current vehicle may need some TLC. A brief trip using ground transportation is possible, but it's more likely you are just running a lot of errands in town.

April 12 brings the new moon, and there is a potential opportunity for you to practice your stage presence. You may be asked to lead a meeting, or you might have the chance to host an event. While this may not be your usual evening activity, you receive quite a few compliments on your performance.

Over the next two weeks, you'll be feeling entirely independent and self-reliant. You may successfully make repairs to a household appliance, or solve a computer problem. You could also test your physical prowess. For those Rat natives who are feeling particularly ambitious, you might go hiking, rock climbing, or even skydiving.

On April 27, the full moon arrives, and Pluto, the planet of power and transformation, goes retrograde. Over the next two weeks, there is good energy for investing in real estate, refinancing your mortgage, or putting a spare room on Airbnb. A work-at-home contract job may become permanent if you move quickly once the offer comes through.

Your intimate relationships improve around the time of this full moon. Those Rat natives looking for love could find themselves involved in a wild romance. While this may not be a lasting relationship, it would undoubtedly be fun for a while. If you're already in a committed partnership, you may explore novel ways of having fun behind closed doors.

May 2021: *May 11 brings the new moon. May 23 has Saturn going retrograde. (Saturn retrograde can cause you to review your career choices and make adjustments. Saturn will be retrograde until October). May 26 is a total Lunar Eclipse. May 29 has Mercury going retrograde. Your High-Energy Days are 1, 7, 13, 19, and 25.*

This month you focus on the family and extended family. There may be special events to celebrate, a milestone birthday, or an addition to the family with the birth of a child or grandchild. While you may not be present for this event, you are there in spirit and communicating with your family.

May 11 brings the new moon and a great deal of activity around your job. There may be some hiccups relating to a bonus or commission payment that need ironing out. But a little due diligence and you'll have no problem getting the money flowing again. You may feel this is a sign to look around and see if there's a better position for you, either within your company by transferring to another department, or with one of your current competitors.

On May 23, Saturn—the planet of reputation and expertise—goes retrograde in the area of your life, including groups and associations. Just when you were thinking of ducking out of a networking group or professional organization, suddenly, you may be asked to lead the charge. Now you have a decision to make on whether this is a good use of your time or if you need to move on to new things. You're only halfway through your seed planting years, and so you may opt to start something new.

On May 26, a total Lunar Eclipse lights up your area of fairness and legal matters. If you're already involved in a lawsuit, this period can bring a verdict or a settlement. However, this is not a good time to initiate legal proceedings. You may also think of creating or signing a contract for something extraordinary in your life, perhaps a business partnership or even marriage. However, wait a few weeks for this knotty energy to clear. You'll likely be attending at least one wedding over the next few weeks.

June 2021: *June 10 is the annular Solar Eclipse. June 20 is the first day of summer, and Jupiter goes retrograde. Jupiter retrograde can indicate a need to relearn things or renew a religious connection. Jupiter will be retrograde until October. June 22 has Mercury going direct. June 24 is the full moon. On June 25, Neptune goes retrograde. Neptune retrograde can draw you back towards habits and addictions from your past; it can also encourage a return to spiritual practices. Neptune will be retrograde until December. Your High-Energy Days are 6, 12, 18, 24, and 30.*

As June rolls around, you find you are interested in tradition and the foundations upon which you base and build your life. You may look back into the past and realize how different you are from even last year—let alone ten years ago. In some ways, you have become stronger and more resilient. Yet, there are still some traditions you have almost forgotten you want to revive—perhaps making time to cook and share some old family recipes, remembering how to grow vegetables in the garden, or sharing stories that have been passed down.

The Solar Eclipse is on June 10 and brings you a hectic couple of weeks. You are rushing to finish up several projects for your home or your job. There's an emphasis at this time on communication so you may send out last-minute emails, invitations, or responding to friends and family. Rat natives can move quickly, but during this period, avoid arguments with neighbors, siblings, or younger relatives as minor issues could be blown out of proportion right now.

Jupiter goes retrograde on June 20 and moves back into your area of friendships. At this time, you might be considering a friend for a romantic engagement. You may find there is chemistry brewing between the two of you. It would be good to express yourself now and see what happens.

On June 22, Mercury turns and goes direct. Now a contract for employment or an agreement for a large purchase finally comes through. Now everyone is in a rush to get the paperwork signed; however, there is still a little time if you wish to start some last-minute negotiations. Read any paperwork over carefully before jumping in, even if you're feeling a push from others.

June 24 brings the full moon and a career opportunity. Rat natives looking for a new job can have some excellent luck. The stars are in alignment for you to talk with your supervisor about a potential opening within your company.

July 2021: *July 10 brings the new moon. July 24 is the full moon. Your High-Energy Days are 6, 12, 18, 24, and 30.*

You are filled with enthusiasm this month, which is good as there are some hurdles to clear. Some people in your life may put minor obstacles in your path. Others are quick to tell you why things will not go smoothly. You feel like a gazelle, gracefully leaping over people's objections and hesitations. A windfall could arrive this month, especially if you're proactively responding to phone calls or emails.

There's some good energy around getting a new vehicle. You may be tempted to spend a little more to get the features you want. Or perhaps you trade in your car for something a little more exciting, such as a motorcycle, scooter, or bicycle.

The new moon on July 10 brings an opportunity for romance. Rat natives already in a relationship may felt more comfortable than ever with their partner. You're in harmony now, finishing each other's sentences and enjoying each other's company. If you're looking for love, the energy is very positive. Over the next two weeks, it's good to respond to online dating requests and also consider going on a blind date set up by a friend or relative.

The full moon comes in on July 24. You may face a situation where you need to display some resourcefulness; fortunately, this is a forte of Rat natives. Your intuitive sense is increased, and you recognize there may be changes in your company. Perhaps a merger is in the works, or some reorganization will bring you extra duties—even a new team. Over the next couple of weeks, there also will be an opportunity to connect with a colleague who has moved on to another position. A job opportunity may open up for you elsewhere.

On July 29, the energy shifts, and you may decide to get back into your exercise routine, or your healthy eating plan. Focus on your well-being by taking up something like meditation, or by enjoying peaceful walks in nature.

August 2021: *August 8 brings the new moon. On August 20, Uranus goes retrograde. August 22 is the full moon. Your High-Energy Days are 5, 11, 17, 23, and 29.*

August brings some faster energy for Rat natives. You may answer an increased number of texts and emails than usual. A friend you haven't seen for a long time may contact you, perhaps even pay a visit. But all this seems to take you away from a project you're trying to finish. The project is likely something big, like your dissertation, your screenplay. Maybe it's something much more mundane, like finally getting the garage cleared out. This month, you may grumble at all the distractions keeping you from finishing up your projects.

Positive money energy is accessible to you, but it's not as easy to access as Rat natives are used to. It's like trying to cut a tomato with a dull knife, and you end up just squishing the tomato. Money will flow when you use some finesse in your request, only to slow or stop if you are too direct. Instead, place Feng Shui cures to attract wealth energy and allow the Universe to bring the opportunities to you.

On August 8, the new moon has good energy for your relationship. For Rat natives who are dating, you might take your relationship to the next level by moving in together. For those already in a love relationship, this could signal a time when you are expanding the family. Fertility energy intensifies. This could mean an addition to the family—a birth, a grandchild, or a new pet coming into the household.

The next two weeks are also an excellent time to make some adjustments in your daily routine. This could mean taking time for a run in the morning before you start work, or adding vegetables to your dinner plate as you subtract the dessert.

August 22 brings an intense full moon, lighting up your area of friendships. Someone may need your help and request more than you expect. While this might temporarily put you in an awkward situation, Rat natives have a reputation for having definite boundaries. Additionally, over the next two weeks, you may meet several new people who could become friends. You may be part of a professional organization or charitable function. You may find intriguing people who find you fascinating.

September 2021: *September 7 brings the new moon. September 20 is the full moon. September 22 is the first day of autumn. September 26 has Mercury going retrograde. Your High-Energy Days are 4, 10, 16, 22, and 28.*

While things have been moving along pretty nicely for the last few weeks, September brings some unfocused energy. Rat natives can be easily distracted by YouTube videos, a Netflix series, or an engrossing novel. You might find hours simply 'disappearing' from your day.

September 7 brings the new moon and a tempting business opportunity for something you've never done before. You have wanted to expand your horizons, and the Universe has been listening. This opportunity will most likely bring increased income in the future. It's time to throw your hat in the ring.

The full moon comes in on September 20 and puts the focus on relationships and partnerships. Perhaps a business partnership provides a boost to your business. A wise person may come along and prove to be willing to mentor you. Look at your marketing plan and move away from traditional methods of promoting yourself. This is where you want to use your creative mind and improve your tech skills to reach your marketplace or find out your resume has risen to the top of the heap.

Around the same time and for the next few weeks, your sweetheart is interested in deepening the relationship you share. This person may be looking for a commitment, whether you're ready for it or not. This could bring talk of marriage or combining finances. Rat natives can often seem calm on the outside when a lot of emotion is going on inside. At this time, it would be a good idea to express your feelings clearly.

On September 26, Mercury goes retrograde, and you may see that your life is out of balance. Too much time spent at work, or perhaps too much time procrastinating at work, leaves you feeling like a change is needed. But over the next few days, you may not make much progress in this area. Next month there will be more positive energy for finishing tasks as well as finding time for leisure.

October 2021: *October 6 brings the new moon, and Pluto goes direct. On October 11, Saturn goes direct. October 18 has Mercury going direct and Jupiter going direct. October 20 is the full moon. Your High-Energy Days are 4, 10, 16, 22, and 28.*

Throughout October, many of the things you want happen start to manifest. By the end of the month, things could be coming in fast and furious. It's good not to procrastinate on essential projects early in the month. Rat natives tend to breeze through tasks. However, you can get tired at times, so try to get things done early in the month while you have the most energy.

On October 6, the new moon comes in, bringing you new insights into relationships. Someone special in your life has been irritating you lately, but they are merely your mirror. You are doing the same thing to those around you that is bothering you! Once you realize what the issue is, the irritation disappears.

For single Rat natives, this is a great time to look at issues you have surrounding the idea of getting into a relationship. You may be hesitant about using online dating sites or match-makers. You're also not sure if your friends and family could introduce you to someone you click with. And so you're stuck with few ways to meet new people. But this just takes some creative thinking and getting over your nervousness. Find groups you can join, take your dog to play at the dog park, or take the leap and do the online dating thing that is helped so many others find love.

By October 18, Saturn, Mercury, and Jupiter are moving forward, and a new employment opportunity can come in. This is a good time for a promotion and a raise. It's good to speak to your supervisor about your future with the company. Rat natives who own a business may be making more sales or expanding their product line. Social media posts could receive more attention now.

The full moon comes in on October 20, and your confidence is high. If you are a Rat native attending school, you may receive some positive recognition or a very high grade on a project. If you seek to acquire a professional certification or licensing, now is a great time to achieve the positive outcome you have been working to accomplish.

Over the next two weeks, you may find you're staying up too late because you're working or distracted by some form of media. Consider changing up your bedtime routine to get more sleep.

November 2021: *November 4 is the new moon. November 19 is a partial lunar eclipse. Your High-Energy Days are 3, 9, 15, 21, and 27.*

November comes around, and your mind is on your finances. This is an excellent time to be checking investments and looking for ways to expand into passive income sources such as real estate investing, stock market, or having your own side business. Rat natives are willing to take risks, but good about avoiding unnecessary exposure to a downside. As you proceed, consider getting some expert assistance from a knowledgeable friend or an older relative who has done well with this type of investment.

November 4 brings the new moon and opportunities for intimacy. Rat natives in a love relationship will want to set aside some time for some sensual fun, which could happen more often in the next two weeks.

Over the next two weeks, you may receive favorable terms on refinancing a house, a debt consolidation loan, or some help with student loans. While likely not your favorite thing to focus on, good energy like this doesn't come along every month, so it would be good to take advantage of it. This is also an excellent time to do some tax planning.

The Lunar Eclipse occurs on November 19, lighting up your house of money and shopping. If the outgo of money has stopped you from accumulating wealth, this eclipse brings the matter to your attention. Now is the time for some changes to happen. There is a possibility of receiving an increase in salary or additional revenue streams. You may have picked up a side job, or one of your side hustles is starting to pay off. You can set new things in motion now, but this energy is more about harvesting what you've been working on for a while.

Near the end of the month, the energy shifts towards optimism and spirituality. This is a good time to consider adding a spiritual practice to your daily routines such as meditation, affirmations, or prayer. You may set up a small altar in the house with crystals and perhaps pictures of spiritual masters. This helps keep you focused on your goals and connects you to the flow of benefits from the Universe.

December 2021: *December 1 has Neptune going direct. December 4 is a total Solar Eclipse. December 19 brings the full moon, and Venus goes retrograde. Venus retrograde can cause you to question what you want and inspires you to look for something new that delights you. Venus will be retrograde until January. December 21 is the first day of winter. Your High-Energy Days are 3, 9, 15, 21, and 27.*

December comes along, bringing strong career energy and opportunities to gain some recognition for something you enjoy doing. This could bring a financial reward such as an increase in commissions, or for those Rat natives who own a business, some additional sales.

December's energy is also excellent for education. If you have tests or projects due in school, you find yourself more prepared to get things done ahead of time. This is because you are focused on the kind of quality work Rat natives are known for doing. As you work on these projects, you streamline the process, leading to better results in less time.

The Solar Eclipse comes in on December 4 and focuses on rules, contracts, and legal matters for you. During the next couple of weeks, you may get challenged to change some rules you have held for a long time. You may find these rules are not benefiting you any longer, and they need reconsidering. At the same time, if you're involved in legal matters, you may need to focus your energy and attention on getting things solved. Let delays happen because this month's resolutions can only occur as a result of compromise. You may have to give away more than you want.

Contracts can also come in for employment, or to sell a large item like a house or vehicle. You may not get the price you want, but the fact that the contract is in your hands is a plus. You can start negotiations from this point. Expect both sides to compromise before the deal is signed.

December 19 brings the full moon as well as Venus going retrograde. This combination can make holiday gift-buying challenging. Everyone will have strong opinions about what they do and do not want. Even when buying for yourself, you may find it challenging to find the exact thing you want, in the color you want, in the size you need. It's a good time to exhibit patience—something Rat natives can struggle with.

January 2022: *January 2 is the new moon. January 14 has Mercury going retrograde. January 17 is the full moon. On January 18, Uranus goes direct. On January 29, Venus goes direct. Your High-Energy Days are 2, 8, 14, 20, and 26.*

January brings the last month of the Metal Ox year, and Rat natives are in the flow. You're making a lot of good connections, especially professional people who could open doors for you in your career in the future.

This month, Rat natives have an opportunity to be on stage. You might be singing a solo with the choir, or asked to lead a company meeting in front of the CEO and other supervisors. If the idea of this brings you some anxiety, it's good to plan ahead and see who you can get to take your place.

January 2 brings the new moon and a career opportunity, something you have asked for. Soon you'll be entering the third of your seed planting years. New opportunities can be expected; however, this new chance may not increase your salary, merely more hours of work! So unless it's entirely in line with your goals, it might be something you want to pass on.

On January 14, Mercury goes retrograde, causing you to rethink some decisions you've made over the past two weeks.

There's still time to renegotiate or to return to something you have done before.

This retrograde energy could also slow down the progress you're making in your love life. Now your two schedules seem to be out of sync, and this could go on for a few weeks. You and your sweetheart may feel like two ships passing in the night.

January 17 has the full moon in your area of home and family. If you have not moved in the last two years, moving energy now becomes very compelling, maybe due to some great opportunities out there in the real estate world. Or, there may be issues around neighbors; even changes in the neighborhood itself can cause you to rethink where you live.

While Rat natives tend to be quick on the draw, this is just the beginning of this energy, so a move doesn't have to happen immediately. In general, it's good to avoid moving on Mercury retrograde—as doing so can cause you to want to move again soon.

Now is the time to rejoice as the energy shifts into Water Tiger, a harmonious time for Rat natives. You can discover many opportunities in the months ahead.

February 2022: February 1 is the new moon and begins the Year of the Water Tiger.

Rat native, you can feel this new exciting Water Tiger energy on the horizon. There will be a lot of opportunities for you if you're willing to move quickly. Success will come through communication and when you implement your plans.

Attract New Love

Love relationships can be intense this year for Rat natives, as you're feeling particularly social this year.

Opportunities for love can be found through friendships, friends of friends, and at social events. You can also meet interesting people through networking groups focused on investing or business.

To meet someone new, consider doing things outside of your routine. In fact, you can go so far as to think of what you would typically do, and then do the opposite. The strongest period is in November when there can be a complete change. During this period, someone may suddenly become irresistible to you. You could likely become the object of someone's affection, perhaps even be pursued.

When attracting a new love, call the right person's energy to you with the sweet sound of a bell. The bell can be made of metal, porcelain, or any material—so find a `bell with a sweet sound. (You don't want to attract love with a bell that's off key.) Hang the bell from a yellow ribbon. Yellow is the color of friendship and mutual understanding.

Put the bell in your bedroom where you can ring the bell at least once a day. (Do not hang the bell where you're going to bump your head into it.) If you want the relationship to start as a friendship and move slowly, hang your bell in the living room. Then move it to your bedroom when you want the relationship to become intimate.

Enhance Existing Love

There is a lot of energy connected to existing relationships this year. Many Rat natives will likely find stronger friendship and mutual respect in your current love relationship. However, if your relationship is weak, you may find yourself going through a period of strife before things get better. It would be good to seek advice from good friends, especially those in successful relationships.

Energy smooths out in the middle of the year, and there is more harmony between you. You lean on each other a little bit more in November when a financial matter has you pooling your resources. Together you can look for creative solutions and doors leading to success.

This year, there are many reasons you may want to add the essence of joy to your home to aid your current relationship. You can do this by adding floral scents to your home either by burning floral incense or using a scented floral spray. A nice floral-scented incense like Nag Champa works very well. Or pick up a variety pack of floral-scented incense and fill the house with the scent of flowers. Add a floral scent to your dwelling once a week or so to keep the energy of love and joy in the home.

Looking to Conceive?

Looking to get pregnant this year? Herd a couple of terracotta elephants into the bedroom. Elephants are considered lucky in many cultures and for a variety of reasons. In India, they are seen as a fertility symbol—specifically when made from red terracotta clay (said to mimic menstrual blood).

If you can find mama and baby elephants with the little baby holding on to mama's tail with his trunk, you have found the ideal pair. Place them in the bedroom so mama is facing the door and so you can see them from the bed.

(From Donna Stellhorn's book, A Path to Pregnancy: Ancient Secrets for the Modern Woman)

Family and Kids

You could feel connected to your family this year as you pursue a variety of activities, perhaps even some business opportunities. You may be pulling together resources to make investments, or maybe you are helping each other out. This year, in the Metal Ox year, Rat natives benefit from going back to family traditions. Perhaps because you're far from your extended family, you now feel more of a desire to cook old family recipes and keep family holiday traditions.

There's positive fertility energy this year, possibly even an announcement of a pregnancy in the family. Your kids are thriving as new opportunities open up for them. Adult children are making good headway in their careers. For the most part, everyone's getting along. There is a bit of stress around November, when it may be challenging to get everyone together; or it could be something minor, like stressing about what is being served for Thanksgiving.

Amber is not a stone, but a fossilized resin from pine trees. Its warm honey color reminds you of hearth and home. Because pieces of amber are genuinely ancient, the energy is about longevity and strength. It's a symbol of the love of a relationship stretching back to the beginning of time and going forward for all time.

Find a specimen of amber to display in your family room or bedroom. It doesn't have to be large, but if it's small, it should be in a place of honor, such as next to a family portrait or on the fireplace mantle. Clear the stone when you get it (see the section at the end of this book on clearing crystals) and then clear it again every few months to renew the energy. This year, you can wear amber to bring positive relationship energy.

Money

2021 is quite an active year for Rat natives to bring in money—especially from alternative sources of income. If you're feeling ambitious, you can certainly find new streams of revenue. Money is earned through your own efforts, but there will also be opportunities to identify alternative income sources, such as investments or having your own business.

Additionally, money derived from career is strong. This indicates that income from regular employment improves. Rat natives who own a business and work side-by-side with their employees can do very well indeed!. The most challenging period is May, when there may be a significant expenditure. This may be for an item you have wanted for some time, which you now see available at a reasonable price. However, be prepared, it is likely to take some careful budgeting to make this happen.

Around the world, seaports are still the most popular places to live and work. Even though we no longer rely on ships for personal transportation, much of the goods we use come into the country via ocean transport. For this reason, a powerful Feng Shui cure is the wealth ship, representing prosperity sailing into your life. This is one of the most potent symbols for attracting what you want.

A Feng Shui ship symbol could be a ship figurine, a picture, or a painting. If you're feeling ambitious and craft-minded, you can build a model ship from a kit. Or if you are so inclined, you can paint a picture yourself of your own wealth ship. Any of these would make a delightful Feng Shui cure.

Job or Career

The new seed-planting energy from last year continues this year, and you may see many changes in your career. Most notably, there are opportunities to shift jobs to make more money. Additionally, you may move outside your comfort zone, but this is the best way to reach your goal destination. This is a year of learning new things, expanding your skill set, and beefing up your resume.

If you stay in your current position, there are indications your current place of employment could go through a merger, or new management replaces the familiar organization. This could change the very core of what you do. Focus on learning how to use technology, especially if this is an area you have struggled with.

During this Metal Ox year, you're working hard, and it's unlikely you will be out of a job for any extended period. This year the energy supports forging fresh paths and making connections to build your reputation and your standing in the marketplace.

The traditional red envelopes are used each year to give presents of money to people, mostly children. These envelopes are glossy red with colorful pictures and prosperity sayings printed on the front. You can use this energy to help you attract new career energy.

Take a traditional red envelope and write down a description of your desired new career. You may name the profession, or you may just describe some aspect of the work ("I get to use my creative abilities", "I work with supportive people", "I leave each day with a sense of accomplishment.", etc.) Place a small amount of money in the envelope and place it near your front door, either on a table or in a drawer. This symbolizes receiving the gift of new employment.

Education

This year is an excellent time to focus on learning new things and exploring new concepts, as you now are in the second year of your seed-planting time. If you feel a desire to go back to school, Rat natives may want to consider online classes or accelerated learning programs. The best topics include learning how to market yourself, sell items, anything to deal with using technology, or how to get your own business going.

You may be learning new software platforms, grant writing, and public speaking. The best time for making decisions on questions about your education—like going back to school or getting funding—will occur in May, June, or December.

Legal Matters

Rat natives have the opportunity to engage in negotiations and complete several contracts during the year of the Metal Ox, 2021. Most of these are financial contracts such as for employment or the sale of large ticket items. Rat natives are generally cautious, so there's no need to allow yourself to feel rushed when executing these agreements. Take a breath and go over each point carefully. Identify what the other party wants more than you do. Any lingering lawsuits may come to a completion this year. Avoid getting entangled in legal matters in May or December.

Health and Well-Being

Rat natives can expect a lot of energy around health and well-being this year, as you take more time to care for your physical self. You may be influenced by friends to change your diet or to begin a new exercise plan. You are making progress on healing a lingering condition and may work with any limitations you had in the previous year. Surrounding yourself with friends and family improves your overall sense of well-being. It's good to share your milestones and successes with them. Use caution around November as you can fall back into old bad habits.

A powerful Feng Shui cure recommended for you this year is the mirror; mirrors have many uses in Feng Shui. A Bagua mirror is a particular kind of mirror recognized as a powerful symbol of protection—much stronger than an ordinary mirror. It is often an octagon-shaped wood frame with a small circular mirror in the center. Hang up this mirror for protection.

Symbols designed to attract the protection energy are carved or printed onto the wooden frame. This type of mirror is never used facing into the house; always use it pointing out of the house. Place or hang the mirror in a window facing outward. Specifically, to help protect your health, hang it in your bedroom or bathroom window pointing towards the outside. This keeps any negative energy away.

Ox

February 19, 1901–February 7, 1902: Yin Metal Ox
February 6, 1913–January 25, 1914: Yin Water Ox
January 25, 1925–February 12, 1926: Yin Wood Ox
February 11, 1937–January 30, 1938: Yin Fire Ox
January 29, 1949–February 16, 1950: Yin Earth Ox
February 15, 1961–February 4, 1962: Yin Metal Ox
February 3, 1973–January 22, 1974: Yin Water Ox
February 20, 1985–February 8, 1986: Yin Wood Ox
February 7, 1997–January 27, 1998: Yin Fire Ox
January 26, 2009–February 13, 2010: Yin Earth Ox
February 12, 2021–January 31, 2022: Yin Metal Ox

Ox Personality

Slow and steady, the Ox is always making progress towards success and prosperity. Ox is the hardest working of all the signs of the Chinese Zodiac. Once they accept a task, they toil and toil until it's done. They like to finish one thing before starting another. Often, new projects will sit and gather dust while Ox completes any previous obligations—no matter how exciting or how profitable the new project may be.

Those born in the year of the Ox are intelligent and resourceful, although these qualities may not be apparent. Ox native is often introverted and shy. The truth is, they're shy until the need arises—then they will stand up in front of a group and take on a leadership role. As one of the largest and strongest animals of the Chinese Zodiac, Ox is never intimidated and rarely at a loss for words.

Ox individuals like a routine. They will stick to a particular way of doing things and may find it extremely difficult to change. In some ways, this is the key to Ox's success. They use tried-and-true methods and hard work to create the outcomes they want to manifest.

Ox never jumps in, or relies on "luck" to succeed in their endeavors (or worse, "wings it"). Tenacity and dedication to a specific outcome brings Ox the most satisfaction and the most success.

Those born in Ox year have patience and understanding with others. They take pride in being a good and loyal friend. However, they are not particularly good at being a romantic partner. It wouldn't occur to them to fly you off to Paris at a moment's notice to enjoy a weekend vacation. However, once Ox does fall in love and marries, they are in it for the long haul. They are faithful and prove to be agreeable partners.

Ox, like buffalo, cannot be stopped once they begin moving. If an Ox person gets angry, expect to be run over. However, the Ox native can get stuck; they can walk the same path, doing the same things for so long they wear a rut so deep they can't climb out of it.

This can occur in the course of their career or daily work, but the same pattern can also show up in their intimate relationships. An Ox can hold on to grievances far longer than any other sign. You can quickly identify an unhappy Ox: they work all the time.

Because Ox is so self-disciplined, they expect similar behavior from other people in their lives. Ox will patiently instruct others, but should someone refuse to listen or pay attention to their excellent advice, Ox will turn away, head out, and never look back.

Ox doesn't believe in shortcuts, not for others, and not for themselves. They build things that last, designs copied around the world. Everything Ox receives, he or she has earned, and no one can say otherwise.

Ox natives do not like to be in debt. They want to settle accounts as soon as possible, preferably never get into debt in the first place! When they receive something as a gift, their gratitude overflows. That being said, Ox is also likely to remember an injustice for a very, very long, long, long time.

Ox: Predictions for 2021

How to use your High-Energy Days: On these days, plan to take action for your most important goals, make vital phone calls, send important emails. Your high-energy days are when your energy and luck are the strongest for the month

January 2021: *Uranus goes direct on January 14. Mercury goes retrograde from January 30 to February 20. Your Lucky Days are 2, 8, 14, 20, and 26. [How to use your Lucky Days: On these days, plan to take significant actions, make vital phone calls, send emails. These are days when your energy and luck are high.]*

The Year of the Metal Rat comes to a close, and for Ox natives, it is the end of your personal 12-year cycle. Next month, you will begin a brand new 12-year cycle, and life will feel like springtime.

This month you may look around and decide to release any remaining old stuff. This is a perfect time to do a deep declutter. Get into the rafters and to the back of the garage, getting rid of stuff you may not have used for years. Selling off stuff can be a source of income for you now, but don't let that get you bogged down. It's better to release excess and open up your space for the coming new energy.

A shift in eating habits is beneficial now. Ox natives may be attracted to a new diet or style of eating. You don't often make a change like this, so when you feel inspired to do so, don't let anyone talk you out of it. Your intuition is speaking to you. Healthy eating can help your body heal in so many ways.

As Uranus moves direct on January 14, you may be planning to change your appearance. Consider a new hairstyle, new clothes, or add jewelry that sparkles.

Your experience at work improves as the changes in management settle down.

If you own your own business, it's good to automate some of your procedures or processes. Plan to outsource some of the tasks rather than to hire new people. Start your hunt by asking "How can this be automated?" or "How could I avoid doing this task?" You will receive some helpful answers and information from the Universe when you become aware you are looking for it. Try to implement changes before Mercury goes retrograde on January 20.

February 2021: *Lunar New Year begins on February 12, the Year of the Metal Ox. February 20 has Mercury going direct. February 27 is the full moon. Your High-Energy Days are 1, 7, 13, 19, and 25.*

The first two weeks of February are still filled with the Metal Rat energy. Ox natives may still scramble around getting things done—especially concerning technological changes at work. Your charisma is robust, and you likely receive some recognition from a supervisor or a complimentary note from a customer.

The new moon comes in on February 12 and marks the beginning of the Metal Ox year. This is your year. Now you will enter the first of three seed planting years. During this time, the more new things you do, the more opportunities will reveal themselves. Ox natives tend to like the well-worn path, but this year, you'll find the old road is boring. You are looking for some excitement, and this itself puts you in harmony with the new change energy.

On February 20, Mercury goes direct. Now things start to go your way. Over the past week, you may have felt like you were swimming upstream, but now communication is flowing again. For those Ox natives who are looking for love, you may receive a few whispers of love from someone you've been dating. If you're already in a love relationship, you and your beloved are now seeing eye to eye on many topics, and there is more peace and harmony at home.

On February 27, the full moon brings a great deal of positive energy around friendships and associations. If you are part of a community group or professional networking endeavor, you receive quite a bit of support from your fellow members. All you need to do is ask.

There's positive energy around finances, especially for Ox natives expecting an increase in salary or a sizable commission check. You're an excellent money manager, and you may want to put some of these proceeds towards future purchases or into long-term savings. Some investments are likely to come up soon, and you would benefit from keeping some of the available money.

March 2021: *March 13 brings the new moon. March 20 marks the first day of spring. March 28 is the full moon. Your High-Energy Days are 3, 9, 15, 21, and 27.*

March begins with a focus on friendships and associations. You may receive several invitations for significant events during the year. But this year, travel may be limited due to your schedule and to external circumstances. It will be wise to make plans well ahead of time.

There is the possibility of a new pet coming into your life. Or you may have some interaction with animals in the neighborhood. A local cat could begin to visit your back porch regularly, gophers may dig up your backyard, or you may come across a stray dog.

The new moon comes in on March 13, and romance energy is all around you. Single Ox native, you may be seeing someone new and enjoying a great deal of fun learning about each other.

If you're already in a love relationship, you may be spending more time together than usual. There could be opportunities to visit with other couples as well. This positive relationship energy extends to people you know as well. One of your adult children may be getting into a relationship that is serious. You may also receive an invitation to a wedding or a milestone anniversary.

There is shifting energy around March 20, and Ox natives may feel like a vacation is in order. You've been going pretty much nonstop for the last six months or more, and you may not have had much time off during that period. Now it's time for a break, even if this means a staycation at home. What's most important is to break up your routine and permit yourself to enjoy a little "me" time.

March 28 brings the full moon, and your energy is restored. Now, you feel you could take on quite a few projects, and you seem to leap through open doors of opportunity. Others seem to be noticing how much more confident and focused you are. You may receive suggestions from various family members and friends, but you have your goals pretty much mapped out. While you are generally a good listener, when it comes to your life path you seem pretty much set in your ways.

April 2021: *April 12 brings the new moon. April 27 is the full moon, and Pluto goes retrograde (Pluto moving backward can cause you to review underlying assumptions about life and to eliminate what is unnecessary. This brings you back into questioning what is essential. Pluto will be retrograde until October.) Your High-Energy Days are 2, 8, 14, 20, and 26.*

This month your internal psychic centers open up; you feel more intuitive than ever before. You may receive some messages about your life path when you meet friends who have been looking for you, and when a family member needs you. It's a good idea to give yourself a little time to explore this hidden talent by making it a regular practice. Consider doing meditation or working with spiritual tools.

As the month continues, on April 12, the new moon comes in, and you feel a burst of energy and a desire to get things done. Additionally, help seems to come in from all sides. The moment you think you need some assistance with your computer, a contract, or keeping up with daily tasks, someone volunteers to help. Ox natives would do well to avail themselves of this help since this positive energy doesn't come along every day.

Over the next couple of weeks, your charisma is powerful. Ox natives hoping to get into a love relationship should consider putting a profile online on any major dating sites. If you're dating already, someone else may be flirting with you, someone who isn't yet your sweetheart. Things could get complicated if you allow this flirtation to go too far without intending to do so.

Around April 19, the energy shifts and becomes much more comfortable for you. You find you have enough time to get many of your projects underway or even completed. Additionally, some of your work has been noticed, and you receive appropriate recognition.

Towards the end of the month, on April 27, the full moon puts a spotlight on partnerships for you. While this can be a love relationship, it also gives you good energy around business connections. Now you can find helpful bankers, mentors, or companies to share cooperative advertising campaigns. Over the next two weeks, the help you receive could change the very trajectory of your career.

May 2021: *May 11 brings the new moon. May 23 has Saturn going retrograde. (Saturn retrograde can cause you to review your career choices and make adjustments. Saturn will be retrograde until October). May 26 is a total Lunar Eclipse. May 29 has Mercury going retrograde. Your High-Energy Days are 2, 8, 14, 20, and 26.*

The month of May brings energy to stabilize a lot of the projects you've been working on. Now things at work start to flow positively and smoothly. An issue that has been bubbling up now seems to resolve itself. You like the people you are working with. Those Ox natives who work at home receive a great deal of support from those who still work at the office. Be sure to vocalize what you're looking for, and help is more likely to come your way.

On May 11, the new moon brings an opportunity for you to shine. Your special qualities are highlighted over the next couple of weeks, as you can now differentiate yourself from the crowd. This may mean you stand on a stage, publish a manuscript, work on your company branding, or receive an award for work you've been doing for a while now.

Over the next two weeks, there are multiple opportunities and good energy for bringing in extra money. This may come from a secondary source, and may not be something you can expect consistently, but the source does bring you the occasional windfall. This aspect is particularly useful for those Ox natives who like to rummage around through stores and garage sales finding treasure.

May 26 brings a lunar eclipse; most Ox natives focus on getting their finances in order. You may find yourself sorting through old paperwork, shredding, and moving things online. Ox natives do like tradition, but perhaps you're ready to go paperless? Decide once and for all to get out of debt. It feels like the right time to create a written budget.

At the end of the month, around May 29, Mercury goes retrograde. Suddenly there's a hiccup in your plans for staying frugal. Maybe you find an unexpected expense—possibly something you have been taking for granted (a cell phone, or water heater?) now unexpectedly needs replacing. You may find your only option is to incur this expense; however, it doesn't mean you are unable to stay on your budget most of the time. Mercury retrograde disrupts the flow, but this doesn't mean your plans are completely derailed.

June 2021: *June 10 is the annular Solar Eclipse. June 20 is the first day of summer, and Jupiter goes retrograde (Jupiter retrograde can indicate a need to relearn things or renew a spiritual connection. Jupiter will be retrograde until October). June 22 has Mercury* *going direct. June 24 is the full moon. On June 25, Neptune goes retrograde (Neptune retrograde can draw you back towards habits and addictions from your past, and it can also encourage a return to spiritual practices. Neptune will be retrograde until December). Your High-Energy Days are 1, 7, 13, 19, and 25.*

June rolls around, and people near you seem to be on pins and needles. While things overall are improving for Ox natives, there are those around you who need your help. This may even be profitable. You have good luck in the area of finances in June. You may receive additional money from your job (or from a second job), and some Ox natives may be changing jobs to receive an increase in salary. Most Ox natives will make a career shift before the end of 2023, but if you're doing it already, you're ahead of the game.

Energy shifts on June 20, and as a result, communication becomes more critical. A longtime disagreement with a sibling or neighbor can now resolve. Even if all parties are not jumping for joy, at least there's some peace, and a better relationship can be the result.

On June 22, Mercury goes direct. Now that Mercury is moving forward, financial opportunities start to open up. You may have been waiting for a check to arrive, or for a customer to sign a contract. It will take Mercury a few days to get up to speed, so you need patience now—something Ox natives are quite good at. This is also an excellent time to have repairs done on your cell phone, laptop, or car.

The full moon comes in on June 24, and there could be a great deal of discussion about living arrangements within the family, redecorating, or doing some renovations. This may not be taking place in your home. Indeed, a family member's dwelling may need some extra care, and they may need help finding skilled workers or pricing out some changes. If so, this could inspire you to do some decluttering at home or finish some of your home repairs.

July 2021: *July 10 brings the new moon. July 24 is the full moon. Your High-Energy Days are 1, 7, 13, 19, and 25.*

The month of July brings both the subject of your relationship and your home into focus. For Ox natives who are dating, this may mean introducing your sweetheart to your family and friends. You may talk about living together or buying a place together. If you're already in a committed relationship, you now enjoy greater harmony and joy at home. Now could be a wonderful time for barbecues on the patio, or simply sitting together enjoying some fine weather.

The new moon comes in on July 10 and brings a sense of relief—as you have faced and cleared up quite a few hurdles over the past few weeks. Ox natives are known for their tenacity, and their tireless focus on pushing or plowing their way through difficulties in their way. You may have been working on important projects which now have come to completion. People may have been standing in your way, but now the road ahead is clear. Over the next two weeks, you benefit from the work you've been doing, perhaps even a financial windfall. New opportunities seem to show up as a result of luck and synchronicity.

The energy shifts on July 22, and for those Ox natives who are working out of the home, you may decide to give yourself a home office makeover. Now is the time to declutter and send unneeded items to charity. It's also an opportunity to connect with older relatives for a time, or even to make plans for a future reunion.

July 24 brings the full moon, lighting up your area of career. Some concerns you have about your company, even perhaps the industry you work in, now require your attention. There may be red flags ahead! You will have time to make some adjustments to your career, but this is not a good time to sit on the information. New opportunities will be opening up for you over the next few months, especially if you take the chance to explore through professional websites like LinkedIn. The next two weeks is a time for collecting information to see whether what you suspect about your company (and the industry) is actually true.

Towards the end of the month, there is an opportunity to spend time with adult children. If you are looking to start a family or expand the household, there is some good fertility energy. This is also an excellent time to be looking into adoption opportunities.

August 2021: *August 8 brings the new moon. On August 20, Uranus goes retrograde. August 22 is the full moon. Your High-Energy Days are 6, 12, 18, 24, and 30.*

The month of August brings some changes to your routine. You're in the first of your three seed-planting years, and it's terrific to be trying new things. Now focus on what you enjoy doing rather than only doing work, tasks, and drudgery. Look beyond the current work/life balance. This time is about finding what brings you happiness. You may decide to sit down at your electric keyboard in the morning before work to play music. You might try writing a few pages of your novel during a lunchtime break. On weekends you could pick up your notebook and make some quick sketches. Even the smallest touches—something like beautifully plating your breakfast—can boost your mood and give you energy for the day.

The new moon comes in on August 8 in your area of foundations and traditions. Ox natives can be attached to their heritage and family history, yet some things from your past are not serving you now. This is especially true of wounds from younger days, even from your childhood. This is the first year of your 12-year cycle. It's time to look back at events and beliefs formed in previous cycles and to let some things go. As you look through your house, you may find that some of the furniture or knickknacks are no longer your style, or they may remind you of negative things from the past. It's okay to box those things up and ship them off to charity.

Around August 20, Uranus goes retrograde. Uranus is the planet of change, eccentricities, and disruption. When Uranus goes backward, it asks you to go back to look at the different roads you could have taken. Those paths can open for you again. Uranus helps you expand your comfort zone. For shy Ox natives, Uranus brings crowds; for traditional Ox natives, Uranus brings newfangled things; but it can also bring you exciting opportunities and new directions to explore. So as Uranus goes retrograde, embrace the new exciting things that can happen. Try new foods, explore unknown places, meet new people, and you'll see future roads open up for you.

August 22 brings the full moon and a new interest in exercise routines and healthy eating. You may be embracing a plan one of your friends is on, or you may go back to something you were doing earlier this year. You can gain significant benefits by paying attention to your health, especially over the next two weeks.

September 2021: *September 7 brings the new moon. September 20 is the full moon. September 22 is the first day of autumn. September 26 has Mercury going retrograde. Your High-Energy Days are 5, 11, 17, 23, and 29.*

September comes along, and you may find it brings a great deal of focus on work. You may have some big projects on your desk. Your company may be making some changes. A new computer system or changing up procedures this month could lead to more work for you and your coworkers. If you're looking for a job, there are a few possibilities, but they may be outside your comfort zone, and not suited to your resume. This is your opportunity to schedule an interview to learn more about the job. Consider applying and don't let the fact that your resume is not an exact fit to hold you back.

On September 7, there will be a new moon, and this brings some attention to your area of children and creativity. If you have kids in school, this energy can be channeled into getting them outfitted and back into their educational routines. You might be going back to school yourself, remembering how to study and get homework done. This is also an excellent time for you to focus on some types of creative projects that bring you joy. Over the next two weeks, try to spend some time cooking, sewing, woodworking, or playing music.

The full moon comes in on September 20 and marks a two-week period where you may focus on endings and letting things go. There are things you want to get rid of; clutter, a couple of extra pounds, etc. There is a chance a friend of yours is moving away and will live at a distance where you may not see each other as often. While this can feel sad, you are excited about the new opportunities opening up for them due to their move.

Towards the end of the month, on September 26, Mercury goes retrograde. This particular Mercury retrograde may be particularly irksome to you as it affects your daily routines and work. You may find people pulling you in different directions; this causes you to have to break your well-established regular patterns. On the other hand, this is a great time to renew your commitment to some good habits. Doing things like exercising or eating healthy during Mercury retrograde can be very beneficial. Lifetime habits can be established by using the retrograde energy because it's likely you will return to these positive habits every time Mercury goes retrograde.

October 2021: *October 6 brings the new moon, and Pluto goes direct. On October 11, Saturn goes direct. October 18 has Mercury going direct and Jupiter going direct. October 20 is the full moon. Your High-Energy Days are 5, 11, 17, 23, and 29.*

In October, your focus turns to relationships. You may be establishing yourself in a new relationship, having just met someone new, and now exploring who this person is and how they fit into your life. Perhaps you have been dating a while, and now you want to make the relationship an exclusive, monogamous partnership. Ox natives in an established relationship may discuss plans as you now look ahead to the next few years to the possibility of a move or career change. Perhaps the two of you can start a business together?

On October 6, the new moon shows up in your house of health and well-being. You may feel it's time to schedule a regular physical at the doctor's office, the dentist to have your teeth cleaned, the eye doctor to have your eyes checked, etc. Mercury will be going direct later in the month, so it's best to schedule these tasks after October 18. This is also a good time to look at matters involving your insurance to settle any disputes you may have with hospitals, doctors, or insurance companies.

As mentioned before, October 18 has Mercury going direct, and now things start to move forward again. Work, in general, flows much easier; medical appointments can be set up, and social connections can happen. Mercury will take a few days to get up to speed. Now you will have many weeks of energy flowing in the right direction.

On October 20, the full moon arrives, bringing you a burst of energy. Over the next two weeks, you can be quite productive, getting things done at work and at home. You may decide to clean out the garage, can vegetables, or paint a room. However, you need to take some breaks as well. Look at your evening routine. Make sure it's peaceful and helps you settle in to a night of restful sleep.

October 22 brings a shift in energy, and you'll feel more harmony in your love relationships. This includes your sweetheart as well as family members and friends. Several may reach out to tell you how much they appreciate you.

November 2021: *November 4 is the new moon. November 19 is a partial Lunar Eclipse. Your High-Energy Days are 4, 10, 16, 22, and 28.*

November can be a challenging month as there will be a Lunar Eclipse, and this can trigger some powerful emotions in the people around you. You'll find that some who are closest to you are easily irritated or themselves attempting to overcome their obstacles. These may be issues you cannot help them with, but you can stand beside them and be supportive, something Ox natives are known for.

On November 4, a new moon lights up your house of relationships. You may meet a new friend and be so taken with this person you want to see them often. Or, you may become very attached to your sweetheart to the exclusion of other people. Since the focus is on relationships, those Ox natives who are looking for love can discover what is blocking you from a great relationship. Now you can clear away any obstacles. You might do this by talking to close friends, or accessing modalities such as self-hypnosis or tapping. Consider placing Feng Shui cures to help you attract love as well.

On November 19, there is the Lunar Eclipse, and this signals a time of change for you. You may be frustrated with your finances and resolve to do things differently to better your situation. At the same time, you may want to change your job(s) to seek a position where you get greater respect and find more supportive coworkers. For those Ox natives who are hesitating about the change, the Universe may start closing some doors in your life to help push you in a new direction. New doors will open to better opportunities.

Even as you feel the energy of change, you are beginning to feel much more confident about your plans. Over the next few weeks, you feel unhurried in various situations; things begin to unfold just as you envisioned they would. It's as if you have a guardian angel on your shoulder, watching over you and guiding your steps.

The energy shifts on November 21, and suddenly you see resources open up for you. If you own a business, you can find a loan at a reasonable rate. A credit card company may increase your limit, or you may qualify for a Small Business Association loan. For Ox natives looking to go back to school, this could mean scholarships or student loans at a good interest rate.

December 2021: *December 1 has Neptune going direct. December 4 is a total Solar Eclipse. December 19 brings the full moon, and Venus goes retrograde (Venus retrograde can cause you to question what you want and inspires you to look for something new that delights you. Venus will be retrograde until January.) December*

21 is the first day of winter. Your High-Energy Days are 4, 10, 16, 22, and 28.

The excitement continues in December, starting with Neptune going direct. Neptune rules spiritual matters but also obfuscation. It can feel like you're walking through a fog bank. But at any time, the fog can clear, and the bigger, more important truth is revealed. That's what is happening now, and over the next few weeks, the fog is clearing, and you will get a great deal of clarity about the path you want to take.

December 4 brings the total Solar Eclipse. Eclipses always bring change, and this one falls in your area of resources you may receive from others. Over the next few months, there may be a significant change in your finances. If you have been working on this by taking charge of your money, investing wisely, and changing jobs to get a better salary, the next few months will be remarkably profitable. But if you have been digging in your heels, and avoiding taking action, the Universe is now going to help you change. You will still have many opportunities, but you will be encouraged to move forward as a result of changes occurring all around you.

December 19 brings the full moon, and at the same time, Venus goes retrograde. Just when you thought you were making progress, things get delayed. This can mean a position you're interviewing for now is on hold. A business deal may get blocked. All directions seem closed. But this energy will shift soon enough. It's good to shift your focus to something else while you wait for this energy to clear.

Just a few days later, on December 21, there is a shift in the energy, and you can already see new resources becoming available to you. If you're an older Ox native, you're familiar with this energy. The tide goes out, then the tide comes back in, and it repeats. You know when there's a block, you just have to wait for it to clear. Younger Ox natives can learn this lesson, and then you can proceed through life more smoothly.

January 2022: *January 2 is the new moon. January 14 has Mercury going retrograde. January 17 is the full moon. On January 18, Uranus goes direct. On January 29, Venus goes direct. Your High-Energy Days are 3, 9, 15, 21, and 27.*

January arrives, bringing the last month of the Metal Ox year. There's been quite a few ups and downs and some challenges for Ox natives. But when you look back, you see many new things are happening in your life. That's a good thing!

On January 2, the new moon comes in, and sometime over the next week or so, you receive some good news. There is an opportunity to gain a professional license or to pass a certification exam. Ox natives who are in school can get some good grades or get through a challenging project. It's easy to get recognition at this time.

On January 14, that pesky Mercury goes retrograde again, and some plans get put on hold. You may have been thinking to speak to your supervisor about a new position, but at this point, you may want to wait for a few weeks until the energy clears. There is also the possibility of traveling to a wedding or special event, but this trip could encounter a lot of delays or interruptions. You may want to arrange travel insurance or allow a considerable amount of extra time to get to where you're going.

On January 17, there is a full moon and Ox natives experience an emphasis on spirituality. You may attend church services more regularly, or begin practicing some spiritual work at home. This could include adding yoga to your daily routine, meditation, chanting, or other spiritual practices. If you haven't done so in a while, dust off your altar or do a space clearing.

February 2022: *February 1 is the new moon and begins the Year of the Water Tiger.*

You can feel the energy shifting as the world moves from the Metal Ox to the Water Tiger. While this is a wholly different type of energy—scattered, and unpredictable—Ox natives know you're going to have a much better year in 2022.

Attract New Love

This is a superb year for new love relationships for Ox natives. At the same time, "... the one you thought had got away..." may come running back to you. Past and future energies could collide as you date new people while thinking about someone from your past. There's also potential for a love relationship to develop unexpectedly at your job. If fraternizing is allowed, you may want to explore the possibilities. This year, finding love can happen as easily as stepping outside your door—especially as you explore new interests or hobbies. Don't hide at home. If by June you're not in a satisfying relationship, it's time to pay attention to what's blocking you. You might want to seek out a relationship coach or a matchmaker.

Traditionally and historically, jade was considered more valuable than diamonds throughout Asia. Jade is most commonly found in the shades of green and purple; green jade represents longevity. Jade can be carved into many things: from lucky charms to fine jewelry. Hang a jade charm in your bedroom to invite in the energy of love and beauty, or find a jade pendant to wear. Jade can be fragile, and if your Jade piece breaks, make sure to replace it.

Enhance Existing Love

This year Ox natives experience intense energy around an existing love relationship. This is a splendid year to marry after a long engagement. There is the possibility of establishing or buying a home together, or starting/combining business interests into a successful business partnership.

But things do not flow smoothly when this much energy exists all around you. Issues in your love life will center around identity and respect. Misunderstandings can occur over jealousy about friendships. Ox natives are slow to anger, so if you're becoming irritated with your partner, you know something's going on. It's a good idea to bring it out into the open and open up a discussion before problems grow into resentment. However, the Ox native who keeps the lines of communication open can experience a peaceful and happy year with their sweetheart.

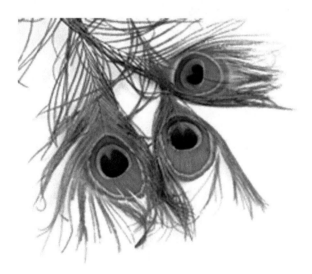

Mysterious and beautiful, Peacock feathers have been prized since ancient times. The feathers represent nobility, but also kindness, glory, and patience. When you display a Peacock feather in your bedroom, you invite sensual and magical things to happen. If you want to improve your existing love relationship, display a single Peacock feather near the head of the bed.

Looking to Conceive?

There are many foods associated with fertility. One is the watermelon—specifically the seeds. You've probably heard the old saying: "Swallowing watermelon seeds can get you pregnant!". Rather than swallowing them, I suggest you take seven seeds, clean them and dry them.

Place the dried watermelon seeds in a small pouch, along with a metal charm shaped like a child (you can find these at party stores, in the baby shower section). Place the pouch under your mattress, so when you lie down, your belly is right over the pouch. This will bring good conception energy.

(From Donna Stellhorn's book, A Path to Pregnancy: Ancient Secrets for the Modern Woman)

Family and Kids

When it comes to your kids and family, this is when harmony abounds in the homes of Ox natives. Everyone seems to be doing their own thing, on their schedule. While everybody else is running around in different directions, you are front and center. You can pull family members and friends together for weekly dinners, game nights, and monthly celebrations. At the same time, your home life is changing because you may have a new job, you're attending a new school, or perhaps renovating the house. The energy seems to be swirling around you and yours, and changes are happening continuously.

When it comes to children, most of the time you're on the same page. Set aside time to have deep, meaningful conversations with youngsters. Listen to how they communicate and what they want to talk about. If they don't want to talk, just sit with them and watch them play a video game, and they will begin to open up.

Sunflower: Add Sunflowers to your home or garden this year to bring in positive health energy. In past centuries people would string sunflower seeds and wear them as necklaces to protect themselves from diseases. Hang pictures of sunflowers or have cut sunflowers in the house, especially in the living room and bedroom. Also, if you have a garden, plant sunflowers along the edges. It's said if you have a little wish, you can cut a sunflower at sunset from your garden, and the wish will come true before the sun sets again.

Money

Income and moneymaking options are promising this year. You can easily connect with opportunities—especially in the form of new jobs and/or helpful people who can open the right doors for you. You have a strong sense of being on a mission this year; that mission is to increase income. You may be working with a budget or an actual financial advisor (like a licensed fiduciary, someone who is legally bound to serve your best interest). The challenging period is during June when, either because of business or other suddenly occurring unexpected expenses, you're not able to keep an eye on the money going out of your hands as carefully as you usually do. The good news is you can get back on track, and you'll likely end the year financially in the plus column.

The Lucky Money Cat is an example of a cultural symbol that is very effective in shifting the energy of a home and bringing prosperity opportunities. The story of the lucky cat tells us of a poor priest, whose job it was to maintain a temple in the woods far from the village. No one came to visit the temple, and so the priest had no income, and yet he dutifully maintained the temple, keeping it clean, lighting the incense and praying. One day a cat came to the temple, and even though the priest had hardly enough food for himself, he divided his dinner each night and fed the cat. So the cat stayed. What the priest didn't know was this was a magical cat.

Months later, a nobleman was riding his horse through the forest to a neighboring town. There was a great storm, and the nobleman got off his horse and took shelter under a tree. In the flashes of lightning, he could see the temple. And on the temple steps sat a little cat. To his surprise, the cat sat up on his haunches and motioned for the nobleman to approach. Intrigued, he left the shelter of the tree and went to the temple. At that moment, lightning struck the tree. The nobleman recognized that he would have died if not for the little cat. And so he spent his life and fortune supporting the cat, the temple, and the priest.

To attract more income this year, place a Lucky Money Cat in your living room or home office. Place it in the far corner of the room and have him face the door. The Lucky Cat has his hand raised to call in money. Often these little statues are banks. Remember to feed him with coins and keep feeding him until the little bank is full. Then dust him regularly to re-energize him.

Job or Career

Considerable changes are taking place in your career in this year of the Metal Ox. But sometimes change can be difficult for Ox natives, even when these shifts move you in the direction you've wished for all this time. Now the contacts and connections you've made over the past come through for you with offers and opportunities.

While you may experience brief disruptions in your career as you shift job title or possibly even change company, you will probably make much more money because you're willing to take a step outside your regular lane. There's an emphasis on doing new things and experimenting with different life directions. This can involve dutting-edge technology you've been learning about. However, your success stems from making good connections with people who can give you a leg up. 2021 can be an enjoyable year as long as you can let go of the desire to keep things the same.

In feng shui, yellow is the color often associated with intelligence, memory, and feeling at home in a situation. Whether you hope to find a great new job or stay in your current position, find a candleholder, and put a yellow candle in it (note: choose a sunny, happy shade of yellow). Find a safe place in your home to place your candleholder on top of your resume or business card. (The candleholder will protect the paper from the flame, but you need to make sure to the items safely away from other flammable items.) Light your candle for a short time each night until the candle wax is spent. This can be repeated throughout the year whenever your career needs a boost.

Education

While some Ox natives may be looking at joining a formal education program this year, many of you will be completing school, and receiving your degree. Now comes the decision about whether to continue studying for a higher degree or to move into the workforce. You may need additional training or learning to find work in a specific field, or you may need to accrue additional hours to be issued a professional license.

There's also a focus on technology. You could be learning proprietary software platforms, or developing skills in more universally used software such as Excel or Salesforce. Overall, continuing to learn is more important than ever this year; being aware of your learning style can help you more quickly understand and gain new skills. You may be a hands-on learner who does well listening to instruction or watching videos while gaining new skills. In May and December, there could be an opportunity to receive scholarships, low-interest loans, or discounts for vocational courses.

Legal Matters

There is harmony in contracts and agreements this year. Paperwork you may have been waiting on for several months (or even years) now lands on your desk. There's a particular emphasis on contracts for employment or real estate (especially buying a new house or renting office space). You are more protected than usual when signing agreements. You can spot points that need to negotiating. This year the other party is more open to negotiating. Unless they are also born in the year of the Ox—then there can be a stalemate. Be careful towards the end of the year to avoid getting embroiled in large lawsuits or class-action legal matters.

Health and Well-Being

Your health is steady and more stable this year; there will be incremental improvements, primarily as you focus on following recommendations from trusted sources. Minor changes in diet can help more than any radical changes that you might pursue for a few weeks, then going back to your old habits. Look to gain wisdom from your ancestors on what to eat. Consider eating as your great great grandmother did.

Exercise centered around group activities—whether it be walking, swimming, or working out in a gym—is good for you. This is your year, Ox native; you may feel a great deal of pressure in your neck and shoulders. Take care of yourself, particularly in November, especially when lifting, carrying, or moving heavy items. Consider removing the color red from your bedroom to help you sleep better this year.

A good cure for clearing negative energy from a space is to use salt. Salt is a potent substance. It takes all forms of energy and returns them to a neutral state. This means salt removes negative energy—and it also removes positive energy—bringing everything back into balance, to neutral. Once energy is neutral, you can then add positive energy by focusing on happy thoughts, playing joyous music, or infusing the air with a floral scent.

To clear a house using salt, dissolve a half teaspoon of salt in warm water; pour the liquid into a spray bottle. Spritz the salty water around the house (taking care to avoid delicate fabrics). Once the entire house is clean, you can add back in the positive energy by burning a scented candle, burning incense, burning sage, or by playing uplifting music. When clearing a house of health issues, pay particular attention to the bedrooms and bathrooms, spray liberally with the saltwater solution.

It is also possible to clear yourself and remove residual energy from a stressful or negative experience by using salt. Just add a teaspoon of sea salt to your warm bath, soak for a few minutes, and think about the good things that will happen in the future.

If you prefer to shower, soak a washcloth in a basin or bowl where you have combined warm water and a teaspoon of salt. Place the bowl and washcloth in the shower, and lift the wet washcloth to squeeze the salty water over your shoulders and body as you stand in the spray from the showerhead. Repeat several times until the bowl is empty. This will cleanse you of any negative energy and help you feel more balanced and peaceful.

Tiger

February 8, 1902–January 28, 1903: Yang Water Tiger
January 26, 1914–February 13, 1915: Yang Wood Tiger
February 13, 1926–February 1, 1927: Yang Fire Tiger
January 31, 1938–February 18, 1939: Yang Earth Tiger
February 17, 1950–February 5, 1951: Yang Metal Tiger
February 5, 1962–January 24, 1963: Yang Water Tiger
January 23, 1974–February 10, 1975: Yang Wood Tiger
February 9, 1986–January 28, 1987: Yang Fire Tiger
January 28, 1998–February 15, 1999: Yang Earth Tiger
February 14, 2010–February 2, 2011: Yang Metal Tiger
February 1, 2022–January 21, 2023: Yang Water Tiger

Tiger Personality

There are two ways to think about Tiger. First and most apparent, consider the beautiful beast in its jungle habitat, hiding in the tall grass, patiently waiting for his prey. A herd of antelope lopes into view, pausing at the local waterhole. The Tiger watches and waits until one not too bright antelope wanders away from the herd. Lunchtime!

But that's only one aspect of the Tiger. There is also an impatient side, the "bounce-bounce-bounce energy" we saw in Tigger, the Tiger of Winnie the Pooh fame. This Tiger is the impulsive, leap-before-you-look energy.

Those born during the year of the Tiger have a personality combining these two aspects. They are both patient and spontaneous. For instance, they can be very patient when they are stalking something they want. But when they find it, they jump in, completely committing themselves to having it, with no thought to the consequences.

The Tiger is a powerful sign, the second most powerful (and second most popular) of all the Chinese Zodiac. People born under this sign are rebellious and unpredictable, but they command our respect. They are ready for anything. Overall, they love life, and they want to experience it fully. Sometimes this sits well with those around them, and sometimes it doesn't.

Those born in the Year of the Tiger are suspicious. They don't trust easily. When their suspicions are confirmed, they are quick-tempered and will say whatever is on their mind. Be cautious of a Tiger's temper—after all, they have sharp claws.

Tiger also has a gentle side. Tigers are very affectionate and devote themselves to those they care about. They can hug, snuggle and purr, just like a soft little kitten.

Tigers are dreamers and artists at heart. At the mere suggestion of it, they are ready to fly off to Bali with you. They will join your band. They will audition when the reality show comes to town looking for contestants. Everything is possible!

Tiger people may spend their entire lives running after exciting adventures. Or they may have short periods of rebellion when they quit their job, leave their relationship, and throw caution to the wind. The rest of us watch and hope the Tiger succeeds.

Tigers are emotional; their highs are really high, and their lows are very low. When the low periods happen, Tiger needs a shoulder to cry on. It will tempt others to offer advice, but Tigers won't listen. As a Tiger, you've learned it's better to stick with who you are, and know that tomorrow is another day.

Tigers can be very charismatic and influence others when they put their mind to it. They make compelling speakers, teachers, and politicians. Tigers are charming; potential lovers fall for their flattery. The passion will burn hot—at least for a while.

But when the initial excitement is over, Tiger can fall out of love just as quickly as they fell into it, and just drift away. If, on the other hand, the object of their attention strays away from them, Tiger is quickly back on the hunt, eager to renew the chase.

Tiger: Predictions for 2021

How to use your High-Energy Days: On these days, plan to take action for your most important goals, make vital phone calls, send important emails. Your high-energy days are when your energy and luck are the strongest for the month.

January 2021: *Uranus goes direct on January 14. Mercury goes retrograde from January 30 to February 20. Your Lucky Days are 3, 9, 15, 21, 27. [How to use your Lucky Days: On these days, plan to take significant actions, make vital phone calls, send emails. These are days when your energy and luck are high.]*

The Metal Rat Year draws to a close, and you feel the approaching energy shift. You will soon enter the last year of your 12-year cycle, one where you'll capitalize on all the experience you've collected over the last decade.

Accumulate money this month towards a bigger goal. It's good to have a written budget, even if you have trouble staying on track. Look at reducing credit card debt. See if you can get interest rates lowered or consolidate debt if possible to aid in paying down balances. Also, find other ways to make money to increase your per-hour take-home pay. Be aware you have acquired a skill set that is valuable to others. You may do consulting or tutoring. Consider all possibilities without deciding ahead of time which one you're qualified for.

It's a good time to lighten the load. Consider decluttering, getting rid of storage units, and clearing out the basement or attic. Tiger natives are rarely materialistic. However, you can sometimes make impulsive purchases and then not know what to do with the stuff. Check in with family and friends to see if you know someone who wants the things before taking it to the donation center.

Love relationships strengthen now. If you have a sweetheart, there will be fun times ahead this month. If you're looking for love, check out places like community centers, shopping malls, and sporting events. Any place lots of people gather is a suitable venue for meeting new people.

February 2021: *Lunar New Year begins on February 12. Happy Year of the Metal Ox. February 20 has Mercury going direct. February 27 is the full moon. Your High-Energy Days are 2, 8, 14, 20, and 26.*

As February begins, there are still a few weeks left of the *Year of the Metal Rat*. As this is harmonious energy for Tiger natives, take these final few days to focus some of your energy on an important goal. It's a great time to get school or work projects done, if you've been procrastinating until now. You can also get assistance from teachers, advisers, or a superstar trainer at your company. This person can provide the information you need to complete your project.

February 12 brings the new moon, and the *Year of the Metal Ox* begins. Now you can feel the energy slowing down. The focus moves from the Rat's desire to survive, to the Ox's desire to rebuild. This begins with you taking stock of what you have and projecting where you want to be a year from now. Mercury is retrograde, so it's a good idea to plan rather than do for the next few days. That's good news for Tiger natives—while you are sometimes spontaneous, you do like to have a plan.

Mercury turns and goes direct on February 20, and the energy feels a little better. It's easier to communicate with people, people respond to your texts, and they answer your emails. You may feel some general restlessness, a desire to move forward quickly, but it will take Mercury some time to get up speed. Good idea to avoid pouncing on people for at least a few days.

February 27 is the full moon, and you enter a lucky period for a couple of weeks. Beneficial energy assists you in connecting with others. It's as if the Universe is watching over you and putting people in your path who will be useful to you on your road to success. This is true if you have issues around education or legal matters. On a different note, you may feel a little sluggish as your energy dips. You may need to take a break. Consider a long weekend sometime soon.

March 2021: *March 13 brings the new moon, March 20 marks the first day of spring, March 28 is the full moon. Your High-Energy Days are 4, 10, 16, 22, and 28.*

March arrives, and your luck continues. You may receive a windfall, and even though the prize isn't exactly what you asked for, it's still nice to receive it. Your luck is strong regarding insights into who you are and your place in the world. Out of the blue, epiphanies about what you want to do over the next few years reveal themselves to you. Explore things you are interested in, or ones obsessively rolling around in your mind.

Along with good luck, your charisma is powerful for the next several weeks. It brings love opportunities for Tiger natives looking for a relationship. You feel attracted to someone who's not your "type." But there's something about this person who has captured your interest. Likewise, they may be interested in you. Tiger natives already in a love relationship may consider getting engaged, perhaps even tying the knot now.

March 13 brings the new moon, this month lighting up your area of career. You may know of some miscommunications or rumors going around about your company. Everything seems to be under a haze of mystery, and underneath the murmurings, you feel that changes are coming. Perhaps a merger taking place, or significant shifts in management. While this could affect your job, it could also open up a possibility of promotion or transfer for you.

March 20 brings a shift in the energy, and for the next couple of weeks, you could spend a lot of time with friends. Someone may come to stay with you, or you have many social events in your calendar. There may also be fundraisers connected to your child's school. Nieces and nephews can knock on your door, asking for your support or financial help.

The full moon comes in on March 28, and a great deal of personal activity begins due to this energy. You feel more energetic and generally productive. Supervisors or upper management notice you. You receive compliments on your work, and at the same time, you may consider starting a side business. It seems you are of two minds right now—not quite ready to commit to either direction.

April 2021: *April 12 brings the new moon. April 27 is the full moon, and Pluto goes retrograde (Pluto moving backward can cause you to reconsider your basic assumptions about life, to eliminate anything unnecessary, bringing you back to what is essential. Pluto will be retrograde until October.) Your High-Energy Days are 3, 9, 15, 21, and 27.*

April rolls around, and your career is still on your mind. Unsettled energy may still vibrate throughout your company, affecting one department after another. Fortunately, you're quick on your feet and aware of the changes coming. You can make the necessary connections to get a better office, newer equipment, or new job description. One downside for you personally is that some of this disruption is affecting your sleep. You may need to take steps to get more rest over the next few weeks. Consider getting a white noise machine, blackout curtains, or a cooling pad to lower your body temperature at night.

On April 12, there is a new moon; things at work become more peaceful. Now you can relax a bit with friends and family, and you may even take some time off work during the next few weeks. Consider hiking, biking, or being out on the water. For some Tiger natives, however, you may finish up school projects rather than finding time to party during Spring Break.

The energy shifts directions on April 19, and you are more intuitive—you may be experiencing a deeper spiritual connection. You are aware of having dreams or psychic impressions. It's easy to feel guided now and find wisdom in the words of spiritual leaders. This is an excellent time to read books and listen to lectures as you seek to learn more about yourself; things like studying astrology can help.

The full moon is on April 27, and now the energy centers on health, well-being, and your routine. Like some Tiger natives, you may have given in to your sweet tooth lately (or other tasty items not included in your healthy eating plan). This may have resulted in weight gain, or just the sluggish feeling of being slowed down. Tiger natives are generally healthy, but you need to take care of yourself by watching what you eat.

May 2021: *May 11 brings the new moon. May 23, Saturn goes retrograde. (Saturn retrograde can cause you to review your career choices and make adjustments. Saturn will be retrograde until October). May 26 is a total Lunar Eclipse. May 29 has Mercury going retrograde. Your High-Energy Days are 3, 9, 15, 21, and 27.*

May arrives with a surge of energy for your career. Someone high up in the company may compliment you. Tiger natives looking for a job can make great connections. You can even receive a tempting offer during the coming two weeks. Headhunters may pursue you, or you may hear from a former colleague who lets you know about openings at the new company where they now work

The new moon comes in on May 11, and love energy is powerful. You receive lots of compliments about how good you look, and the charm of your winning smile. There is the possibility of a secret admirer or a secret romantic rendezvous. Those Tiger natives in a love relationship may enjoy increased fun between the sheets, and more cuddling on the sofa.

Energy shifts on May 20 and several long-awaited opportunities now show up. You may want time to think things over, but it would be a good idea to hasten to secure what you want.

You'll have at least one opportunity to make a great deal—if you let the other side know you're ready to walk away if you do not get what you want.

May 26 brings the Lunar Eclipse, along with a strong possibility of change in your life. For some Tiger natives, this can mean you enter a long-term love relationship. You might move in together with your significant other or to become engaged. If you're focused on business relationships, this can be a time when you enter a necessary business arrangement—potentially with a new supplier, banker, or angel investor.

Towards the end of the month, on May 29, Mercury goes retrograde, and projects get stalled. You may be waiting for someone's signature, approval, or their part of the information. Everything seems on hold now, and this could have you pacing with impatience.

June 2021: *June 10 is the annular Solar Eclipse. June 20 is the first day of summer, and Jupiter goes retrograde. (Jupiter retrograde can indicate a need to relearn things or review your beliefs. Jupiter will be retrograde until October.) June 22 has Mercury going direct. June 24 is the full moon. On June 25, Neptune goes retrograde. (Neptune retrograde draws you back toward habits and addictions from your past.) It can also encourage a return to spiritual practices. Neptune will be retrograde until December). Your High-Energy Days are 2, 8, 14, 20, and 26.*

As June arrives, you have a list of things you need to finish up soon. You may struggle to find help with parts you can't accomplish on your own. Possibly the house requires repairs, or a particular piece of equipment you need for your job has been back ordered. Other departments in your company may be holding back information you need. All of this can cause you to feel a little on edge, possibly even ready to snap.

The Solar Eclipse comes in on June 10, and the changes you have been expecting are starting to happen. Maybe you are planting seeds as part of your plan to expand your career, launch a new product, or release a creative project (such as your first solo album.) This can be an extraordinarily successful time for you. Over the next two weeks, the more action you take—especially to make connections with influential people, influencers, or potential mentors—the more opportunities will roll in. While Eclipse energy brings dramatic and unexpected changes, lightning cannot strike a moving target! It's best to be in motion.

The energy shifts somewhat on June 20, and your focus turns to finances. You may become aware you've been spending a great deal lately and decide now is the time to plug the holes. There are just a couple more items you want, but consider creative solutions to pursuing a desired outcome, rather than buying more stuff.

On June 22, Mercury begins to move forward again, and you breathe a gigantic sigh of relief. Now everything can continue forward. That troublesome cell phone starts working again; your car stops overheating... It will take Mercury a few days to get up to speed, but you can already feel the beneficial energy.

The full moon comes in on July 24, bringing a powerful surge of love and intimacy. Expect happy, romantic communications with someone special, perhaps whispers, innuendos, and generally sexy fun. For those Tiger natives who are single and happy, this can be a great time for barbeques with friends, or sitting on the patio, just watching the world go by.

July 2021: *July 10 brings the new moon. July 24 is the full moon. Your High-Energy Days are 2, 8, 14, 20, and 26.*

July finds you up early in the mornings, perhaps as much as an hour or two before your usual time. You might go for a morning run, or practice Tai Chi in the park. You feel energetic and enjoy a greater sense of freedom and personal strength. In general, there's a feeling that things are going your way.

July 10 brings the new moon. Over the next two weeks, enjoy good relations with siblings or younger relatives. You may receive a visit from one or more relatives, or travel to see family members. Maybe it's been quite a while since you've taken a trip, and you now really savor every bit. Even if you stay in your home town, explore new restaurants and activities, and rediscover some out-of-the-way corners you rarely see.

Around July 10, someone special in your life may ask you for a commitment. You can find yourself involved in a serious conversation about raising children; or discussing plans for what you plan to do together in retirement. You may have a discussion about a job opportunity one of you is considering, yet which might take both of you to a new place in the country, or even to a foreign land. You may itch for a change now, but you're in the last year of your 12-year cycle, so things you discuss now may not unfold until 2022.

The energy shifts on July 22, and communication becomes very important. You may be asked to give a presentation or to take the stage in some capacity. Typically, Tiger natives fear nothing, but for some reason, this particular presentation causes you to feel nervous. Get some coaching, or at least good advice from a friend who has more experience.

The full moon comes in on July 24; there's a lot of activity on the home front. Perhaps you're considering a move or putting your house up for sale. The change at home may not happen for some time, but suddenly you look around and think, "I have too much stuff!". It's a good time for general decluttering. Also, look at the Feng Shui remedies you have in place. Moving them to a new location can re-energize them. Switch things around, and you'll discover renewed energy.

August 2021: *August 8 brings the new moon. On August 20, Uranus goes retrograde. August 22 is the full moon. Your High-Energy Days are 1, 7, 13, 19, 25, and 31.*

As August begins, Tiger natives may hang back a little bit. You may work behind the scenes on a big project, putting the final touches on it. Or, you may be at the point where you are getting ready for school and having a last fling before the coming semester begins. This month you are at a transition point, a time when some things are ending, and some are just beginning. It's a good reminder if you're waiting for something to begin, you may first need to clear out something from the past.

On August 8, the new moon comes, highlighting communication. Tiger natives can be impulsive when expressing their feelings, and now people are paying attention. Notice how what you post affects others. This energy continues for a few weeks, and feedback becomes more positive towards the end of the month. Take professional tests for licensing or certification.

The positive side of focusing on communication is you can reach an agreement on something you've long hoped for. This can be in the context of a new job or an offer to sell your business. However, your home is also highlighted at this time. You may be planning an addition or expanding your space, renting a new apartment, or finding a vacation rental.

August 22 marks the full moon, and you're highly visible for the next couple of weeks. You may be on stage in some capacity, whether to lead a meeting or perform for an audience. You may launch a product for your business or sending your screenplay out for a critique. Your YouTube or Instagram channels may show a burst of new followers.

At the same time, Tiger natives receive a lot of attention at home from the smaller audience there. You may host a family get-together or a backyard barbecue. This can be a good time to re-arrange the furniture or lay new floors. Tiger natives who are dating may talk about living together.

September 2021: *September 7 brings the new moon. September 20 is the full moon. September 22 is the first day of autumn. September 26 has Mercury going retrograde. Your High-Energy Days are 6, 12, 18, 24, and 30.*

Now in September, romance energy is in the spotlight. Opportunities abound for single Tiger natives to meet someone new—perhaps a chance meeting at a coffee shop, or while you are involved in physical activities like hiking or walking.

September 7 brings the new moon. Some Tiger natives will be unpacking from a recent move or putting the last touches on a home renovation project. But most Tiger natives will be dealing with their current housing situation. You may suddenly be the focus of your neighbors, or there may be noise complaints relating to construction in the area. While your current neighborhood may still be a fine place to live for a time, you now have an underlying awareness that it may be time to move in the next year or so.

As the full moon comes in on September 20, Tiger natives can receive a favorable project evaluation at work. You might be given a new desk with a window, or be offered a work-at-home opportunity you've been hoping for. If you own a business, you or your company may be the recipient of highly favorable publicity at no cost to yourself.

The energy shifts, and on September 22, your thoughts focus on love and romance. If you've met someone recently, you will probably be seeing more and more of this person, enjoying their company, and introducing them to friends and family. Some Tiger natives may be dating more than one person and juggling their calendar.

On September 26, Mercury goes retrograde, and a business opportunity or risky investment comes back around as if to see if you're interested at this time. If this happens for the second or third time, and you've reviewed the same or very similar information the previous times, you may want to pause to consider why this opportunity keeps coming back to you. Maybe the offer isn't quite right for you in its current form. Perhaps it needs to be molded into something you would prefer. You have a lot of positive energy at this time. If you want to take a calculated risk, consider reading through the agreement one more time, and discussing likely future outcomes or possibilities with knowledgeable people.

October 2021: *October 6 brings the new moon, and Pluto goes direct. On October 11, Saturn goes direct. October 18 has Mercury*

going direct and Jupiter going direct. October 20 is the full moon.
Your High-Energy Days are 6, 12, 18, 24, and 30.

October is here, and at the beginning of the month, everything seems to be moving in slow motion. You keep pushing in every direction, trying to get others to respond—and all you hear is crickets. You'll have to cool your heels until this energy shifts. It will do so towards the middle of the month.

The new moon is October 6, and for the next two weeks, you can focus on having fun. If you have kids, you may be doing fun activities with them, going to their sporting events, or watching them in a school play. You could be arranging some festive projects yourself, perhaps hosting a wine and painting party, or a board game night with your friends. Explore Meetup groups to find others interested in writing or playing music.

On October 18, Mercury moves forward again. Now you hear from the businesses and important people you've been waiting to connect with. If you asked someone special out on a date, the answer is likely to be "Yes!" (even if you've had to wait for a bit). It's also possible someone interesting may have suggested you go on a date with them a couple of times in the past, and now you agree the time is right. A romance could be forming.

The October 20 full moon brings an emphasis on friendships and associations in general. If you belong to a professional networking or charity group, they may ask you to help with a fundraising event, possibly to run for a seat on the board. Join organizations, even virtual ones like Facebook groups, so that you can connect with like-minded people.

On October 22, the energy shifts towards productivity. You notice how often you're distracted or pulled away from tasks and projects which could benefit you in the future. Over the next two weeks, you are likely more mindful of how you use time. If you want to work on your side business, your novel, or your YouTube channel, but keep getting caught up in busy-work and things bringing no value to your life, you'll find the next few weeks most helpful!

November 2021: *November 4 is the new moon. November 19 is a partial Lunar Eclipse. Your High-Energy Days are 5, 11, 17, 23, and 29.*

November rolls around and, Tiger native, you may be considering how to celebrate the upcoming holidays. There may be an opportunity for you to travel to see family members living far away, even possibly in another country. You may not have done any traveling for some time, so this can be quite exciting. There's also the possibility of making the trip using ground transportation, perhaps an RV, a bus, or a train. Of course, every door swings both ways, and relatives may be planning to visit you in the next couple of months. Plans may be firmed up and reservations made in the next two weeks or so.

On November 4, there is a new moon, and you find work is busy, busier than you generally prefer. You may receive vague instructions from management, which leaves you feeling somewhat perturbed. At the same time, your side business is heating up as well. Your kids need more help with homework and projects. Your calendar is filled.

The Lunar Eclipse on November 19 ushers in some particularly intense energy for Tiger natives. Eclipses can bring change, but fortunately, Tiger natives are experts at pivoting and re-directing their focus. New modifications may be applied to your job. These are sufficiently substantial for you to consider whether or not you want to stay with the company in the future.

You make changes in your daily routine as well. You may start on a new diet or exercise plan to transform your health. Whatever adjustments happen now, know that in a few months, you will be happy they occurred. In the meantime, stay flexible and be prepared to leap when the opportunity appears.

There is an energy shift on November 21, and now relationships are highlighted. With all the changes that have happened in the past few days, now is the right time to have a serious conversation with your partner about how all of this is going to affect your lives. Indeed, it may be the right time to convene family meetings or talk things over with your extended family. All the important people in your life need to be informed. This way, they can be aware of how changes in your life may ripple into theirs.

December 2021: *December 1 has Neptune going direct. December 4 is a total Solar Eclipse. December 19 brings the full moon, and Venus goes retrograde. (Venus retrograde can cause you to question what you want and inspire you to look for something new that delights you. Venus will be retrograde until January.) December 21 is the first day of winter. Your High-Energy Days are 5, 11, 17, 23, and 29.*

December begins, and a great many Tiger natives are focused on relationships and partnerships. This may surprise you, since you possibly prefer to be more of a hermit this month. You may want to revert to your usual independent self, finding your own solutions, and making your own way in the world. But this month, you need to relate with other people—they hold keys to the opportunities you're searching for. You may decide to launch a business with a friend or a business partner, and need to be involved in long, detailed discussions. Or, this may be a perfect time to have a conversation with your sweetheart about the future. Additionally, you find so many opportunities for interactions with your friends.

December 4 brings the Solar Eclipse, and the vibrations of change now shift to the people in your life. Your significant other may be going through a job change that could end up moving the family. Your best friend may have decided to move back to their hometown. Tiger natives who are dating can discover their sweetheart may want to leap forward into a more committed relationship (an engagement or a move together?) with you. Decisions will have to be made together with these other people in your life.

December 19 brings the full moon, and at the same time, Venus goes retrograde. It's when the energy can smooth out somewhat, as decisions are made, and things are settled. Now is a time of adjustments, time for you to re-envision the parameters of your recent decisions to see if a greater change of direction is still necessary.

Love and romantic relationship energy remains strong, especially on the intimate side. With Venus retrograde, you could spend the night with somebody you don't know well, and then have some regrets the following morning. Use caution when it comes to these types of decisions now. For some Tiger natives, it's a time to be getting back together with someone from your past.

December 21 reveals the shifting energy, and life takes on a more serious tone. Study an overview of your financial activities during the past year and outline your intentions for the new year. It's time to look at your investment and debt repayment plans. Talk to your tax professional about end-of-year planning.

January 2022: *January 2 is the new moon. January 14 has Mercury going retrograde. January 17 is the full moon. On January 18, Uranus goes direct. On January 29, Venus goes direct. Your High-Energy Days are 4, 10, 16, 22, and 28.*

January begins as some of the dust settles from the changes of the past month. Tiger natives who are dating can now move toward a committed, monogamous relationship. Happiness grows as you focus on communicating with each other and having fun together. For those Tiger natives in an established relationship, positive energy abounds—especially in every aspect of your intimate life. There is a lot of fun behind closed doors.

January 2 brings the new moon, and you may be impatient for the fresh new energy to begin next month. However, you're in the last month of the Metal Ox year, and it is time to finish up the little bits left from the previous 12-year cycle. It's a good idea to project possibilities and plan where you want to be a year from now, three years from now, and five years from now. Sit down with trusted friends (choosing some of the more or most adventurous ones) and talk about your plans.

On January 14, Mercury goes retrograde, slowing down the energy. Now, be careful about leaping too soon. You're still in the planning stages for the future, and so even if you want to jump into a business or a new relationship, now is the time to be patient. (It's rare when things move as quickly as a Tiger native wishes!)

There is a full moon on January 17, and if you're in school, things are in full swing. You pay a lot of attention to your projects right now. Consider investing and passive income sources. You could make money by getting a real estate license or other professional certification.

On January 19, the energy shifts, and your luck is very strong now. You feel the synchronicity as things come together. However, it may still not exactly be the energy you're wishing or waiting for. Perhaps a job comes your way, but it may not offer the right pay or the actual duties or type of work you're looking for. You may have to wait just a few more weeks to find yourself in the full flow of Tiger energy in 2022.

February 2022: *February 1 is the new moon and begins the Year of the Water Tiger.*

At the end of the month, your big year officially begins. Water Tiger year will bring you many new opportunities. The Universe sees the plans you've made over the past few weeks and will send signs to light up the road ahead of you. It's going to be an exciting year.

Attract New Love

The fun is in the chase, right? Well, there is some chasing going on in 2021. When you get tired, you can stop running, and the other person will chase you. It can be lots of fun until it's not. Keep the spark alive and make things interesting by being unpredictable and downright eccentric from time to time.

Look for alternative places to go and things to do you've never done before. You might feel quite at home in Meetup groups with devoted hobbyists or lifetime learners. They can show you how commitment to a person, place, or thing can make life better. May can bring an opportunity for love; a love from your past may come back into your life. Around the holidays is the most likely time for you to be solidifying a relationship and perhaps taking it to the next level.

We are more sensitive to scent than any of our other senses. Odors influence our emotions and behaviors. Scent triggers memories in our brains and associations with those memories. Then we take action, even if we're not conscious of the reasons. Those small actions add up, bringing us closer to our goals.

The scent of vanilla is wonderful for attracting new love. You can find Vanilla extract in most grocery stores. Place a drop or two on cotton balls and place these in your bedroom. Place them behind a picture or on a small dish on your bedside table. You can also spray vanilla-scented air fresheners; however, the more natural the scent, the better. Or place a small amount of vanilla in a pot of boiling water on the stove and allow the aroma of vanilla to fill the house. While you do this, visualize the love relationship you want coming to you.

Enhance Existing Love

You enjoy a great deal of compatibility in your existing love relationship this year. You seem to get along better than ever. While you both have strong opinions about politics, your faith, and who knows the answer to this week's sports trivia question, there is still lots of laughter. Adventure is possible when you shrug off slights and don't take things personally (it's not something you do anyway).

This is a good year to travel together or study something side-by-side. Things you do as a couple can strengthen the bonds of your relationship year. It's desirable if you want to explore other spiritual paths to see what they have to offer, or if you want to delve more deeply into the faith you share by bringing it into your daily lives.

If you're in an existing relationship and want to increase the fidelity energy and overall happiness, place a pair of Mandarin Ducks on your bedside table or dresser. These ducks mate for life, and they are a symbol of marital bliss. They can be so attached to each other that when separated, they will pine away and die.

Mandarin ducks are primarily used, because they are considered the best of the species in intelligence and beauty. Their energy symbolizes felicity. They often display them with the lotus blossom, which emerges from the mud pure.

Looking to Conceive?

Pine cones are a great fertility symbol. Think of how a little seed grows between the hard petals of the cone. You can display a basket of scented pine cones in your family room or bedroom to promote conception energy. Eating pine nuts is also said to bring on good sexual relations, leading to a future joyful event. You can add the nuts to a salad or create a decadent dessert with honey and increase your odds of getting pregnant.

(From Donna Stellhorn's book, A Path to Pregnancy: Ancient Secrets for the Modern Woman)

Family and Kids

There's a great deal of positive energy for Tiger natives in home and family. Most everyone seems to get along. There is a lot of activity at home, perhaps because of construction projects, or preparation for a move in the next year. People who live with you come together to pool resources for larger projects and the success of the household. Starting a family business together can now be a good idea.

Fertility energy is intense, and there may be an addition to the family through birth or adoption this year, or early in 2022. Children excel at school, even though they spend a lot of time on their electronics. Adult children may discover that they want to go back to school, or to look at some licensing options in order to provide a boost to their career.

Your symbol of protection this year is the Dragonfly. Dragonflies are associated with harmony, good luck, power, and adaptability. When dragonflies are in your life, they remind you of joy and letting the wind guide you. In ancient Japan, dragonflies were a symbol used by Samurai warriors to represent agility and victory.

Find dragonfly symbols to place near your front door. You can place them inside the home or on the front porch. The dragonfly motif can be in wind chimes, painted on pots or metal sculptures hung so they seem to fly on their own. You can use one or many. Odd numbers are best.

Money

This year you have quite a few monetary opportunities; however, you can feel some impatience due to the delay between the time you learn of an opportunity and manifest it. Your impatience could overturn some positive outcomes, so take a deep breath and allow things to unfold in the time they take. As often is the case for Tiger natives, you find many opportunities when you explore new technology, new directions in your industry, or learn new things you can apply to your current job. Many of the opportunities will manifest in the second half of the year. In the meantime, it's good to focus on the connections you can make in your industry, as you improve your skill set.

One Feng Shui cure to attract positive career energy is the gemstone citrine. Citrine is a form of quartz with a gold or yellow color. Find one in its natural form or polished smooth. Either will be an excellent choice for this purpose. Place your citrine specimen on the desk in your home office or on your desk at work. You can also place a small citrine gemstone in your car to bring positive financial energy to your everyday tasks.

Job or Career

As you come to the end of your 12-year cycle, you may find your current job causes you to feel a little stuck. You feel ready to leap into something new, but an established landing pad isn't in place yet. This can cause some slight frustration as you impatiently envision a better future. It's also possible you're completing your education. It can take a little more time until the diploma is in hand before a new job appears.

For Tiger natives, there are a lot of opportunities in healthcare, creative fields, and entertainment. Any field where you have a vision for something bigger, where you want to reach more people, and make a large impact on the world will work well with the energy this year. Putting effort into your own business is good, but it's ideal to find a business mentor to guide you.

Sometimes in Feng Shui, we combine multiple symbols to create a powerful cure. The symbol of a bowl is to "welcome something new into our space." If the bowl is made of brass, we have the energy of success and prosperity.

So, for this cure, place a small brass bowl on your entryway table. You can leave the bowl empty or put coins and crystals in it. You can also place a list of your wishes describing your new, awaited career.

Education

There's a lot of emphasis on education this year, especially on completing a program begun a while back. You may have to make some changes to your school plan if they do not offer the classes you want this year. You may also think about changing your major or looking into an accelerated program. All of this is a good idea. Self-directed or self-study programs are perfect for Tiger natives this year.

Stick with educational programs you're interested in, rather than those you think are popular or moneymakers. If you lose interest in the subject, you could end up wasting money. There are some funding opportunities available for you this year, but finding them will take focused investigation. Enlist relatives and friends to help you look for scholarships or grants.

Legal Matters

This is the year of a lot of energy and activity in the area of your life affected by contracts and agreements. You may sell large items, your business, or even your home. It's tempting to hastily finalize contracts, but this can cause you to miss important points—especially regarding the time outlined in the agreement, or details about interest payments.

It will be a good idea to sleep on agreements before signing them. May, June, and December are when it's most likely you can change your mind after signing. So if you're executing an agreement during one of these months, take extra care that you are happy with all the various aspects of the contract before you finalize everything with your signature.

In this Year of the Metal Ox, the temptation or need to begin a lawsuit will arise. This will probably be a small claim, and can be settled out of court with some quick action.

Health and Well-Being

Tiger natives have extra energy this year. The Metal Ox year's rhythm could energize you more than usual, especially later in the day, even if you typically are a morning person. You may have to adjust your schedule during the year until this rhythm smooths itself out. There can be benefits in changing your diet, focusing on a more healthy diet. You might also switch to a more mindful way of dining. Slowing down your meals will also help.

For Tiger natives, traveling can affect your health this year. You want to take extra precautions when you're on the road. This is particularly true in November. When adding exercise into your routine, try to combine exertion with a little bit of adventure—add rock climbing, hiking, or surfing into your workouts.

The leaves of the eucalyptus tree have long been recognized for their healing qualities. Even smelling the leaves helps.

Branches of eucalyptus are available in craft and florist shops. Find six to nine cuttings from a eucalyptus tree and bring these into your home. Place them in a vase (vases represent peace in Feng Shui).

Display your eucalyptus near where you cook or eat, maybe in the kitchen or dining room. About once a month, gather the leave and branches and go outside to give them a good shake. Remove excess dust throughout the month. Keeping your eucalyptus plant looking beautiful will help attract positive energy to your home.

Rabbit

January 29, 1903–February 15, 1904: Yin Water Rabbit
February 14, 1915–February 2, 1916: Yin Wood Rabbit
February 2, 1927–January 22, 1928: Yin Fire Rabbit
February 19, 1939–February 7, 1940: Yin Earth Rabbit
February 6, 1951–January 26, 1952: Yin Metal Rabbit
January 25, 1963–February 12, 1964: Yin Water Rabbit
February 11, 1975–January 30, 1976: Yin Wood Rabbit
January 29, 1987–February 16, 1988: Yin Fire Rabbit
February 16, 1999–February 4, 2000: Yin Earth Rabbit
February 3, 2011–January 22, 2012: Yin Metal Rabbit
January 22, 2023–February 9, 2024: Yin Water Rabbit

Rabbit Personality

It may surprise many, but I consider Rabbit one of the strongest Chinese Zodiac signs. Most imagine him as a fluffy bunny, an animal who cannot speak, has no claws, and short little legs to hop away with. But the Rabbit sits between the Chinese Signs of the Tiger and the Dragon in the Chinese Zodiac wheel, and he alone keeps these two powerful forces apart.

Rabbit (also called Hare in some translations) generally serves as the sign of kindness and sensitivity. People born under this sign have good manners, common sense, and the ability to soothe and comfort others. For this reason, Rabbit often winds up in a leadership position.

The Rabbit personality is neither forceful nor rash, and they have a way of bringing people together. Rabbit is the perfect arbitrator, networking expert, negotiator, or diplomat. They always have something positive to say about and to everyone.

Because of Rabbit's love of peace, people mistakenly view them as weak, or even self-indulgent. Rabbit prefers to apply brain over brawn and will avoid a confrontation whenever possible. Often perceived as thin-skinned, Rabbit is merely cautious—after all, they don't want to be on anyone's menu! Rabbit can be a treasured friend, adept at keeping secrets and offering very sensible advice.

Rabbit people run in the best circles. They enjoy the finer things in life—everything from the restaurant's best table to the best parking space at the mall. Rabbit natives seek the easy way to do things, and often this leads to the best side of town. They tend to be a little flashy at times, which helps them fit in perfectly with their A-list friends.

Rabbit is realistic, yet sympathetic. They will listen to your troubles, and while they offer brilliant advice, they never push an agenda. As a parent, they are neither the disciplinarian nor are they given to criticism. They are optimistic and rarely embarrass their children in public.

In business, Rabbit's quiet, unassuming air can cause others to think they are not paying attention. But there's more to Rabbit than meets the eye. Before you know it, you have signed the contract or sealed the deal—with Rabbit taking the lion's share of the rewards. Despite this (and because of Rabbit's impeccable manners), you come away feeling grateful Rabbit was even willing to do business with you.

Rabbit: Predictions for 2021

How to use your High-Energy Days: On these days, plan to take action for your most important goals, make vital phone calls, send important emails. Your high-energy days are when your energy and luck are the strongest for the month.

January 2021: *Uranus goes direct on January 14. Mercury goes retrograde from January 30 to February 20. Your Lucky Days are 4, 10, 16, 22, 28. [How to use your Lucky Days: On these days, plan to take significant actions, make vital phone calls, send emails. These are days when your energy and luck are high.]*

Finances are the highlight this month, and you may receive a small windfall from a passive income source. You may sell something, or money owed to you finds its way back into your pocket. Still, if you overspent during the past few months, you may now feel the pinch.

Now, at the end of the Metal Rat year, you have an opportunity to bring in more money as a result of your creative thinking or actual creative work. Consider your talents and see what you can produce, something others may want, or tell you they want. This is also a time to sell off excess stuff. Rabbit natives can be exceptionally sentimental, but that doesn't mean you need to hold on to your great aunt's dishes if you're never going to use them.

Work is going well. Your team is melding together nicely. If you were behind on a deadline before, you're catching up now. If you own your own business, a new system or piece of tech is working out well. Consider automating more systems in your business.

You have grown a lot spiritually and emotionally this year. You have this last month of Metal Rat year to clear out a little more emotional gunk. You can do this through journaling or perhaps a burning ceremony with friends where you each burn little pieces of paper on which you have written down what you want to release.

A friendship can turn into a romance now. If you're looking for love, this can be a great opportunity. If you're already in a love relationship, you may want to think twice before jumping into this sack.

February 2021: *The Lunar New Year begins on February 12, Happy Year of the Metal Ox. February 20 has Mercury going direct. February 27 is the full moon. Your High-Energy Days are 3, 9, 15, 21, and 27.*

February brings opportunities related to assets and resources you receive from others. Several people are stepping up to help you, but not actually doing the things you asked them to do. While gratified that they are willing to help you out, you may have to restate what you want. In the first two weeks of this month, we are still in the Metal Rat energy, so being direct about stating your desires is pi.

The new moon and the year of the Metal Ox begin on February 12. The energy shifts to a much more harmonious pace for Rabbit natives. Soon, you feel a stronger sense of community, people coming together to help each other. As you go through this year rebuilding your life after the events of 2020, you see others connect with you significantly. Over the next two weeks, a person may step forward to inform you about grants, loans, or government programs that can help you.

On February 20, Mercury goes direct and begins to move forward again. Now is an excellent time to make progress on debt repayment as well as applications for financial accounts. You're more likely to connect with bankers or decision-makers who can help you with the process. Help is now available for those who are saddled with student loans.

Intimacy increases now, and you have both energy and time to spend with a special other. They are also feeling an increased interest in spending time with you. This can mean a dating relationship grows much more personal. A connection can go from platonic to downright sexy during the next couple of weeks! For those Rabbit natives in an established relationship, you can enjoy some extra fun behind closed doors.

The full moon comes in on February 27, highlighting contracts and legal documents. Communication of all kinds gain importance now, but it's good for Rabbit natives to pay particular attention to the written format. Use caution signing agreements, especially if you're feeling rushed. This is particularly true for contracts involving employment or related to your business.

March 2021: *March 13 brings the new moon. March 20 marks the first day of spring. March 28 is the full moon. Your High-Energy Days are 5, 11, 17, 23, and 29.*

In March, you may find it easier to do things yourself rather than wait for others to help you. Additionally, when you work with colleagues or other people in professional circumstances, they may not fully understand what you want to accomplish. Therefore, they offer you results that are not helpful. That said, you have a great deal of positive energy around forging ahead on your own. This is true when it comes to working with technology, launching a new product for your business, or getting your resume ready to apply for a new job or project.

The new moon comes in on March 13 and draws your attention to matters related to education, licensing, and certifications. You may be completing a certification course, which might be useful in your current job or a future career opportunity. This final exam could be a high hurdle, but you can clear it. You may find yourself procrastinating instead of studying, but now is the time to keep your eyes on the finish line.

The energy shifts on March 20, and you may receive recognition from a manager or someone you respect at work. Post this for all the world to see on professional websites like LinkedIn. You may also receive a letter of recommendation to use for future job hunting.

On March 28, there is the full moon and a great deal of emphasis on your home. The house needs some repairs, chiefly around windows, air conditioning, heating, fans, or anything involving air flow. You show good luck finding competent service providers, but scheduling can be a little tricky. You may have to give up a fun outing with friends to have the right service provider over to make the needed repairs.

Your intuition is elevated during this time. Consider taking a class on improving psychic ability or the skill of psychic self-defense. It can be an online course or arranged through a group you already belong to.

April 2021: *April 12 brings the new moon. April 27 is the full moon, and Pluto goes retrograde. (Pluto moving backward can cause you to reconsider your basic assumptions about life and to eliminate what is unnecessary, bringing you back to what is essential. Pluto will be retrograde until October.) Your High-Energy Days are 4, 10, 16, 22, and 28.*

Along comes April, and there's a great deal of energy around your health and well-being. You may focus on your exercise plan, seeking something more enjoyable, or an activity to motivate you. Consider doing something involving dance or continuous light movement, such as cycling for pleasure, walking, or skating.

The new moon comes in on April 12, bringing a focus on career and success. Others notice topics you are posting about on social media sites. Your reputation is expanding, and others realize how valuable your ideas are. At the same time, you can sometimes be hesitant about putting your ideas out into the world. However when your heart centers on helping others, your information is received with pleasure.

The energy shifts on April 19, and you get to spend some time catching up with friends. Someone you haven't spoken to in a long time may reconnect with you; the initial contact may take place on social media. It might surprise you to hear they now live much closer to you than you thought, and you may begin to think about a time in the future when you may be able to get together.

The full moon lights the night sky on April 27 and begins a high activity period, which will last for the next couple of weeks. During this time, you may take some risks—possibly in the area of love. Cupid's arrow could possibly strike rabbit natives who are dating! A situation where you thought you were not interested at all may now cause you to feel quite "over the moo." The energy flows in both directions, so you may find yourself chased by love as well.

May 2021: *May 11 brings the new moon. On May 23, Saturn goes retrograde. (Saturn retrograde can cause you to review your career choices and make needed adjustments. Saturn will be retrograde until October). May 26 is a total Lunar Eclipse. May 29 has Mercury going retrograde. Your High-Energy Days are 4, 10, 16, 22, and 28.*

During May, you are likely to feel more confident. Opportunities abound for you to pursue, all of them connected to your most important goals. The future is spread out in front of you, and now you just need to take some action. There's no reason to wait for others, even if they have promised to open doors for you. You can move forward on your own. That said, once you start to move in the right direction, others do show up to help guide and support you.

May 11 brings the new moon, right along with the possibility of receiving an increase in salary. This may be due to you receiving an offer from another company, or as a result of you stepping up to remind your supervisor you are overdue for a raise. There's also the possibility of a greater amount of sales, thus an increased commission payment. If you own a business, you are likely enjoying an increase in revenue as well.

The energy shifts on May 20, and, Rabbit native, you may need a break. You have been hopping pretty much continuously for months now. Plan to take some time off, even if it's just a long weekend. Try some alternative methods to see if you can enjoy more restful sleep by changing a few things in the bedroom. Consider adjusting the airflow in the room, getting a fan, and allowing the white noise to lull you to sleep.

On May 26, a Lunar Eclipse triggers some changes at your job. There can be some changes in personnel directly affecting your work. Someone on your team may leave the company, or there could be an addition to your team, along with added duties distributed by higher-ups. At the same time, you're working behind the scenes on significant projects. This is especially true if you're in school. Eclipses often bring change and so you can see the changes as they begin happening; however, this year is different from last year. Many of the changes you observe are happening to people around you. You're affected by the ripples rather than the changes happening directly to you.

June 2021: *June 10 is the annular Solar Eclipse. June 20 is the first day of summer, and Jupiter goes retrograde (Jupiter retrograde can indicate a need to relearn things or a time to review your personal rules. Jupiter will be retrograde until October). June 22 has Mercury going direct. June 24 is the full moon. On June 25, Neptune goes retrograde. (Neptune retrograde can draw you back towards habits and addictions from your past. It can also encourage a return to spiritual practices. Neptune will be retrograde until December). Your High-Energy Days are 3, 9, 15, 21, and 27.*

Now it's June, and there is vital energy for completing projects or things hanging over your head for some time. You may feel a great urge to clean out the garage, pantry, and walk-in closet. You're trying to simplify your life, to let go of anything holding you back. This may include entire categories of things—even hobbies you intended to pursue but don't enjoy anymore (needlepoint? car repair? collecting stamps?).

June 10 brings the Solar Eclipse. Over the next two weeks, you may experience increased intuition and a deeper spiritual connection. The Universe may be sending you signs in a dramatic, hard-to-ignore way. It's an excellent time to open up the lines of communication with your higher self through meditation or journaling.

On June 20, the energy shifts, and everything feels more harmonious. Things start to come together with much more ease. You feel more confident, and others offer compliments on how you look and how lovely your smile is. Start a new exercise routine, one that involves walking or swimming.

Mercury goes direct, moving forward again on June 22. A project you've been working on for some time is completed. Now it's off your desk, and you have more time for rest and relaxation. Now you have time to enjoy an art project or catch up on TV shows you've been missing.

On June 24, there is a full moon, and it highlights relationships. If you're already in a love relationship, you may notice that you are becoming much closer. You are more likely to finish each other's sentences and to agree on most things. If you're dating, you may begin discussing whether or how to move your relationship to a new level—perhaps moving together or getting engaged. If you are not in a happy relationship, consider how you might be blocking romance due to difficulties you experienced in the past. As you recognize how much you have grown since then, you realize you have more reasons to feel confident. Now you can move forward and meet new people.

July 2021: *July 10 brings the new moon. July 24 is the full moon. Your High-Energy Days are 3, 9, 15, 21, and 27.*

Starting in early July, Rabbit's attention centers on finances and spending habits. You may have some additional expenses this month (or you're doing some extra shopping). At the same time, you may notice some slight tremors in your career path. You may hear rumors from others in the company about changes coming from upper management. This is related to a potential merger or shift in the org-chart. While your job looks pretty secure, you may be saddled with additional responsibilities and feel you're not making progress on your career path.

July 10 brings the new moon and one of the most significant two-week periods of your year. There is powerful relationship energy happening. Rabbit natives looking for love should let friends and family know that it's okay for them to fix you up on dates. If you're using online dating sites, start frequently logging in to monitor who is viewing your profile.

Also, during these two weeks, your confidence continues to increase. It's a good idea to put yourself forward in all kinds of social situations. If you'd like to lead your local Parent-Teacher Association or join the choir, now is the time to let your wishes known.

The energy shifts on July 22, and in the next couple weeks, you may receive a windfall in the form of cash or items. You may have mentioned in passing that you want something, and now a friend or family member is stepping forward to make it happen.

The full moon happens on July 24, and there's considerable energy around investments, credit cards, and banking. You may review passive income strategies or do some retirement planning. This is a favorable time to get your paperwork in order, shred old records, and maybe go paperless. During this time, you may discover some errors in your files. Now you can take steps to remedy this situation.

August 2021: *August 8 brings the new moon. On August 20, Uranus goes retrograde. August 22 is the full moon. Your High-Energy Days are 2, 8, 14, 20, and 26.*

August arrives, and for Rabbit natives, it highlights money derived from a career. There could be some changes in your salary. Positive changes come from making career shifts or transferring within your company. Be aware of whether or not the underlying financial prospects of your current company are healthy—there could be pay cuts in the future. Overall, your financial success options are good, but if the company you work for is not doing well, you'll need to make a change to protect yourself.

On August 8, there is a new moon and, not surprisingly, an emphasis on finances. Now you can call in money from several sources. Perhaps you sell items you no longer need, or your side business is starting to take off. Stick to a written budget to keep track of what is coming in and going out. Finally, you can do a little money magic, re-energizing your Feng Shui cures by dusting them off or moving each item to a new location.

On August 22, there is a rather intense full moon. This energy is about intellectually knowing that something is finished, but continuing to hang on emotionally. Over the next two weeks, you may be unwilling to let go because you still hope things will work out even if there is every sign indicating the contrary. Rabbit natives can be willful, and while you have no problem making changes, you don't like to be pushed. If someone else is suggesting you should let go, you might hold on even tighter.

At this time, consider some of the decisions you're making; see if you're on the right track. Rabbit natives, known for their quick thinking, can rapidly pivot when necessary. Now you can remove internal blocks. Obstacles fall away as though made of dust. You could mow make the most significant leap forward of the entire year.

September 2021: *September 7 brings the new moon. September 20 is the full moon. September 22 is the first day of autumn. On September 26, Mercury goes retrograde. Your High-Energy Days are 1, 7, 13, 19, and 25.*

Here comes September with a strong emphasis on communication. This could involve siblings or younger relatives. You may have a chance to get together with a relative you haven't seen in some time. They may be coming for a visit, or you're traveling to see them. While the plans are being made, you have a chance to talk with one another and build a closer relationship.

On September 7, there's a new moon highlighting your area of contracts and agreements. Something you have been waiting for now becomes available to you. Some negotiation is needed to get it right. At the same time, you don't want to wait too long, as Mercury will go retrograde towards the end of the month. This deal could bring you a windfall. However, be sure to read the fine print because you have an opportunity to negotiate some of the finer points before this deal is put to bed.

The full moon comes in on September 20, and education becomes the focus. You may be going back to college, or your kids are back in school, and everyone is trying to get into a new routine. Studying can be challenging right now; there can be a lot going on at home or lots of noise in the neighborhood. Find a quiet spot in the house to dedicate to studying whether you're in school or not. Having a comfortable place where you can concentrate can bring lots of benefits.

On September 22, the energy shifts, and there's a lot of activity at home. There may be visits from friends, or you may be getting ready for an event. The home goes from being tidy to disheveled and then back to tidy. You're very aware of clutter right now.

On September 26, Mercury goes retrograde. You may receive a contract for a new job position. If you usually work contract jobs, signing during a retrograde is no problem—future retrogrades can bring another contract. Otherwise, generally, it's not lucky to sign contracts for the first time during the Mercury retrograde period. You might regret taking the position, or the position becomes temporary.

October 2021: *October 6 brings the new moon, and Pluto goes direct. On October 11, Saturn goes direct. October 18 has Mercury going direct and Jupiter going direct. October 20 is the full moon. Your High-Energy Days are 1, 7, 13, 19, 25, and 31.*

October brings your attention back to your finances, as income increases, and you make plans for what you will do with the extra cash. You may be paying down debts or funding your retirement accounts. You could be learning about investing, whether in stocks and bonds or real estate. It's essential to be very familiar with the investment method you choose. Only learning a few things halfway by watching a few videos will not bring you success.

On October 6, the new moon brings a lot of energy around the family. Someone in the family may need your help and call on you for assistance. This may pertain to a financial matter, but they more likely need your guidance. Rabbit natives don't mind giving advice, but you can feel bad when your advice is ignored. In this case, this person may not listen (but they still love and respect you).

There is energy around your dwelling. For Rabbit natives moving this month, experience challenges getting your items from one place to another without breakage. Consider buying extra insurance, at least for things that are very near-and-dear to you.

October 18 has Mercury going direct. Now you can sign an employment agreement and start the job. If you've been holding off on starting projects, now is the time to engage—full steam ahead. On an unrelated note, Mercury moving direct could trigger a special someone to start calling you again. You may have wondered about their silence, but, likely, they have just been extremely busy. Now, this relationship can pick up again.

On October 20, there's a full moon and an emphasis on your career. Your reputation is strong, and other people are noticing the good job you're doing. You may receive some accolades from the boss, and you can use these when you are seeking a promotion or a raise. It's also possible your company is moving, and they will offer you a work-at-home position or a new office.

October 22, the energy shifts, and there is a great deal of interest in children and creativity. If you enjoy creating art, you now have a few weeks to indulge in your passion. This is a splendid time to participate in an art show or put your artwork online. Fertility energy is also increased at this time. You find helpful people who can aid you in getting fertility treatments or moving an adoption forward.

November 2021: *November 4 is the new moon. November 19 is a partial Lunar Eclipse. Your High-Energy Days are 6, 12, 18, 24, and 30.*

Now November is here, and things are going on in the neighborhood. You may be friends with some neighbors who have decided to move away. While you will miss them, you're happy for the new opportunities they are gaining. Let the Universe know what kind of neighbors you want in their place.

On November 4, there's a new moon with an emphasis on love and romance. For those Rabbit natives looking for love, this is a great time to be putting yourself out there. Consider attending charity events to add to the usual social activities you enjoy. This is a great time to find a matchmaker or sign up with an online dating site. Invite your friends and family to set you up on a blind date. You've been doing a lot of work on yourself, and now you are ready to find someone extraordinary to have in your life.

On November 19, there is a Lunar Eclipse. Lunar eclipses bring a desire to make changes in your life. You may feel you're not having much fun, not spending the amount of time with your friends as you would like, and it's time to remedy that situation. Think about the tasks you do daily and see what you can streamline, delegate, or even eliminate. As you free up more time for yourself, you can make a point of connecting with friends who, in turn, feel excited about spending more time with you.

The energy shifts on November 21, bringing an urgent matter at work to the forefront, a task which takes up a chunk of your free time, perhaps even your weekend. The office may be short-handed, or there's just more work coming in. If you own your own business, this sudden burst of activity can benefit your bottom line. Still, it does have you working some extra hours. You might feel that just when you were ready to enjoy more free time, you've become busier than ever. However, this is a temporary situation that will clear up in a week or so.

December 2021: *December 1 has Neptune going direct. December 4 is a total Solar Eclipse. December 19 brings the full moon, and Venus goes retrograde. (Venus retrograde can cause you to question what you want and inspire you to look for something new and delightful. Venus will be retrograde until January.) December 21 is the first day of winter. Your High-Energy Days are 6, 12, 18, 24, and 30.*

December is here, and you're likely enjoying your home. If you've recently moved, it's good to finish unpacking. During this month, you may complete some renovations or touch-ups. You may shop for some new furnishings to brighten up your space. Your place is ready to be the family destination for the holidays.

On December 4, there's a Solar Eclipse that could affect your working environment. Now and more comprehensive changes are happening around your job. It's possible a key person is leaving the department or the company, and you may be stepping into their role (not as an official promotion but as an interim person). There can be even bigger changes for you if the company where you work is small and financially unstable. The company may be going into bankruptcy protection, or another company could even acquire it. To stabilize your position, check in with favorite managers to see if you can obtain more information about what is happening at the top. You have good opportunities for job change at this point. But often, Rabbit natives remain in a difficult situation out of a sense of loyalty.

The full moon comes on December 19, and at the same time, Venus goes retrograde. The energy settles down quite a bit from the previous month. Many of the expected changes rumored to be taking place within your company may get delayed until January 2022. You may have already made a job shift and are all set to start very soon. You're busier than usual with your job and the activity at home.

When Venus is retrograde, holiday shopping can be difficult. The things you look for may be hard to find, and you can struggle to locate the right gift for the people you care about. Even when shopping for yourself, it may be difficult to find what you want at the price you're willing to pay. Try not to stress during this time, if possible. When you need to shop, give yourself more time than usual, or do your shopping online.

On December 21, the energy shifts towards relationships and love. For single Rabbit natives, you may have a wonderful date for Christmas or to celebrate the New Year. If you're already in a love relationship, you can feel loved and admired over the holidays. Not only your sweetheart, but others in your family are lining up to tell you how important you are to them and how much joy you add to their lives.

January 2022: *January 2 is the new moon. Mercury goes retrograde on January 14. January 17 is the full moon. On January 18, Uranus goes direct. On January 29, Venus goes direct. Your High-Energy Days are 3, 9, 15, 21, and 27.*

January is the final month of the Metal Ox year, and it brings good relationship energy for Rabbit natives. This means you can connect with new friends and find suitable business partners. Those Rabbit natives currently in a love relationship enjoy an abundance of harmony at home. And if you're looking for love, it can come from a surprising direction, or as a result of a chance meeting or a blind date.

On January 2, there's the new moon and a lot of connections with friends. People are calling you out of the blue, looking to reconnect. Invitations come in, and you may connect with many people you haven't seen in some time.

On January 14, Mercury goes retrograde and brings an emphasis on your finances. It's now time to evaluate what has been coming in and what has been going out. Check your bank statements and make sure there's been no fraudulent activity on your accounts. (You may want to pull your credit report and see how you're doing on that front.) This is an excellent time to take classes in investing.

On January 17, there's a full moon, and you feel more confident and self-assured. You have been working hard on relationships and doing a great deal of inner work on yourself. You've been through a lot over the past two years, and you have every reason to be proud of how you've grown. You find you're more confident when doing job interviews and interacting with others in general. This attracts a lot of positive attention and, for those Rabbit natives looking for love, this can make finding the right someone much easier.

On January 19, the energy shifts, and you may receive a windfall or financial benefit from investments. This is an excellent time to consider how you can expand passive income sources or build your own business. This is not a time for taking big risks; it's about doing what you know how to do and allowing more money to flow in. This is a great time to refresh your Feng Shui cures to bring in prosperity.

February 2022: *February 1 is the new moon and begins the Year of the Water Tiger. February 3 has Mercury going direct. February 16 brings the full moon.*

Now the Water Tiger takes the stage, and the energy starts to speed up all around you. However, this has little effect on you. You continue to move to the beat of your own drummer. As you look ahead, you see many opportunities, so it's time to make some plans.

Attract New Love

Love is available to you, Rabbit native, as soon as you're clear about what you want. It may be necessary to let go of the past, including a love relationship you felt "could have been great," to embrace someone new this year. Sexual and romantic compatibility are likely with this new person. This relationship may start as a friendship and turn romantic. You may get an introduction from a friend of a friend. Good places to meet a soul connection are at investment meetings, real estate gatherings, and spiritual health seminars. A change in your workout routine in May could bring someone with whom you have great chemistry, and a new relationship can begin.

Make the act of finding new love easy and fun by displaying dolphins in your bedroom. You can hang a painting or a photograph, or place a statue, or even toss a couple of cute stuffed dolphins on your bed. If you choose a picture, hang it where you can see from your bed. Choose an image that has more than one dolphin. If you want a lot of love opportunities, choose a picture of a school of dolphins. But have at least two dolphins in the room to represent you in a relationship.

Enhance Existing Love

In the year of the Metal Ox, Rabbit natives enjoy harmony in relationships on many practical levels. But some emotional disconnects happen this year from time to time. Remedy these by spending a little extra time explaining what you need. There is excitement in the bedroom, harmony in financial matters, and vacations are joyful. What may be missing are the little comments you make showing the other person you're paying attention, and that you are grateful this person is in your life. This energy flows both directions, so you don't feel appreciated at times as well. These little hurt feelings can grow into a mighty storm. Don't let things get blown out of proportion over a few missed opportunities.

The sweet, soft sounds of a flute have been used in Feng Shui for ages to bring harmony to the home's energy. This year, create harmony in your existing love relationship by hanging flutes. Simply take a pair of wooden flutes and hang them in the bedroom. Use a piece of red ribbon or string and tie the ends around each end of the flute. This will give you an easy way to hang the flute. See the diagram for hanging flutes below.

Looking to Conceive?

For those born in the year of the Rabbit, it's a year to deepen your existing love relationship. You are independent, but everything is easier with someone who cares about you. This year, find some pearls to bring into the bedroom. It can be a strand of pearls or a single pearl. Pearls have been worn by people in many countries to increase happiness in marriage. Pearls are said to increase loving vibrations in the people around them.

(From Donna Stellhorn's book, A Path to Pregnancy: Ancient Secrets for the Modern Woman)

Family and Kids

You can enjoy many good times at home, even though family members scatter in different directions and seem to focus on doing their own thing. You can bring everyone together for special events, often through family dinners, game nights, or backyard barbecues. This will help you support each other. A financial venture could bring extended family members together to contribute wisdom and resources. Investments made on the house itself through renovation or room additions can be quite beneficial. This is a good year for happy relationships with children. Adult children may visit more often or even move home for a little while. Fertility energy is also intense. You may welcome an addition to the family through a birth of a child or adopting a pet.

The lotus flower is a sacred symbol of wisdom, purity, and spirituality. Use this symbol to bring protection and harmony into your home. You can use pictures of lotus flowers or find a figurine of a beautiful lotus blossom to place on a table in the family room or living room. It's also said that a lotus flower can unlock a locked door. This symbol is to help you unlock better relationships with everyone at home.

Money

Careful Rabbit natives can e9xpect an outstanding financial year—one where you can see lots of growth and opportunities. The only caveat is you will need to think outside your comfort zone just a little bit. Some investment opportunities will feel more experimental. In that case, you should just put your toe into the water and avoid investing heavily. On the flipside, you should not pass up opportunities to work with others, to pool resources, to consider long-term investments. You may have incurred some debt over the past few years, and now you have the opportunity to catch up and get things paid down—notably towards the end of the year. As with most things, rewards come when you pay attention and are mindful of your finances. This year, count your pennies, and you will accumulate dollars.

When we experience the energy of change around money, we need to prepare for the worst and focus on the best. Think of what genuinely wonderful thing could happen this year concerning your income. Then think of something even better. Write the thought (your vision) on a small piece of paper and place it under a Diamond Energy Crystal. Place the Diamond Energy Crystal on a table near the front door or on your desk in your home office. Once a month, dust the crystal or wash it in water. When the wish you have written on the piece of paper is fulfilled, write a new wish and place it underneath the crystal.

Job or Career

Your career looks steady, in fact, quite busy. The issue may be that you have reached the top of a pay grade. It may be challenging to find ways to increase your income if you remain on this career path or stay at a specific company. You can find a variety of passive income opportunities, or you may create a side business. But if you want to focus on a traditional career, it may take some serious networking to find ways to increase your salary substantially. That said, work looks very steady, and you're in high demand. There are opportunities to transfer or shift teams in May, and at the end of the year around November or December. It's good to be ready to take one of these openings. Keep your resume current, and have lots of coffee meetings with colleagues who have moved on to better positions, either within your current company or with a competing company.

Lapis has been called the gemstone of kings. It's a blue, opaque stone with flecks of pyrite that sparkle like gold. It's often made into jewelry, but you can also find small, tumbled pieces to carry your pocket or purse. Wear or carry the stone to remind yourself of your value and worth. Wash the stone with soap and water about once a week to clear it. This will help re-energize the stone. You can also carry this stone with you when you're going on job interviews to give you a boost in that area. If you prefer not to carry the stone with you, place it on your desk at work or at home or put it where you do financial matters.

Education

Formal education may not be a huge focus this year. If you are in school, you may have trouble concentrating on your studies. You may be thinking about taking a gap year, or wondering whether you should shift your major. You may be doing a year of study consisting of more prerequisites than the subjects you truly want to study. This is a good year to check out alternative schools where you can design your course of study. Also, schools centered on a practical application of knowledge — such as studying to be a building contractor or nurse practitioner—are excellent choices for you this year. If you want to add skills to your resume, consider studying independently through Internet courses, as some offer a certificate of completion. That said, there are many education funding options available for you this year, especially if you think outside the box. It's worthwhile to do a little digging to find financial assistance for your education.

Legal Matters

This year you may have to wait a little longer for contracts or agreements to reach you. Rabbit natives may not feel very patient with this process. You may be waiting on a contract for employment or your business. But delays can work out in your favor, giving you more time to review materials and negotiate some of the finer points.

Avoid individual lawsuits, though you can engage in class action suits with some success (the financial rewards will take a year or more to manifest). Some legal matters could involve employment, child support, or matters concerning an estate. But most of the legal matters you will pursue this year are financial and for opportunities around business and the sale of items.

Health and Well-Being

You may take a more intuitive approach to your health this year, perhaps cleaning up your diet is one of those aspects.

Adding more root vegetables can help with your overall sense of vitality and energy. Healthy foods can help you feel more grounded, as well. This year it's okay to have a stop/start approach to diet and exercise. If you fall off the wagon, that's okay. Allow yourself to get back on track the next day.

When it comes to exercise, you may want to assemble a home gym or get some equipment you can use in the privacy of your own home. Your nighttime routine is much improved this year, and you could be getting more restful sleep. June may be an excellent month to replace your bed or redecorate your bedroom. May and December are good months to avoid risky situations such as participating in extreme sports or spending time around many ill people.

Consider adding the fragrant flower, jasmine, to your front yard or place a picture of jasmine in your bedroom if this is not possible. You can also have cut jasmine flowers in the bedroom about once a month. Artificial or silk flowers will work energetically for a few months but need to be cleaned or replaced to renew the energy. This pretty, night-blooming flower is said to bring sound sleep and prophetic dreams. In the morning, you will feel both rested and have an inner knowledge of what the day will hold.

Dragon

February 16, 1904–February 3, 1905: Yang Wood Dragon
February 3, 1916–January 22, 1917: Yang Fire Dragon
January 23, 1928–February 9, 1929: Yang Earth Dragon
February 8, 1940–January 26, 1941: Yang Metal Dragon
January 27, 1952–February 13, 1953: Yang Water Dragon
February 13, 1964–February 1, 1965: Yang Wood Dragon
January 31, 1976–February 17, 1977: Yang Fire Dragon
February 17, 1988–February 5, 1989: Yang Earth Dragon
February 5, 2000–January 23, 2001: Yang Metal Dragon
January 23, 2012–February 9, 2013: Yang Water Dragon
February 10, 2024–January 28, 2025: Yang Wood Dragon

Dragon Personality

When considering Chinese Zodiac animal qualities, it helps to examine the animal's traits, behaviors, and personality—except there are no dragons to study (at least not anymore). Dragons are listed in the Shuo Wen dictionary (200 AD), and it describes this creature: The Dragon has "the will and power of transformation and the gift of rendering itself visible or invisible at pleasure."

It is said there are three types of Dragon: one, the most powerful, inhabits the sky; the second lives in the ocean, and the third resides in dens (or caves) in the mountains. Some say a dragon can shrink to the size of the silkworm, or expand in size, lie down and fill up an entire lake! These powers describe the traits belonging to Dragon and explain why so many people envy the Dragon native.

The Dragon seems not to be of this world, and likewise, Dragon natives are seen to exist "above it all." They have big ideas and the power to make them happen. Even when young in years, Dragon will take on and carry enormous burdens and responsibilities.

Dragon natives can tap into a seemingly endless supply of energy, and they are eager to talk about their ideas. The Dragon has the potential to accomplish great things—or simply to fly around in the heavens, never allowing his or her feet to touch the ground.

Despite all of this magical power, people born in the Year the Dragon can have violent tempers (and explosive temper tantrums) when things don't go their way. Sometimes a Dragon is not diplomatic. They would much rather say what they want to say than tell others what they want to hear. When a Dragon breathes fire, everyone in the vicinity gets singed!

The Dragon native requires a clear purpose in life, a cause to champion, a wrong to right. No matter what Dragon does for a living, they will have their pet projects and dreams. Without these, Dragon becomes listless and depressed.

The Dragon is very skillful in finance and management. Dragon sensibly looks at long-term investing to protect their assets. Good at spending money, Dragon is always on the lookout for an innovation to adopt. Dragons rise to the top of whatever field they choose. They are often chosen to be the leader, even if they're new to the organization.

Dragons hate to be trapped, with no options for change. If stuck behind a desk or saddled with a long list of rules, Dragons will revolt. For all their seeming confidence, the Dragon can feel insecure on the inside. There is a constant struggle between the desire for success and the fear of success. They're status-conscious and don't like to fail, especially in the eyes of others. This causes them sometimes to shoot for small goals, rather than pursue big dreams.

Dragon is by far the largest personality of the Chinese zodiac. As the only mythical animal of the twelve, a Dragon can take on many forms.

Traditionally, a Dragon could manifest as a creature the size of a gigantic cloud formation to one as small as a butterfly. Because of this remarkable ability, Dragon holds the vision for our future in this world. They see where we are heading and are aware of where we should be going.

Dragon's confidence is as big as its personality. They motivate everyone around them. They undertake the greatest adventures, eager to experience wild success—or will endure crushing failure. There is no stopping a Dragon once their mind is made up. They will push right to the edge to see if they can make something happen. If things go wrong, well, that's when Dragon truly shines as a leader, the one to lead everyone out of danger.

Dragons have nothing to hide (Why should they? They have nothing to fear!). Their feelings are out in the open for everyone to see. Dragons do not keep secrets. After they share the news, the Dragon will tell you they were right to reveal everything. So, if you keep a Dragon as your confidant, be aware that whatever you have told them will come out, eventually.

Dragons are sensitive to the climate. Calm in pleasant weather, when a storm comes they become rattled or irritated. When a storm is on its way, it's time to steer clear of Dragon! Dragon doesn't mind either way—although nearly always surrounded by friends, they are perfectly happy spending time alone.

Dragon natives need a mission or a life purpose. When their life purpose is clear, Dragon can soar to heights other animals couldn't even dream of reaching. Dragon is very decisive. Once they've chosen a path, it's tough to dissuade them from continuing along it.

However, sometimes Dragon is not particularly smart in the realm of business. They don't pick up on the cunning of others. Dragon natives are often unaware of the plots and schemes surrounding them. Dragon is more concerned about reaching their goal and not willing to play the petty games of others.

The most challenging thing for a Dragon is the stubborn desire to do everything on their own! They never call for help, never ask for support. Dragon is powerful and can be intimidating; natives have a fiery temper and a fixed idea of the ways things should be. Dragon often speaks without editing, letting people know exactly what they think.

Dragon: Predictions for 2021

How to use your High-Energy Days: On these days, plan to take action for your most important goals, make vital phone calls, send important emails. Your high-energy days are when your energy and luck are the strongest for the month.

January 2021: *Uranus goes direct on January 14. Mercury goes retrograde from January 30 to February 20. Your Lucky Days are 5, 11, 17, 23, 29.*

As the Lunar year comes to a close, you're a little more emotional, even sentimental, than usual. The positive energy combined with Dragon native's natural luck has brought you some real benefits. There have been some challenges, but you've grown during this Metal Rat year, and so has your status in the world.

You may have a job opportunity land unexpectedly in your lap. It could come from a former colleague who now wants to bring you on board their new company. You need to discuss this with the entire family if it means relocating the household.

Romance is in the air, and your powers of attraction are high. If you're looking for love, you can meet new, intriguing individuals in places where people have fun, such as shopping malls, amusement parks, arcades, and sporting events. Consider going to a fun conference to explore a hobby of yours in more depth. You will meet new friends and admirers.

A child provides you with a reason to celebrate. You can be proud of the influence you've had in their decisions.

You are looking for the change in the energy, a change you can celebrate at the time of the Lunar New Year. You probably want to change your hairstyle, alter your fashion choices, buy new clothing, or add a new tattoo. Consider doing something bold before Mercury goes retrograde. Also, look into a fun class. Take singing lessons, painting, or jewelry making. Add some bling to your life.

February 2021: *Lunar New Year begins on February 12. Happy Year of the Metal Ox. February 20 has Mercury going direct. February 27 is the full moon. Your High-Energy Days are 4, 10, 16, 22, and 28.*

The first two weeks of February bring the tail end of the Metal Rat year. Consider completing things hanging on for the past 12 months or so. You may be de-cluttering somewhat, or perhaps letting go of items of a more emotional nature. The general focus this month will be on relationships, and this shifting energy can help you enjoy better connections with some of the most influential people in your life.

This month, changes at work are also possible. New rules may come down from very high in the company. Even if you disapprove of them, this is not a fight you can win. Instead, consider this time a sign of where the company is heading. Now you can assess whether you want to continue as part of this team. This doesn't mean you are changing jobs immediately; it's more likely, Dragon native, you are envisioning future possibilities.

The new moon is on February 12, marking the start of the Year of the Metal Ox. Dragon natives in a love relationship may take action to solidify your partnership. Perhaps you announce your relationship with friends and family, or maybe go one step further and become engaged. You can expect a lot of support from the people around you. People are lining up to congratulate you.

On February 20, Mercury moves forward again. There is positive energy connected with negotiations for a new car or for making some other large purchase. It will take a few days for this energy to get up to speed, but now you will see some forward motion. Likely within a week, you can receive the paperwork or the contract you've been looking for.

March 2021: *March 13 brings the new moon, March 20 marks the first day of spring, March 28 is the full moon. Your High-Energy Days are 6, 12, 18, 24, and 30.*

As March arrives, your focus shifts to available resources. Resources likely encompass a range of things, including other people's expertise, information, and the actual funding for your projects. Start approaching people to talk about what you are looking for. Formulate your queries, including the question, "Who can help me with this?" Some intriguing opportunities will arise from inquiries like this.

It's March 13, and the new moon draws your attention to the part of your life, which enjoys intimacy and sexy fun. If you're in a committed love relationship, you and your honey can expect to be spending more private time together. This is a useful aspect if you're seeking a romantic relationship, as you are likely to attract a match where both of you enjoy the pleasure of good physical chemistry. It's possible to meet someone you find exceptionally physically attractive. While this match could end up a long-term relationship, be aware there will be more relationship opportunities later.

The energy shifts on March 20 to highlight education. If you're in school, this may bring you some positive recognition from a teacher or assistance from an educational consultant. This is also an excellent time to apply to a university or to pursue continuing education options. For those Dragon natives not in school, this energy is about taking tests for professional certification or filling out licensing applications.

On March 28, there is a full moon. This puts a spotlight on risk-taking and creativity. You may consider doing something outside the norm of the things you usually prefer. You may decide you want to go on stage or launch a website showcasing your art, or put your music on YouTube. You're likely going to be a little nervous as this particular energy is about doing something you've never done before. Stretch yourself. You can achieve more and hit your success goals much more quickly when you take steps to launch your creativity out into the world.

April 2021: *April 12 brings the new moon. April 27 is the full moon. Pluto goes retrograde. (Pluto moving backward can cause you to re-consider your basic assumptions of life and eliminate anything you deem unnecessary, re-focusing on what is essential. Pluto will be retrograde until October.) Your High-Energy Days are 5, 11, 17, 23, and 29.*

April brings an emphasis on spirituality and how you connect to your higher self, to God and the Universe. In the past, you may have attended services at a church or temple. This energy is more about your relationship with your spirituality. Perhaps you practice meditation, prayer, or reading spiritual texts. Now is the time to be in harmony with the rhythms of the Universe. You will show up at the right time, take action just at the right moment—putting you in the path of the right people. This is important energy this month, so it's a good idea to allow time for it.

On April 12, the new moon is elevated in your chart, and you become much more noticeable to others than usual. It's a favorable time to meet new people, to form close and even loving relationships. Over the next two weeks, you may be invited to attend special events like weddings or anniversary celebrations. These types of events offer opportunities to meet new people. You may also make contacts through classes—even online courses—as you break out to chat with someone you find interesting. The energy is harmonious for you, and it is an impulsive energy. Over the next two weeks, go with your gut instinct, as it's likely it's the correct move.

The energy shifts on April 19, and you can be recognized for how you have been doing at your job. Over the next couple of weeks, you will hear how things are changing with your company or the industry you are employed in. In the past, you could have dismissed what you heard as "just talk," but this time, you hear the underlying importance or meaning of what's said. You receive some vital information which will help you decide about the future of your career. The Universe is sending you a message.

On April 27, there is a full moon, and you notice an increase in energy related to your home and family. Someone in the family may need your help. If you cannot help them with something, you may need to hire a professional to step in. Possibly there are home repairs you are trying to complete, or you may get some help with the computer or the network. Adult children may need advice (though they may not take it once they hear it). Younger children may need help with a presentation they're doing for school, or want you to work with them on their lines for the school play. It's a busy time, but quite enjoyable.

May 2021: *May 11 brings the new moon. On May 23, Saturn goes retrograde. (Saturn retrograde can cause you to review your career choices and make adjustments. Saturn will be retrograde until October). May 26 is a total Lunar Eclipse. May 29 has Mercury going retrograde. Your High-Energy Days are 5, 11, 17, 23, and 29.*

In May, Dragon natives have more than one opportunity to receive recognition or even accolades for your work, creative projects, or for just being you. During this month, you may have someone from your past reach out to you with a job opportunity, or you may find a former boss asking for you to come back to work for them. There's beneficial energy as you put yourself forward as a team leader or as you take the microphone and center stage.

On May 11, a new moon is bringing new projects, especially ones putting you in the public eye. It's an excellent time to launch your podcast or upload your novel on Amazon over the next two weeks. The challenge during this period will be the inclination to procrastinate. You may be telling yourself that you're just taking some extra time to perfect or improve your work. But with this positive energy, it's better to post now and make changes later.

The energy shifts on May 20, when fun and romance play a more significant role in your days and nights. A friend could become a romantic interest, or a new acquaintance may ask you out on a date. Dragon natives in an established relationship may find this energy a little more challenging as your partner wants to be serious while you would like to have more fun. This may take some negotiations. But Dragon natives are always charming, and you can win your sweetheart over with some loving words and understanding.

On May 26, there is a lunar eclipse lighting up your area of children and creativity. If you have kids, they may need more attention than usual. And while you are always there for your kids, you may be scrambling to fit everything into your schedule. There's also powerful fertility energy at this time if you're looking to add to the family.

Creative projects can go well over the next two weeks. It's a good idea to carve out some time for your art or content creation projects. This is a good time for gallery showings, launching a new product, or posting your YouTube videos.

June 2021: *June 10 is the annular Solar Eclipse. June 20 is the first day of summer. Jupiter goes retrograde. (Jupiter retrograde can indicate a need to relearn things or review your beliefs. Jupiter will be retrograde until October). June 22 has Mercury going direct. June 24 is the full moon. On June 25, Neptune goes retrograde. (Neptune retrograde can draw you back towards habits and addictions from your past; it can also encourage a return to spiritual practices. Neptune will be retrograde until December). Your High-Energy Days are 4, 10, 16, 22, and 28.*

June brings a lot of energy around change. It's a good idea to examine your habits and routines and discover which of them no longer serve you. Avoid settling for minor changes; instead, do something completely different. Keep in mind now can be the time to plant your seeds for doing something bigger later in the year. You might even consider a complete lifestyle change—like moving into a tiny house or moving out of the country. You may change how you define yourself. If you tell everyone you're not good with technology, it doesn't help you get better at PowerPoint, Instagram, or Google calendar integration. But if instead you say, "I'm a lifetime learner," your mind becomes willing to bring in new information.

On June 10, there's a Solar Eclipse signaling more change. There can be a change of career at this point. If you have already started this process weeks ago, this celestial event can bring you an interview, even an offer. You may give notice within a week or two. If, however, you have made no changes in your career lately, the Universe may bring you signs of a new door opening soon. What's notable about eclipses is that even if there are difficulties at the time of the eclipse, a few months from now, you will be happy all of this happened. You will recognize the benefits of the changes you've made.

On June 20, the energy shifts, and you could use a break. Go hiking where there are lots of trees or sit out in your backyard and enjoy your garden. This is a fine time to get extra sleep and not stay up late watching TV or playing video games.

On June 22, Mercury goes direct, and now contracts can come in, new jobs or projects can be started. New opportunities will flow in. A person could return a favor you did them a while back. A payment you have been long expecting can now arrive.

On June 24, there is a full moon and positive energy to shift your diet and exercise plan in a more healthy direction. You may only need a few small tweaks in your routine. Add a few more vegetables to your plate or find an exercise you enjoy. Dragon natives are generally healthy. When you increase healthy eating and exercise, even just a little bit, you can quickly see the benefits overall.

July 2021: *July 10 brings the new moon. July 24 is the full moon. Your High-Energy Days are 4, 10, 16, 22, and 28.*

The month of July shows Dragon natives needing a break. You have been flying through your days, weeks, and months getting things done and connecting with people. Now you need some "me" time. This can be something you do at home where you shut off your connections to work at a specific time each day to avoid being on call 24/7. Go camping, rent a cabin overlooking a lake, or take a cycling trip with your honey. This month you'll find some fun things to do.

On July 10, there's the new moon, and your intuition is strong. You might intuit or discover messages in your daily life about your life path and changes you need to consider. Your charisma is strong, and you meet some fascinating people. With this combination, you're able to read the motivations of others and the subtext in their words. This can help you establish new friendships, even a new relationship, if you're looking for one.

On July 22, the energy shifts, and you have a sudden burst of vitality, energy, and confidence. This is a great time to interview for jobs or approaching your supervisor about a position opening within your company. Now you can take a leadership role within your social group or a professional organization. If you own a business, this is a great time to consider hiring someone to help you with the administrative work or outside sales.

On July 24, there is a full moon, and relationship energy is highlighted. If you're already in a love relationship, you may celebrate a milestone anniversary or adding more romance into your daily life. You'll see the benefits of being in this relationship, and your partner is generous with their praise. For those Dragon natives looking for love, this is an excellent time to search for a long-term relationship. You may use a matchmaker's services to help you find a monogamous partnership, leading to commitment and even to marriage.

August 2021: *August 8 brings the new moon. On August 20, Uranus goes retrograde. August 22 is the full moon. Your High-Energy Days are 3, 9, 15, 21, and 27.*

The month of August is one of your strongest months all year. You can see what you want and take direct action to get it. Other people show you deference. They are aware of your potential. You may field several offers from jobs, business possibilities, beneficial partnerships. As you do these things, you may spend a bit more money than usual. That's the only warning this month. Monitor your checkbook, as it's easy to overspend.

August 8 brings the new moon; there is an interest in getting back into shape. You may join a gym, or perhaps you have taken up an enjoyable pastime like basketball, baseball, or hockey. Any activity you can enjoy doing with others—even one like playing golf—brings real benefits to your physical self.

On August 22, there is a full moon and a strong desire just to let go. You may be compelled to remove excess from your life. You want to finish up projects, or if you can't finish them up in the course of the next few weeks, you may let the project go entirely. Not that you're giving up, but you realize you have moved on. Now you're on a different path and may no longer be drawn to finishing that quilt, restoring grandma's rocking chair, or writing the screenplay (the one in your head for ten years). By letting go, you allow yourself more space to bring in new opportunities. At some point, this past project may come back to you, which will be a sign to give it another try. But for now, open your hands and release.

The full moon also highlights relationships for you. You can meet or connect with someone who becomes pivotal in your life. It may be the words they choose, their philosophy about life, even their productivity hacks; your eyes are opened. They may open doors for you, but more likely, they reveal more of the inner you.

September 2021: *September 7 brings the new moon. September 20 is the full moon. September 22 is the first day of autumn.*

September 26, Mercury goes retrograde. Your High-Energy Days are 2, 8, 14, 20, and 26.

September arrives, and your focus is on finances. You may attract an additional revenue stream or increase your current salary. However, this is out of your comfort zone—which for a Dragon native says something! While you deserve the increase, some negotiations may be involved. Likely you must present a valid case to secure this financial windfall you deserve.

On September 7, there is a new moon and your luck increases in your career. Seeds you planted months ago (or even a full year ago) now blossom into opportunities. This may mean you receive a promotion at your current job or with a competing company. If you own a business, you may do some cooperative advertising or finding a great sponsor for your products. This energy is so natural and comfortable; it can be easily overlooked. Make it a point to keep your eyes open for new opportunities.

On September 20, there is some sensual, romantic energy available for you to play around with. If you're already in a love relationship, you need only make time for you and your sweetheart to spend together. If you're looking for love, you'll have ample opportunities to find an attractive and intriguing someone, and this can lead to a great romance.

On September 22, the energy shifts, and there is a lot of activity around siblings or younger relatives. It may be time to mend a rift in a relationship that happened a long time ago. Now you can communicate more openly and even talk about getting together—even though you may not have seen each other. It's best if you can talk with them, rather than putting things in writing. Avoid sending letters outlining your feelings as Mercury will go retrograde soon.

On September 26, Mercury goes retrograde, and communication slows to a crawl. You may be waiting for contracts or sales agreements. Suddenly, the other party wants to go back to the negotiating phase. While usually, Dragon natives are confident about moving ahead and are ready to take action, it may be better for the time being to hang back. It will take great effort to influence the speed of how things unfold over the next few weeks, so it's best to step back and wait for the other side to make a move.

October 2021: *October 6 brings the new moon, and Pluto goes direct. On October 11, Saturn goes direct. October 18 has Mercury going direct and Jupiter going direct. October 20 is the full moon. Your High-Energy Days are 2, 8, 14, 20, and 26.*

Now, as October begins, you may find you have a lot of energy for handling communications or paperwork; there may even be some travel. You might look at getting a new vehicle. However, Mercury is still retrograde for the first part of this month. Mercury retrograde can wreak havoc with automotive related transactions, so wait until the end of the month. This month's energy is so intense you may find yourself bouncing off the walls. Vigorous exercise or playing sports can help channel and focus your energy.

On October 6, there is a new moon, and you may take a brief trip to see friends. There are some celebrations possible, maybe a birthday or anniversary. A friend of yours may give birth (or have adopted a puppy). While there is abundant positive energy around, you feel the pull to get back to work as soon as possible. Projects are piling up, and a deadline is looming.

On October 18, Mercury goes direct, and things begin to move forward again, especially in contracts. If you have been waiting to sign paperwork, now things will run much more smoothly. This is also an excellent time to clear up any miscommunications that may have happened over the last three weeks.

October 20 brings the full moon, lighting up the top of your chart. Many people may see and hear things you post on social media and communicate with others. If you want to boost your social media numbers, it's a good idea to post often over the next two weeks. However, stay positive as controversial topics could bring a backlash. Your actions at work are visible. By staying positive, you can attract recognition from a supervisor.

The energy shifts on October 22, bringing happy times at home. Everyone is getting along better. Some Dragon natives may move in with a sweetheart, settling together into the new dwelling. This is a good time to enjoy being at home.

November 2021: *November 4 is the new moon. November 19 is a partial Lunar Eclipse. Your High-Energy Days are 1, 7, 13, 19, and 25.*

In November, you are likely to see a lot of activity around family and extended family. Someone may travel to see you for a visit. Also, a family member may call upon you to help them move. Take care of repairs in the home, especially ones related to water (such as leaky faucets or slow drains). Home is your sanctuary and it's a good idea to make it more comfortable and safe.

On November 4, there is a new moon, and you have some new ideas. These could blossom into significant changes in your life. You no longer feel held back by what you believed in the past. Old patterns from younger days seem to dissolve away. You have grown, and now you can more easily pursue your goals.

On November 19, the Lunar Eclipse lights up the area of your career. Eclipses often bring change, adjustments you've been looking for, but these may unfold differently than you were expecting. The company you work for may make some top-down changes, and you can take this as a sign you should make some changes yourself. You've been getting ready to launch yourself into something new for quite a while. Around the time of this Lunar Eclipse, you may meet with your supervisor, who lays it all out for you. But even as the Lunar Eclipse closes a door, another will open for you. This can be a transfer within the company, a transfer to an out-of-town office, or perhaps you move to a new company entirely.

At the same time, it may be time to say goodbye to a friend who is moving some distance away. Perhaps they are returning to the place they were born or moving closer to their spouse's family. While you will miss them a great deal, this gives you another place to plan to visit.

On November 21, there's a shift in the energy, and suddenly things become easier, and the path forward seems much clearer. You feel supported by friends and family members. They have rallied around to help you pursue your goals. For those Dragon natives looking for love, the time is now ripe to meet new people and to expand your thinking into what you consider is your "type."

December 2021: *December 1 has Neptune going direct. December 4 is a total Solar Eclipse. December 19 brings the full moon, and Venus goes retrograde. (Venus retrograde can cause you to question what you want and inspire you to look for something new that delights you. Venus will be retrograde until January.) December 21 is the first day of winter. Your High-Energy Days are 1, 7, 13, 19, 25, and 31.*

Good times, fun, and laughter abound in December for Dragon natives. You are likely invited to many parties or plan to throw a few gatherings of your own. People travel to see you, and many will tell you how much they wish they could be around you for the holidays. For those Dragon natives who have adult children, there could be a family reunion this month.

On December 4, there's a Solar Eclipse. This could bring an addition to the family by marriage, pregnancy, or adoption. This can even be an unexpected event. Your son or daughter may walk in with a new spouse. The puppy you got may come with a sibling. While this can mean a lot more work in the future, it brings a lot of joy now. For those Dragon natives looking for love, it's an extraordinary time to meet new people or go online on popular dating websites. Envision the person you want to meet and then allow the Universe to connect you up.

On December 19, there's a full moon, and at the same time, Venus goes retrograde. (When Venus turns backward in relation to the Earth, Now is the time to question what you want in your life. Look at the things you purchase or use without thinking and see if these are things you still genuinely enjoy. Of course, this can make holiday shopping a little difficult, even when shopping for yourself. Make sure you can return anything you buy.

The energy shifts, and starting on December 21, you become busy. There's a lot to do at work, and there are family obligations as well. You may take on some seasonal work, and suddenly, you have a last-minute burst of activity. However, these days look quite enjoyable. You may meet many people, making a lot of money, or both.

January 2022: January 2 is the new moon. January 14 has Mercury going retrograde. January 17 is the full moon. On January 18, Uranus goes direct. On January 29, Venus goes direct. Your High-Energy Days are 6, 12, 18, 24, and 30.

On paper, January looks a lot like a new beginning, but the old energy of the Metal Ox is still lumbering along for the entire month. For Dragon natives, there's a focus on putting paperwork in order, de-cluttering, organizing the garage, and rearranging things— striving to make life better. You may change your diet by eating healthier meals and perhaps doing more cooking at home.

January 2 is the new moon, and the energy is split between finishing up old projects and starting brand-new things. You may wrap up seasonal work or organizing things for your job (like taking the annual physical inventory). At home, there's similar energy involved in putting away the holiday things and cleaning up after extended holiday visits.

There's an abundance of new energy all around you. Single Dragon natives may meet someone new and quickly fall in love. This person seems so familiar to you, and it feels comfortable to slip into a serious partnership. If you're already in a love relationship, you discover more wonderful things about each other—helping to draw you closer together.

On January 14, Mercury goes retrograde, possibly derailing a lot of resolutions and plans. Fortunately, Dragon natives can change directions pretty quickly. You will hear many people complaining and griping because things they wanted to do are delayed or canceled entirely. This is an excellent time to stay flexible and adapt.

On January 17, the full moon introduces an excellent two-week period for Dragon natives. Now you can expand your circle of friends and supporters. This is an excellent time to find mentors, teachers, or advisors. If you see someone you're interested in working with, don't hesitate to send them a message.

The energy shifts on January 19, and now it's time to evaluate your current work-life balance. You may have to delegate or even eliminate some tasks in your life so you can enjoy some much-needed quality free time. When you have free time, make sure you are spending it mindfully, not merely frittering it away on something that brings you nothing of value.

February 2022: *February 1 is the new moon, beginning the Year of the Water Tiger. February 3 has Mercury going direct. February 16 brings the full moon.*

Dragons like excitement, and here it comes with the Water Tiger energy. Time to think big again and meet opportunities head-on. For Dragon natives, this is your year to spread your wings and fly.

Attract New Love

Love is ready and waiting if you'll slow down for two seconds to notice. You're off to the races and not seeing the loving glances coming your way from someone special. If you're interested in love, consider pausing long enough to take a deep breath, and start a conversation. This is one of the best charts Dragon natives have had in quite some time for love relationships. You can meet someone through a friend or family member. Also, matchmakers can help. You can meet interesting people at conventions where technology, science, or the creative arts are discussed. May and December are the most vital months for a new connection. These months are also robust for fertility, so if you don't want an addition to the family, take precautions.

Traditionally, one of the best flowers for attracting love is a rose. Its wonderful scent attracts, while its sharp thorns warn, "Be careful not to wound me!". From the perspective of a Feng Shui cure, the rose is the perfect flower to choose when you want to attract new love, and you still want to be cautious, protecting your heart.

Grow roses outside your front door to attract love energy. If you can't grow them in this location, consider placing a miniature rose plant in your bedroom. If you are not confident about taking care of a live plant, find a beautiful picture of roses (in your favorite color) and hang or place it in your bedroom.

Enhance Existing Love

In some years, your relationship grows stronger and closer, and this is one of those years. It notably can happen when one person is very committed to making the relationship work. This energy and interest can swing back and forth like a pendulum. During this Metal Ox year, you and your partner both feel committed to making your relationship work, but at different times during the year. While you focus on your career, your partner may support you by taking care of the finances. At other times, you're able to support your sweetheart as they go back to school or change jobs by caring for the kids. There is abundant energy for strengthening this relationship, understanding that being in a true partnership means you have each other's back.

Dragon natives who are dating and want to move the relationship forward can find this is a good year to move in together or get married. There is positive energy for romance and also fertility energy for when you want to build a family.

Amethyst is the purple quartz stone of peace. It's said to raise hopes, calm the mind, and bring soothing energy to your life. Amethyst can help you be more intuitive and connect spiritually. This is a good gemstone for Sheep natives, who are looking to improve their love relationship.

Place a specimen of amethyst in your bedroom. Place it on the dresser or on a table where you can see it from the bed. You can also wear amethyst jewelry this year to connect with your partner in a deeper, more meaningful way.

Looking to Conceive?

When you're hoping to conceive, it's good Feng Shui to place a representation of what you want near where you sleep. This year, place a figurine of a sleeping child (or children) playing on your nightstand or dresser. Choose a figurine you like, one that brings joy to your heart. Or ask a relative, one who has kids, if they have a favorite figurine you could borrow. A borrowed figurine would have phenomenal fertility energy.

Place the figurine in your bedroom where you can easily see it from the bed. Picture the energy of the symbol entering your body and your life. Wash or dust the figurine regularly to increase the energy of this classic Feng Shui remedy.

(From Donna Stellhorn's book, A Path to Pregnancy: Ancient Secrets for the Modern Woman)

Family and Kids

Relations with family members are very positive this year as everyone seems to get along, working together, and supporting each other. The family seems to be growing larger. This can occur because of a marriage, pregnancy—or adult children bringing home their significant others. There may be a family reunion or large family get-together sometime during the year.

Close friends are also feeling more like part of the family, maybe hanging out at your home. There is increased energy for expanding the family this year. This can happen because of a marriage, birth, or adoption. The primary time for this intense energy is in May and December.

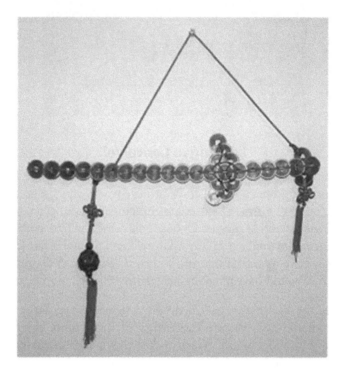

The coin sword is a classic Feng Shui cure for bringing both protection and prosperity to a home. This a "sword" crafted out of Chinese coins. It can be small, just a few inches long, or more than a foot long. It's hung from a red ribbon tied at the hilt and the sword tip. Hang the coin sword in the living room with the point facing the front door. You can also use a coin sword in your office or home office. It will help with sound financial decisions and protect your profits.

Money

Sometimes Dragon natives can attract money easily. However, this year, you are aware of the sources of money, so you can put effort into creating new revenue streams. Beneficial partnerships can happen, bringing you monetary opportunities, sometimes directly and sometimes indirectly (these could be passive income sources). There are a few stressful periods when Mercury is retrograde, where you could lose some ground and have to put out more money than you are taking in. But after these periods, you get back on track quickly and speed ahead. Most financial opportunities this year will be related to communication, technology, as well as interpersonal relationships. You may invest with family members or your partner in a business or real estate.

To capitalize on your luck in 2021, I recommend those born in the Year of the Dragon to create a "Money Tree." You can make one using any large house plant. Using pipe cleaners or twist ties, attach dollar bills like leaves to the plant. You can also hang Chinese coins (the coins with the square hole in the center) from the branches.

As you decorate your Money Tree, choose an odd number of bills or coins. From the perspective of Feng Shui, odd numbers are more potent than even numbers. You can select bills of any denomination, but dollar bills work just fine.

Display the money tree in your home office, your living room, or in view of your front door. Make sure you take care and water the plant—you want it to stay healthy and happy.

Job or Career

You are excited about your career this year. You can rise to a higher level than the average worker in your field. This year your skill set is more in demand. Finding a mentor or business partner this year is relatively easy. Others believe in your ideas and your ability to follow through. One possible limitation is your tech skills, which might need improvement. It is also possible that your company is upgrading its system, and you don't want to be left behind.

Mostly, your job looks stable. But with all the changes that happened the past year and those you can see coming, Check your company—and your entire industry—to make sure that everything is still stable and the forecasts are positive. Quite a few shifts are coming, but with your skills, you can make a beneficial change. A job opportunity arises around November. If you're looking for a new position to come in earlier in the year, it is a good idea for Dragon natives to do some networking.

When considering a new career or a new job, you sometimes want to draw the energy in quickly. The traditional cure is to take ground cinnamon (the kind in your spice cabinet) and sprinkle a bit on your porch—specifically on top of your welcome mat. A single teaspoon of cinnamon should suffice for the whole porch. This will attract positive career and financial energy. Repeat every couple of days until you have the job you want.

Education

Education proves to be challenging this year. You may be in school, and if you have a tough semester, you may consider whether or not school is right for you at this time. If you're not in school, you may think it's time to go back to complete a degree that was interrupted in the past. Success can come when you're honest with yourself about what you want to do. Ask yourself if the career you're planning requires more schooling, or if there's another way you can gain the knowledge or skill necessary to get a good job. It's not a great idea to just follow your friends off to school, but rather to seek knowledge. Should you attend formal classes at college or university, and that's the direction to go; if you'd do better going through a trade school or an apprenticeship, that works, too. That said, in this Metal Ox year, one-on-one studying is ideal for Dragon natives. This can mean self-directed programs, online studies, on-the-job training, or finding a tutor/mentor to get you through the practicalities of your future career.

Legal Matters

There's a lot of positive energy around contracts and agreements when you move quickly and decisively this year. The emphasis is on business partnerships and contracts for employment. These agreements are possible with contractors or other outsourcing services your company needs you to be involved in. There are also indications of a potential marriage contract. If you are already engaged or soon to be so, you will probably get married during the Metal Ox year.

Overall, it is not lucky to sue anyone this year; particularly avoid individual suits. There is a little better energy for class-action suits. You may encounter some challenging energy in November concerning agreements and lawsuits. Try not to initiate or sign anything of great importance during this month.

Health and Well-Being

Dragon natives enjoy much better year health this year than you have in several years. You can see much improvement in your overall vitality, as well as some improvement in pre-existing conditions. There is still a need to overhaul daily habits, especially around snacking or binge eating on weekends. Find a friend to exercise with. Suitable forms of exercise this year would be walking, cycling, and dance.

After the turmoil of the previous year, Dragon natives are much more calm overall this year. Even if circumstances aren't entirely back to normal, you have found that you are more resourceful and able to handle what life throws at you. Knowing this helps you sleep better and be calmer overall.

This year, to best shelter and safeguard yourself and your family, place seashells on your bedroom window sill. Seashells represent protection, a comfortable home, and a sense of safety. This will attract positive energy for health and vitality.

Snake

February 4, 1905–January 24, 1906: Yin Wood Snake
January 23, 1917–February 10, 1918: Yin Fire Snake
February 10, 1929–January 29, 1930: Yin Earth Snake
January 27, 1941–February 14, 1942: Yin Metal Snake
February 14, 1953–February 2, 1954: Yin Water Snake
February 2, 1965–January 20, 1966: Yin Wood Snake
February 18, 1977–February 6, 1978: Yin Fire Snake
February 6, 1989–January 26, 1990: Yin Earth Snake
January 24, 2001–February 11, 2002: Yin Metal Snake
February 10, 2013–January 30, 2014: Yin Water Snake
January 29, 2025–February 16, 2026: Yin Wood Snake

Snake Personality

When considering a Chinese Zodiac animal's qualities, it's a good idea to examine the animal's traits, behaviors, and personality. At first glance, it may seem Snake is at a disadvantage, having no hands or feet. But Snakes use their sense of smell to track their prey. Their sense of smell comes from using their forked tongue to collect airborne particles. You may already be aware your sense of smell is more acute than the average person. This is one of your advantages.

The scales covering a snake's body allow them to grip things tightly and to move swiftly along the ground. These scales are shed off periodically, revealing new skin beneath as the snake literally crawls out of its old skin. This means you can reinvent yourself whenever you want. When your life needs to change, you can change it in a big way.

People born in the Snake Year rely on their intelligence and wisdom to make their way through the world. They have a very keen intuitive sense of other people. They easily attract people and keep them near for as long as they need. Snakes can also enjoy spending time alone when they wish.

Snakes cope well with making significant life changes. It seems they can renew themselves at will. They may change careers or move to a new city, leaving everything behind. They are reborn. Snakes admire power and look to gain power for themselves. When Snake realizes they're stuck in a situation, or they feel limited in their choices, they will move on.

Snake is the wisest of the zodiac signs and relies on their own judgment. They're excellent with money and have a good sense for investments. They have a computer-like brain that never stops calculating. They are incredibly tenacious when they want to achieve something. They never forget a broken promise. Some say the Snake is paranoid, but that doesn't mean people are not plotting against him/her.

While Snake natives always have money in the bank, they are cautious about speculating and should avoid gambling. If they gamble, they need to make safe bets.

Snakes are passionate lovers (not necessarily limited to one person). Snakes are loyal, but they will wander if they suspect the other person is not entirely devoted. When wronged, they like to crush their enemies completely. Snake natives will strike without warning, although they can be patient until the time for revenge is right.

People born in the Year of the Snake keep their feelings a well-guarded secret. Often seen as detached and cool, but in reality, Snakes feel things deeply. If surrounded by negative people, it breaks their concentration, and Snake becomes wary. But

Snake has the power to win people over, and many fall into line with whatever Snake wishes.

Snake: Predictions for 2021

How to use your High-Energy Days: On these days, plan to take action for your most important goals, make vital phone calls, send important emails. Your high-energy days are when your energy and luck are the strongest for the month.

January 2021: *Uranus goes direct on January 14. Mercury goes retrograde from January 30 to February 20. Your Lucky Days are 7, 13, 19, 25. [How to use your Lucky Days: On these days, plan to take significant actions, make vital phone calls, send emails. These are days when your energy and luck are high.]*

As the Metal Rat year comes to a close, you are already starting to feel the new positive Metal Ox energy on approach. Things in your life are going more smoothly, and the pieces are starting to fall into place. You are getting more help around the house. People around you are offering to share resources with you. Things are getting easier overall, and they will continue to improve.

See what you can do about getting more restful sleep—maybe doing some renovations in the bedroom to make it more of a sanctuary. You may need a new mattress or pillows. Consider a white noise machine or some blackout curtains. The more restful sleep you enjoy at night, the more productive and happy you will be during the day.

Your relationship is in a good place; you enjoy more harmony at home. You feel you and your partner are on the same page regarding the kids and extended family. You may be adding some new décor to the house or finishing up a renovation project. Keep the budget in mind. What you want may be found at a cheaper price if you do just a little research and are willing to accept a slightly longer delivery time.

You're busy at work, but you have more work/life balance now, which feels good. The people you work with, for the most part, are pulling their weight. They often come to you to ask for your opinions and insights into what's going on. You impress others with your decisive nature and quick wit. You being there makes the office a better place for many.

February 2021: *Lunar New Year begins on February 12. Happy Year of the Metal Ox. February 20 has Mercury going direct. February 27 is the full moon. Your High-Energy Days are 4, 10, 16, 22, and 28.*

The first two weeks of February still hold the harmonious metal Rat energy and Snake native; you can access the energy to finish up some important projects. If you're in school, there may be some last-minute changes to your schedule, or the school report you're working on. Make sure your materials are backed up. If you're working on a team, it's good to help everyone agree. With the positive Metal Rat energy, success is likely.

On February 12, we enter the Metal Ox year. You will be offered many opportunities during the year. It will be essential to differentiate between something you want to do and something that seems profitable. At first, the shift into Ox energy could cause you to feel out of sync. Still, in actuality, your highly intuitive nature is picking up the vibes from the people around you. No one can adapt as readily as a Snake native. You recognize the boundary between your own feelings and the way other people deal with their lives.

The energy shifts on February 18, and your focus turns to relationships. You may wonder how your love-interest feels about you. Perhaps you are receiving mixed signals from them. You may not be clear about whether you want to move this relationship forward. Now you feel as if there is a spotlight on your love life; answers to your relationship questions will be forthcoming.

Mercury goes direct on February 20, and now it is easier to get a response to your emails and phone calls. Communication is easier in all aspects of your life. A contract arrives in relation to possible new employment, or potential investment opportunities.

February 27 brings the full moon and much attention to you personally. Others notice you at this time. This can be beneficial for you, Snake native. Whether you're looking for a love relationship, or you'd really like to differentiate yourself at work, the next two weeks can bring quite a few opportunities.

March 2021: *March 13 brings the new moon; March 20 marks the first day of spring; March 28 is the full moon. Your High-Energy Days are 6, 12, 18, 24, and 30.*

In March, your natural clairvoyant abilities are working overtime—especially in regard to your career. A manager or a key supervisor could dig in their heels on some particular aspect of your job you know should change. This can signal a change in employment may be in the stars for you in the next few months. This is especially true if you've been in a similar situation at the same company before.

March 13 brings the new moon and the opportunity to connect with friends you haven't seen in a while. Supportive people surround you. These are people who have, over the years, proven themselves time and time again.

There's good energy for meeting someone new in your love life during the last two weeks of the month. You're more magnetic than usual, and there could be attractive others lining up at your door. If you're already in a love relationship, there are powerful signs indicating enhanced intimacy and fun between the sheets. However, there is still a lot of variable energy circulating around for many of the other zodiac signs, so it's a good idea to maintain a flexible schedule in order to accommodate your partner.

The energy shifts on March 20, and a significant resource becomes available to you. Snake natives have a natural ability with money. You often go out of your way to avoid borrowing or lending funds, but sometimes a project or person in your life requires some outside funding. Over the next week, you have luck negotiating with bankers or investment managers.

The full moon falls on March 28, putting a continued focus on your finances. Someone you know well (perhaps a relative) may ask to borrow money. Snake natives have good boundaries, and this ability will be important in the current situation. Find alternative ways to help without opening your wallet.

At the end of the month, Snake natives can bring in an additional source of income. This source could become a permanent flow. This may be connected to a side job, or a personal project which is becoming profitable.

April 2021: *April 12 brings the new moon. April 27 is the full moon, and Pluto goes retrograde. (Pluto moving backward can cause you to review your basic assumptions of life, to eliminate what is unnecessary, bringing you back to what is essential. Pluto will be retrograde until October.) Your High-Energy Days are 5, 11, 17, 23, and 29.*

The month of April is an interesting time for Snake natives. While you are independent and an expert at critical thinking, outside advice is beneficial this month. This is especially true if you're considering a business merger, or thinking about a career change. You may consider taking a survey among your friends to see what their opinions are. After you've collected their advice, you can still go your own way.

The new moon falls on April 12, and a financial windfall is possible. You could receive a gift of money such as a grant or a prize, but this financial bounty could also come in the form of a low or delayed interest loan. While you are flush with cash, there may be some temptation to spend, but most Snake natives are pretty savvy with their money.

The energy shifts on April 19, and paperwork or legal matters become the focus. You might be applying for a license or building permit. You may have government paperwork to complete for a business program or school scholarship. Most of this happens over the next few weeks. Avoid procrastinating on these tasks, or you'll miss this positive energy.

The full moon is on April 27, and for those Snake natives in school, this is a hectic time. You may have a standardized test to take, project due, or you could be catching up on your studies. It's also possible it's your kids who are the students, and you are helping them with homework or getting them ready to take a big exam.

The last week of April is very strong for your spiritual life. Consider going back to church or doing a spiritual practice privately in your home. Meditation, lighting candles, or chanting can bring you multiple benefits.

The end of the month may bring increased contact with a sibling or younger relative, possibly visiting town. Or, they may confess a secret to you in a late-night phone conversation.

May 2021: *May 11 brings the new moon. On May 23, Saturn goes retrograde. (Saturn retrograde can cause you to review your career choices and make adjustments. Saturn will be retrograde until October). May 26 is the total Lunar Eclipse. May 29 has Mercury going retrograde. Your High-Energy Days are 6, 12, 18, 24, and 30.*

The month of May brings some positive energy to Snake natives. You can quickly get answers to questions, and feel the synchronicity of the Universe's helping hand as it guides you towards your goals. You may find you have the most luck this month when making connections with influential people.

The new moon on May 11 brings you additional charisma, and Snake natives looking for love can find a splendid match. This could be through an online dating site, or you can meet someone through a friend. Let others know you are looking for love, and allow them be your emissaries. Snake natives are adaptable in relationships. This is an excellent year to explore a love connection with someone who's not necessarily your "type." If you're already in an established relationship, you may travel together to visit distant family members or friends.

The energy shifts on May 20, and over the next couple of weeks, you could be in line for a promotion or a beneficial shift in your career. For those Snake natives looking for a job, this is a great time to post your resume, interview, and accept a position. There is extra good luck around jobs involving communication, transportation, or coaching.

There is a lunar eclipse on May 26, and suddenly a block you've been quite aware of gives way. Now opportunity is in your hands, but it may be much more than you were expecting. Careful Snake natives might feel hesitant, as this could mean taking on more responsibility, or agreeing to be in charge.

Mercury goes retrograde on May 29. A door to opportunity, allowing you access to something you've done before could open, allowing you to move back to something you've done before. You must weigh the choice of moving forward or staying with something familiar.

June 2021: *June 10 is the annular Solar Eclipse. June 20 is the first day of summer, and Jupiter goes retrograde. (Jupiter retrograde can indicate a need to relearn things or to review your beliefs. Jupiter will be retrograde until October). On June 22, Mercury goes direct. June 24 is the full moon. On June 25, Neptune goes retrograde. (Neptune retrograde can draw you back to habits and addictions from your past. It can also encourage a return to spiritual practices. Neptune will be retrograde until December). Your High-Energy Days are 4, 10, 16, 22, and 28.*

This month, there are plenty of fun opportunities to interact with friends—though your work schedule may not give you the extra time you want. Block out some time for activities like hiking, water skiing, or cycling.

On June 10, there is a solar eclipse triggering some disruption in your area of career. Often, solar eclipses will cause one door to close, and some significant ending. But the Universe always opens a new door for you, offering an alternative way forward. This eclipse may bring changes in your company, possibly within your entire industry. Pay attention to long-term trends when an eclipse hits your chart's career area. It gives you a heads-up that a change would be in your best interest.

The energy shifts on June 20. Certain trends may be revealed to you, and you can see how your life is flowing in a particular direction. As you look ahead, you can see whether you are sailing towards your goals, or if you're off course. The Universe is sending you messages.

Mercury goes direct on June 22, and now, if you're considering taking a new job, it would be good to start after this date. Beginning a new job during Mercury retrograde can lead to some interruptions in your career later (possibly resulting in you getting laid off, or just not liking the job).

The full moon falls on June 24 and lights up your personal area of risk-taking. Risks can come in many forms. Perhaps you're interested in asking a special someone out on a date. You may be reaching out to an influencer or potential mentor. You may be launching a side business. Now is the time to expand your world and step out of your comfort zone. Snake natives are known for taking their time making decisions, but when action is called for, you move with great alacrity.

July 2021: *July 10 brings the new moon. July 24 is the full moon. Your High-Energy Days are 4, 10, 16, 22, and 28.*

July has you working hard on your work/life balance and enjoying some excellent results. You've been applying yourself to tasks at work, and this is paying some dividends. Snake natives are good at creating systems and streamlining procedures, so work takes less time. July also brings a lot of luck when you work on your relationship. When you make an effort to understand your partner and make their life easier, you reap substantial rewards. Your intimate life improves; and you enjoy a lot of fun behind closed doors.

July 10 brings the new moon, and a potential secret admirer may come into your life. Snake natives are the most sensual sign in the Chinese zodiac. You have charisma and magnetism and can attract potential partners. Now the energy is here to enjoy a sensual liaison, perhaps a secret rendezvous with someone who is attracted to you. There is positive relationship energy for those Snake natives already in a committed relationship, too. You may want to get a hotel room with your sweetheart, as the change of scene can inspire some sexy fun.

The energy shifts on July 22—Snake native, you quite simply need a break! You've been working hard, helping friends and family. You need some "me" time. In the next week or so, see if you can't carve out some time for yourself, perhaps a visit to a spa is in order, or some camping in nature without the sound of traffic in the background; even simply staying home in your flip-flops or lounging in the backyard can feel like a chance to re-wind and re-charge your own batteries.

On July 24, there is a full moon, and Snake natives have the opportunity to find a new health regimen or exercise routine that really works for you. This could indicate a change of diet; perhaps you're going vegan or trying keto. You may get a personal trainer to help you work out, or a new piece of exercise equipment. Snake natives enjoy taking care of their health, and this period can be quite beneficial to you.

August 2021: *August 8 brings the new moon. On August 20, Uranus goes retrograde. August 22 is the full moon. Your High-Energy Days are 3, 9, 15, 21, and 27.*

August begins, and you are ready to spring into action. You have more energy than you've had in some time. This could be because of some changes you have made in your routine. Additionally, many aspects of your life are going well now, causing you to pop out of bed in the morning, ready to take on the day. There's a mix of energies this month, you may be completing some projects and starting some new ones. Consider letting go of some old home decor items you have held onto for a long time, but which are no longer your style.

August 8 has the new moon, bringing you increased intuition and a desire to connect spiritually. You may be dreaming dreams (and hopefully logging them in your dream journal). You may feel increasingly more intuitive than usual (which is saying a lot, as Snake natives are naturally psychic). This is the time to put spiritual ideas into practice. You may try things like automatic writing or astral projection. Consider learning how to read the tarot or do numerology. Any of these spiritual modalities can help you uncover answers and reveal the truth when you need to know what's really going on.

On August 22, the energy shifts, as the full moon shines in the night sky. Once again, the Universe puts you on notice: it's time to let go of whatever no longer serves you. If you have unopened boxes from a previous move, consider now that you haven't needed those things in months (or years), and maybe now is the time to release them. See how you can pare down your belongings in order to make your life easier.

Towards the end of the month, there is a change in your relationships. A friend may move away, pursuing a better opportunity, or seeking to live in a place where housing is less expensive. Instead of feeling like you're losing a friend, consider you're gaining a place to stay somewhere else in the world. Letting go is still hard; Snake natives are known for how close they keep their friends. But if you think about it, you'll see the advantages your friend will have if they move on. You, of all people, understand the importance of focusing on a future goal.

September 2021: *September 7 brings the new moon. September 20 is the full moon. September 22 is the first day of autumn. September 26 has Mercury going retrograde. Your High-Energy Days are 2, 8, 14, 20, and 26.*

Your high-energy continues, and your confidence increases. You are likely finishing more than one extensive project during the month of September, which will certainly give you a confidence boost. This may be related to your education; or perhaps you are applying for a professional license. When you take the time to study, you breeze through tests. It's true, you're juggling a lot, and Snake natives, you rarely like dealing with all the boring everyday stuff. But this serves as a means to an end, and getting a large project off your desk this month will feel terrific.

September 7 brings the new moon and a lucky period for the next two weeks for Snake natives. This is a time to push yourself forward. Reach out to people you want to partner with, even if they enjoy a celebrity status you do not. You may make find you make a personal contact unexpectedly, rather than have your messages read by an assistant. Now you can make some headway on an important goal. You don't want to miss taking advantage of this lucky period.

On September 20, there's the new moon. Now relationships or partnerships solidify. You may receive a contract to review, good news, there's still time to do some negotiating to get what you want. Work will be busy, and you may find you're falling behind on the paperwork. It's a good idea to prioritize and make sure you can work on your most important goals now, rather than allow yourself to become bogged down in busywork.

September 22 brings a change of seasons, and over the next few weeks, your finances show improvement. You may receive an increase at work, or a side business may bring additional profits. Snake natives are good with money. When you discover a financial opportunity, you can take hold of it and make a success of it.

Mercury goes retrograde on September 26. This can cause some delays, especially with regard to receiving a windfall, or other amount of money you were expecting to receive. But after a phone call or an email from you, things start to happen again. It's businesses as usual. However, if you're thinking of selling property or buying a new car, put this project on hold for a few weeks, as the retrograde Mercury can disrupt the buying and selling process.

October 2021: *October 6 brings the new moon, and Pluto goes direct. On October 11, Saturn goes direct. October 18 has Mercury going direct and Jupiter going direct. October 20 is the full moon. Your High-Energy Days are 2, 8, 14, 20, and 26.*

In October, the focus on finances continues, and you may see financial opportunities all around you. Snake natives are creative. If you have an idea for a type of content to make, even an invention, it would be a good idea to set aside some time to work on it.

October is also marked by the ability to differentiate yourself with your growing skillset. Something you know how to do can become a desired service or commodity—either in your work or among your friends. They may ask you to take a leadership role in a professional group or for a local charity because of your particular abilities. While this means taking on additional responsibility, and losing more time out of your busy schedule, it may be in line with your life path and your heart's desire.

October 6 brings the new moon and extremely high energy to your week. Seeds you planted weeks ago now all seem to ripen at once. It's harvest time. Take action as projects arise; otherwise, this harvest will be gleaned by someone else.

On October 18, Mercury and Jupiter begin to move forward. What you experienced as delays and interruptions in your communication over the last few weeks, now begins to dissipate. Now it feels like you are being shot from a cannon; nothing is holding you back. You can launch yourself toward your goals.

This is also a time you could pretty easily blow your budget. Something you've wanted for a long time is offered to you at an extraordinary price. You may find a used item, or receive an offer through a private party, but it feels like something you don't want to pass up.

The full moon on October 20 brings romance, and you may have a last-minute get together with your sweetheart that lasts all night. For some Snake natives, this can mean cuddling on the sofa or spending Sunday morning spooning with your favorite person.

The energy shifts on October 22, and for the next few weeks the emphasis is on all kinds of communication. You may be be busy writing reports, sorting and doing paperwork. A contract can come in, an agreement you've been waiting for. You may find an increase in email correspondence, or receive a lot more texts than usual. Mercury is direct, so if you want to get a new phone or laptop, now is a good time.

November 2021: *November 4 is the new moon. November 19 is a partial Lunar Eclipse. Your High-Energy Days are 1, 7, 13, 19, and 25.*

The month of November can bring some unexpected changes for Snake natives. You usually prefer your life to go according to plan, however, that said, you're very good at adapting to new circumstances when the need calls for it. It's said, "No one can push a snake.", but if you see the benefit of making a change, you will jump in with enthusiasm.

November 4 brings the new moon, and changes center on receiving resources from others. One source of income may be coming to an end, and a new one is beginning soon. There may also learn of changes in credit terms, or the stipulations of a loan. You will see this coming, you may even initiate these changes. Now, you have more control over the circumstances. This is better than allowing these things to happen on their own.

November 19 brings a lunar eclipse, and now you become people begin to notice you, to pay attention to you and what you are saying or doing. Snake natives looking for a relationship may find more than one interested person is pursuing you. Some Snake natives will choose this time to get engaged or move an existing relationship forward by introducing your sweetheart to friends and family. You may announce you are moving in together. While this is a good time to make major changes in your relationship, this lunar eclipse won't be easy for everyone. Recognize that some of the people in your life may not adapt as quickly as you do to the changes you suggest.

On November 21, the energy shifts, putting a lot of emphasis on home and family for the next few weeks. This provides an opportunity for you to help your significant other feel comfortable in your family. You may move someone into your home, which creates changes for the other people living there. This can also occur due to bringing a pet into the house. A new addition can turn the house upside down for a little while.

December 2021: *December 1 has Neptune going direct. December 4 is a total Solar Eclipse. December 19 brings the full moon, and Venus goes retrograde. (Venus retrograde can cause you to question what you want and inspire you to look for something new that delights you. Venus will be retrograde until January.) December 21 is the first day of winter. Your High-Energy Days are 1, 7, 13, 19, 25, and 31.*

December is marked by powerful desires and wishful thinking. You may feel obsessed about having someone or something you've wanted for a long time. This can be centered on an object, but it's more likely your focus is on an individual, someone with whom the chemistry works. You may have trouble getting this person off your mind. Simultaneously, something is limiting your ability to communicate—perhaps because of your schedule or the other person's circumstances. As you wish for things to be different, the Universe sends some assistance.

December 4 brings a total solar eclipse. While this energy generally brings change, this eclipse is more likely to affect other people in your life, and you experience the ripple effect. There could be changes with a partnership, or perhaps your sweetheart gets a job offer on the other side of the country. As their life changes, so does yours. This can reverberate throughout the entire family, but many are looking to you for your wise counsel. Snake natives are known for their ability to observe and make assessments of the surrounding circumstances.

December 19, the moon is full, and Venus, the planet of desire, starts to move backward. Suddenly, a relationship you thought was going well seems to hit the rocks. Maybe it's something something you've said, or something they have said, but now a disagreement can arise. Avoiding this will take some very thoughtful, heartfelt communication. On the other hand, you learn about something about each other and how to deal with bumps in the road.

On December 21, there is a change of seasons, and the energy turns more harmonious for Snake natives. You have a lot more fun over the next few weeks. There are people around to laugh and share good times with. At the end of the year, you could have a very close, warm holiday season, creating positive memories for the future.

January 2022: *January 2 is the new moon. January 14 has Mercury going retrograde. January 17 is the full moon. On January 18, Uranus goes direct. On January 29, Venus goes direct. Your High-Energy Days are 6, 12, 18, 24, and 30.*

The month of January brings one of the best relationship periods of the year for Snake natives. If you are looking for a new relationship, find someone you connect with beyond the surface attributes. You can find a special person to share true compatibility with you. It's a good idea to put yourself out into the world in as many ways as possible during this month in order to capitalize on this energy. This could mean going on online dating sites, letting friends and family know that you're looking, or even contacting a matchmaker.

January 2 brings the new moon, and your creative, courageous energy is very high. You recognize all you've been through, and how you've weathered storm after storm. In a sense, you are now an expert sailor. So as things come up, you can remind yourself you've been through storms before, and you will get through this one as well.

January 14 has Mercury going retrograde. It's imperative to make sure work projects are securely backed up. If you are carrying a company computer, keep an eye on it. On a positive note, a big opportunity could come back into your life. You may be selected to lead the team this time.

January 17 brings the full moon and emphasis in your personal realm of money derived from career. You will probably receive recognition. Be sure to use this opportunity to ask for a raise. You may get a "No," but it's more likely you'll get positive feedback.

On January 19, there's a shift of energy, and your thoughts turn towards health and well-being. You may have started the year with some resolutions, and possibly found it was difficult to follow through. But now information about an alternative method of taking care of yourself through diet or exercise comes to you and piques your interest. This can be centered on martial arts, or some sort of dance.

February 2022: *February 1 is the new moon and begins the Year of the Water Tiger. February 3 has Mercury going direct. February 16 brings the full moon.*

February 1 brings the new moon, and the year of the Water Tiger begins. Tiger and Snake energy can be rather combative, but you're up for the challenge. No more sleepy Ox energy, now opportunities come in leaps and bounds. Buckle up; this is going to be a wild ride.

Attract New Love

You and love connect this year. If you are single, you have a very strong possibility of connecting with a significant other, someone with whom you enjoy a deep and meaningful relationship. This can be a person you work with, or one who has a similar profession. You may meet this person through professional contacts, or in the course of your day-to-day business. At first glance, you may not feel sparks flying, because this year Snake native, you are generally focused on business. But by the second meeting, it starts to get steamy, and the relationship can form quickly. In May and December, you have an opportunity to change your living arrangements due to a love relationship. You might move in together.

The peony, especially the pink peony, is a flower used in Feng Shui to represent love and romance. It has a wonderful sweet scent and beautiful appearance. It's said to inspire beauty in life. Hang a picture of a peony near the entrance of your bedroom. This can be inside the bedroom or in the hallway leading to the bedroom. This is a Feng Shui cure best used to attract new love. Once you're in a happy relationship, remove the picture and give it to someone looking for love.

Enhance Existing Love

While there is a good connection between the two of you, there could be a temporary separation this year, caused by one person working in a different city, or perhaps you need to spend more time with extended family members. This can result in little time to spend talking with with your partner, much less playing together. The lack of time or separation may also be due to an addition in the family—one that keeps one partner more sleep deprived, and the other focused on career and being out in the world. It will take sensitivity on both sides to recognize when you have to stop the action and have a good conversation.

Fortunately, Snake natives are highly intuitive and can sense when words are needed. Towards the end of the year, difficulties clear, and you come together stronger than ever.

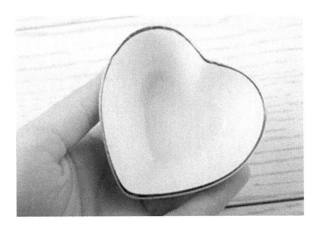

To attract lots of love possibilities, get a heart-shaped bowl. The bowl can be made of wood, stone, or fabric. Choose red or hot pink. Avoid pastel colors as this can attract a very passive partner. Write your wishes for a new love on small pieces of paper and place them inside the bowl. This list can include the qualities of the person you're trying to attract, what a new relationship will mean in your life, and how you know that you've found the right person. Then place this bowl on your bedside table to attract love and romance.

Looking to Conceive?

Wheat is a symbol of fertility and an affirmation of life. This may surprise the growing number of gluten-free people, but good news—you don't have to eat wheat to benefit from the positive fertility energy. Try growing wheat-grass as a house plant. Using a square or rectangular pot, plant wheat seeds, and place it in a sunny bedroom window. The wheat will grow into tender blades of grass. If you don't have adequate light in your bedroom, move the planter each day to a sunny window, and then move the planter back to the bedroom at night. *(From*

Donna Stellhorn's book, A Path to Pregnancy: Ancient Secrets for the Modern Woman)

Family and Kids

There is a lot of activity around the home and family. There could be a big push to organize stuff, clean out the garage, or declutter in general. In May or December, possible changes can be expected for a potential move or renovation. There may be a need for home repairs. In December, there could be a dispute with the neighbor over property lines or some other matter.

Overall, the family comes together to support you. Your children may start school and find changes to their schedule a little overwhelming, but soon, they excel through hard work and effort.

Use a Feng Shui cure this year to add an extra layer of protection to your home. Choose a convex mirror. (A convex mirror is shaped like the back of a spoon.) Such a mirror can reflect negative energy back where it originated more forcefully than a flat mirror can. This adds additional protection for you and your family.

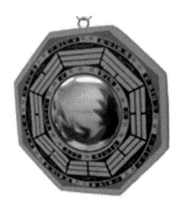

Hang your convex mirror in a window near the front door, in your bedroom window, or—if you have a difficult neighbor—you can point it at their home. This can result in them moving within a couple of months. Use only one of these mirrors at a time, as they are powerful. Too many convex mirrors, and you will block even positive energy from reaching you while simultaneously blocking the negative energy.

Money

This year is financially beneficial; money seems to drop into your lap. As you visualize, you can observe your vision manifest. Follow the rules of the law of attraction, or the principles of "like attracts like." That said, some sweat needs to happen in order to make good profits, and to access the many opportunities. Don't neglect your homework when looking into investments, or due diligence if you're interested in buying a business. This year most money comes from your skillset—something you are continually improving. Consider your favorite hobby. How can you monetize what you enjoy doing?

This year, to stimulate monetary flow, add a picture of moving water to your home office or entryway. Position the picture so that the water seems to be flowing into the house. The picture can be large or small, it can be a photo or a painting, and it can be of the ocean, a river, or a waterfall.

Job or Career

You're busy this year with many opportunities for your career, perhaps even more than you can count. You are in high demand, which is a help when you ask for more money, or for an opportunity to achieve a higher position. If you like what you do, it's a good idea to stay in your current position. However, there will also be contract opportunities for working a side job, or expanding your own business.

Communication will be key this year. The more people and connections you make, the more directions you can go with your career. There can be shakeups in your company in June, when it may be purchased or go through a management shift. Get ready to write your own ticket when the new management comes in and needs your help.

A good Feng Shui cure is to use Chinese coins in your home or employment or business place. Because Chinese coins have a square hole in the middle of them, they can be strung together in a display. And since on an energetic level, "Like attracts like!", hanging coins attracts both money and new job energy. The Chinese characters inscribed on the coins identify when the coin was cast. Most coins you find today are replicas.

Find strings of coins hung on red cords (choose strings with three coins, eight coins, nine coins, or 18 coins). Hang a string on the doorknobs in your house—especially the front door. Each time you use the door, your hand will touch the coins bringing the energy of opportunity right to your fingertips.

Education

There is a great deal of focus on education this year. You may have made a change last year to a new institution or changed your major. You may have found your enthusiasm for finishing your degree is waning. Education this year can be expensive, and it's wise to look for ways to help pay for it. But this awareness also enables you to focus on your studies, and be effective in getting through classes and completing projects. Hands-on classes are best this year. If you are studying construction, cosmetology, or anything that lends itself to an apprenticeship, you can find success. But even if you are in a long-term program or pursuing a regular university degree, you could do very well this year. Be aware that in November, there will be a decision to make. This might be about dropping a class, or applying yourself to a difficult topic.

Legal Matters

While there is considerable luck in contracts and agreements for Snake natives this year, especially with regard to career moves or employment, you may encounter a difficult energy with lawsuits. You should be careful not to need to sue anyone, and to avoid engaging in individual or class-action lawsuits. These types of suits could end up costing you more money than you could be awarded. It's also possible that last-minute evidence or a reversal can happen. This is especially true in November. If you have a lawsuit coming to court in November, see if it can be postponed. That said, contracts, especially for work, living arrangements, and purchasing a vehicle, are beneficial this year. Don't be afraid to negotiate for better terms.

Health and Well-Being

You are usually healthy throughout the year, even though a variety of energies pull you in different directions in the context of your health and well-being. You may be under more stress and, therefore, not sleeping as well as before. There may be disruptions in your daily routine. Some snake natives will seem out of sorts. It's important to get daily exercise and to eat well. New information can come to you through an educational or spiritual source; this information forms the basis for the dramatic shifts in your diet or exercise plan. So while you may make some changes this year, overall, this is a positive health year for Snake natives.

To clear old energy out of your home and bring in positive family energy, consider using Smudge Spray this year. Smudge Spray, also called Sage Spray, can be made by making a tea from white sage leaves and putting it in a spray bottle. This spray will stay fresh in your fridge for about three days. Smudge Spray you make yourself will smell very woodsy like sage. You can also find commercially sold Smudge Spray created by some very good herbalists. This Smudge Spray usually has an alcohol base and a light floral scent. It lasts a long time and need not be refrigerated.

Use the spray at least once a month. Spray around door-ways, especially the front and back door. Also, use it in the bedroom. Be careful spraying around delicate fabrics. Using Smudge Spray will help you clear the energy and bring in positive health vibes.

Horse

January 25, 1906–February 12, 1907: Yang Fire Horse
February 11, 1918–January 31, 1919: Yang Earth Horse
January 30, 1930–February 16, 1931: Yang Metal Horse
February 15, 1942–February 4, 1943: Yang Water Horse
February 3, 1954–January 23, 1955: Yang Wood Horse
January 21, 1966–February 8, 1967: Yang Fire Horse
February 7, 1978–January 27, 1979: Yang Earth Horse
January 27, 1990–February 14, 1991: Yang Metal Horse
February 12, 2002–January 31, 2003: Yang Water Horse
January 31, 2014–February 18, 2015: Yang Wood Horse
February 17, 2026–February 05, 2027: Yang Fire Horse

Horse Personality

When considering a Chinese Zodiac animal's qualities, it's a good idea to examine the animal's traits, behaviors, and personality. There are many myths and legends about horses in our culture. Humans domesticated horses around 3000 BC. Many cultures have horse stories and traditions that help us identify these beautiful animals' specific traits and behaviors.

Horses are sensitive creatures; they can sense danger and know how to flee. They can sleep standing up, giving them the ability to run at a moment's notice. Even baby horses—foals—can run soon after birth. Horses have enormous endurance and are highly intelligent.Those born in the Year of the Horse are attuned to the moods and motivations of others. They are quick to take offense and can explode with anger. But once Horse feels safe again, they quickly forget their rage. Horses want to move things forward, sometimes rushing others. They become impatient when results manifest too slowly.

They prefer things done their way. While they believe in the pursuit of happiness for everyone, their way is the best. They will become aggressive if you try to block them or pull them off their chosen direction.

Horse natives are great at business—primarily from the perspective of sales and promotion. They are sociable beings, eager to connect people for the benefit of all. However, they're not good at sticking to a schedule, nor do they like adhering to procedures. The more stimulating the job, the better! Once involved in their tasks, Horse much prefers to keep working on a project until it's done, then take time off to play.

Horse natives are better at short-term projects; they may not have the staying power to tackle lengthy processes. Break goals down into quick steps. Horses are great at solving problems. They love to get things done—no endless projects, please! Horses are curious and enthusiastically interested, or not interested at all. Once they lose interest, they're out the door. (This goes for love as well as business.)

Horses need both mental and physical exercise. They are graceful and elegant in their movements (and in their decision-making). They can be defiant nonconformists. When you try to put them in a box, they become hot-tempered and headstrong.

Their biggest problem is their lack of focus and their readiness to jump to another project when things seem to move too slow. They will abandon the original goal and wonder why they are not making much progress.

Horse natives excel at making money. They are strong leaders, but allow people the freedom to work on their own. They can be extremely generous with their time and energy, but if Horse doesn't like what you're saying (or doing), he won't think twice about trampling you.

Horse: Predictions for 2021

How to use your High-Energy Days: On these days, plan to take action for your most important goals, make vital phone calls, send important emails. Your high-energy days are when your energy and luck are the strongest for the month.

January 2021: *Uranus goes direct on January 14. Mercury goes retrograde from January 30 to February 20. Your Lucky Days are 1, 7, 13, 19, 25, and 31. [How to use your Lucky Days: On these days, plan to take significant actions, make vital phone calls, send emails. These are days when your energy and luck are high.]*

The Metal Rat year comes to a close, and you may already feel the new energy of the Metal Ox year approaching. This year is when you have had to stomp your feet a little harder to get the attention you deserve. Now, in the shifting energy, you find you've learned much about how to promote yourself and your work. This will be beneficial in the new year.

A person from your past returns. If this was a lover, they might want to get things going again. If they were a close friend, they might move back to your area. Either way, this could be interesting.

Your child or a younger relative may come to you for help with school or finding a job, but they may be more interested in having you listen to their side of the story than hearing your advice.

If you're in a committed relationship, it's a good idea to get together and have a conversation about finances. When the two of you are on the same page, you can create some real prosperity. You can make progress this month by talking about your goals to repay debt or accumulating retirement savings.

Renovations or repairs on the home front may have to be postponed. Mercury is retrograde at the end of the month, and you may have trouble finding reliable service people to help. Or you may want to wait until this energy clears, and you are sure which changes you want to make to the house. You may also be interested in selling or downsizing. It's a good discussion point, but wait to take action until after Mercury goes direct in February.

February 2021: *Lunar New Year begins on February 12. Happy Year of the Metal Ox. February 20 has Mercury going direct. February 27 is the full moon. Your High-Energy Days are 6, 12, 18, and 24.*

February begins with the final weeks of the Metal Rat energy. Use this energy to finish up projects and declutter. Put this ending energy to use by reviewing what you've been working on for some time and consider if you need to continue or if it's ready to be completed. If you have been procrastinating on a project, it may be a sign that it's time just to let it go.

February 12 brings the new moon and the year of the Metal Ox. This is improved energy for Horse natives even though there are considerable differences between an ox and a horse. The horse and the ox live on the farm but have different jobs. The ox toils away day after day, while the horse is engaged for pleasure rides or to pull a cart filled with children. The ox moves slowly and deliberately, whereas the horse can race ahead and turn quickly. So think of 2021 as a time to make adjustments. There will be many opportunities, not all of them will be a perfect fit. This is where adjustments can be necessary.

The new moon also brings Horse natives some opportunities for romance. Over the next two weeks, you can connect with an interesting person. If you're already in a love relationship, you may find the two of you have more fun, break out of your routine, and enjoy each other.

There's a shift in energy on February 18, and Mercury goes direct on February 20. Career energy improves. If you own a business, you may be ready to take a calculated risk, expand your territory, or launch a new product. Horse natives who work for someone else may get extra hours added to the schedule, or be asked to lead a team.

On February 27, there is a full moon, and over the next two weeks you'll focus a great deal on routines and habits. This is a great time to add spiritual practices to your daily routine, such as meditation, yoga, or journaling. You may want to stimulate the energy by moving your Feng Shui cures to new locations.

March 2021: *March 13 brings the new moon, March 20 marks the first day of spring, March 28 is the full moon. Your High-Energy Days are 2, 8, 14, 20, and 26.*

As March begins, you find you are choosing between something you need and something you want. There may be a way to find a compromise to have both. Consider some gray areas, rather than just looking at everything in terms of black-and-white.

March also brings the ability to dissolve boundaries. In some cases, boundaries create limitations. You can think outside your blocks right now. You can see a way forward that didn't seem to exist even a month ago.

March 13 is the new moon, and for those Horse natives in school, you could be extremely busy with homework or preparing for tests. Assistance with schoolwork is easy to find now. Also, you can get help from school administrators or educational consultants.

March 20 brings new energy to your relationships, including your close friendships, business partnerships, and love relationship. If you want to expand your circle of acquaintances and friends over the next few weeks, positive energy surrounds your efforts. You'll find more synchronicity than usual as you reach out to people, even in simply connecting with them at the first attempt. Horse natives are naturally adept at social interaction. You're generous, enthusiastic, and fun to be with.

March 28 brings the new moon, and you can heal an essential connection in your life. You may help others to get along better. Through good communication, you can find a point of common ground with just about anyone now. This may be one of the high points of the year.

April 2021: *April 12 brings the new moon. April 27 is the full moon, and Pluto goes retrograde. (Pluto moving backward can cause you to review your basic assumptions of life and eliminate what is unnecessary, bringing you back to what is essential. Pluto will be retrograde until October.) Your High-Energy Days are 1, 7, 13, 19, and 25.*

April begins with more positive relationship energy. You may be tempted to reengage with someone you used to date. Someone from your past comes back into your life and tells you they've changed. And they may have, but you have as well. Often it's better to move forward, but this month you can find yourself encountering temptations from the past.

April 12 brings the new moon, and there is a great deal of focus on home and family. You could make some significant changes at home, transforming the house through construction or redecorating. You may do a deep decluttering. These changes at home may be due to someone moving out, and as they take their belongings and furniture, it seems like parts of the house echo with emptiness.

You may be tempted to fill up the house again quickly. Horse native, you have an opportunity to make money through your home during this time. You could consider getting a roommate, or setting up a home office. While this can lead to good things, the process can feel a little chaotic at first. Allow the possibility you may not quite feel at home where you are now. The disruption at home can leave you feeling out of sorts; however, things will feel better soon.

There is a significant shift in energy on April 19, and a possible financial windfall could land in your lap. This could be a zero-interest loan, or you may receive some object of value. This activity brings your thoughts to your finances in general. Over the next few weeks, you might take steps to change how you handle money, where you go for investment advice, or where you bank.

April 27 is the full moon, and your focus on finances continues. Now is an excellent time to look at how many resources you have available to you, and how you can capitalize on them. You may investigate investing, or perhaps you considering a stock purchase plan through your company. There may be online groups where you can learn about real estate investing or get into bitcoin. Over the next couple of weeks, you can start on the path of making more money and see success by the end of the year.

May 2021: *May 11 brings the new moon. May 23, Saturn goes retrograde. (Saturn retrograde can cause you to review your career choices and make adjustments. Saturn will be retrograde until October). May 26 is a total lunar eclipse. May 29 has Mercury going retrograde. Your High-Energy Days are 1, 7, 13, 19, and 25.*

May comes in bringing with it a lot of determination and focus for Horse natives. Financial opportunities may show up from several directions. While some of these could be one-time windfalls, there are streams of income forming a steady flow of money coming your way. If you have been focused on paying off debts, it's a good idea to channel some of this money toward that end. This month, visualize what your life would be like if you were wealthy. Give yourself a compelling vision, and doors will start to open.

On May 11, there's a new moon. The focus for Horse natives moves to spirituality, contemplating just how are interacting with the Universe. You often have an optimistic view of life, and this allows you to see opportunities. Over the next two weeks, you can increase your spiritual work by praying, meditating or attending spiritual classes. Consider attending a conference with motivational or spiritual leaders. Consider limiting time spent watching the news, and look for more uplifting and inspirational messages.

The energy shifts on May 20 to focus on education. You may finish up a school year with all that entails. You could look at short courses on practical matters such as video editing, social media marketing, or home repair. You might consider a subscription to an education website. If you already have one, you may find renewed interest in the content.

There's a lunar eclipse on May 26, and on May 29, Mercury goes retrograde. Over the next two weeks, there could be some delays in receiving a contract or getting agreements signed. You may get an offer for a job or promotion, but starting during the Mercury retrograde period can be problematic. Look at how you can delay your start time, perhaps by drawing out negotiations.

Towards the end of the month, you are showing increased activity with siblings and neighbors. A solution can be found to a long-term disagreement, or the two of you agree to disagree.

June 2021: *June 10 is the annular solar eclipse. June 20 is the first day of summer, and Jupiter goes retrograde. (Jupiter retrograde can indicate a need to relearn things or a review of your beliefs. Jupiter will be retrograde until October). June 22 has Mercury going direct. June 24 is the full moon. On June 25, Neptune goes retrograde. (Neptune retrograde can draw you back towards habits and addictions from your past. It can also encourage a return to spiritual practices. Neptune will be retrograde until December). Your High-Energy Days are 6, 12, 18, 24, and 30.*

June brings some changes, but in general, there is harmonious energy. You may have been wishing for some new opportunities, and now they appear. It's good to recognize how the Universe weaves together the gift you've asked for with the lesson your soul needs. This doesn't mean you need to accept everything being offered by the Universe. Each opportunity should be considered carefully before you jump in.

June 10 brings the solar eclipse. For those Horse natives dealing with legal or contract issues, this eclipse energy can bring a breakthrough. However, know that the Universe prefers action. If you are working on your case or contract, you have a much better chance of having a positive outcome from the eclipse energy. That said, eclipses can bring disruptive energy. You do want to avoid initiating lawsuits or signing contracts around this time.

The energy shifts on June 20 and highlights the top of your chart. Now you may receive recognition at your job. If you have been looking for employment, this is a great time to be posting your resume or reaching out to hiring managers as you are more visible. For the next few weeks, you have an opportunity to make a great connection. Additionally, Mercury goes direct on June 22, and this helps communication flow more freely.

On June 24, the full moon highlights a lot of activity at home. You may set up a home office, but it's more likely the family is coming together to spend time with you. Out-of-town guests may visit, or older kids come home from school. You the grandchildren may be visiting. Horse natives enjoy a lot of activity, so a bit of noise in the house can be comforting.

July 2021: *July 10 brings the new moon. July 24 is the full moon. Your High-Energy Days are 6, 12, 18, 24, and 30.*

The month of July brings calmer energy, and Horse natives can breathe a sigh of relief as everything settles down into a routine. If you have a new job, you may start feeling more comfortable in the role. The additional people in the house have blended in, and now everyone's feeling more at home. For single Horse natives, thoughts can turn to love, as someone you've known for some time expresses interest in you romantically. While you may have some hesitation about this individual, it's still fun to play with possibilities. Your charisma is high, and you can be admired by many this month.

July 10 brings the new moon and a great deal of focus on your reputation. You have accepted certain responsibilities, and now others are counting on you. If you are a member of a group, it's possible you will be offered a leadership position in the organization. At work, you may find you've been tapped to lead the team. Or it's possible you merely need to step forward and take over some aspect of your job to show managers you are capable of doing it. Remember, this is a Metal Ox year where hard work is lauded. By stepping forward and volunteering, your reputation is elevated.

On July 22, the energy shifts and Horse natives just want to have fun. It may have been a while since you've had any sort of time off, and had the chance to be social. This is a good time for a vacation or just a weekend getaway. If work and obligations keep you home, it would be good idea to invite some friends over for socializing or spending time in the backyard around the pool.

The full moon is on July 24, and romance is back in the picture. Someone from your past, or someone very familiar to you is likely to be knocking on your door. Those Horse natives looking for love would do well to ask friends and family for assistance to meet new people; and more importantly, make it possible to let go of relationships from your past. Free yourself to be with somebody new. If you're already in an established relationship, now is the time to become closer to your sweetheart. You seem to be more connected than ever, finishing each other's sentences and reading each other's thoughts.

August 2021: *August 8 brings the new moon. On August 20, Uranus goes retrograde. August 22 is the full moon. Your High-Energy Days are 5, 11, 17, 23, and 29.*

For Horse natives, August brings a renewed sense of feeling connected to nature and to the people around you. You may do more walking or hiking. You may visit the ocean or a lake. Consider daily meditation or spend some quiet time listening to the messages of your heart and the Universe. There's a lot of love energy around you. You may slip off to spend time with your sweetheart, share long intimate conversations, or spend time in each other's arms.

The new moon comes in on August 8 and brings a celebration. This might be a birthday or an important anniversary. You may attend a wedding or a baby shower. Horse natives love to be social, and you have lots of friends, some of whom you haven't seen in a long time. This is an excellent opportunity to reconnect with people you care about who can't wait to see you.

The middle of August is also a time when you need to make some adjustments in your schedule to accommodate other people. Fortunately, Horse natives are good at pivoting and making quick changes. You adapt quickly, which helps if your significant other suddenly has to work the night shift, or if the beginning of school now means everyone's getting up much earlier.

The energy shifts with the a new moon on August 22, and the good energy for relationships continues. During this time, several people may comment on how good you look. This is because you are taking care of yourself, either physically or sartorially. It's possible someone close to you is moving away. This could be an older child going off to school or a friend who is moving back to their hometown. It's both a happy and sad moment, where you wish them well but you'll miss them.

Financially, there's some good energy around taking calculated risks. If you have been thinking about starting a business and have worked out the details, now is the time to launch. Or you may consider doing a side business that takes a small investment. In the Metal Ox energy, you want to move slowly and deliberately, but know that forward movement is supported now.

September 2021: *September 7 brings the new moon. September 20 is the full moon. September 22 is the first day of autumn. September 26 has Mercury going retrograde. Your High-Energy Days are 4, 10, 16, 22, and 28.*

September brings some busy energy, and you may work some overtime hours. A lot is going on behind the scenes as you may be putting together reports or streamlining procedures. What you're doing may not be noticed or appreciated by supervisors, so it's essential to speak up. It's not the usual way you draw attention to your work, but this is one case where it's good to have your name in big, bold letters on the report you're submitting.

For Horse natives in school or who have kids in school, you are getting back into a routine and dealing with homework and tests. It's a good idea now to take a little time to develop systems for getting school work done. Find a dedicated place to study within the home where all the tools you need are organized, as well as adequate lighting.

On September 7, there's a new moon, and all this rushing around has you feeling pretty tired. If you haven't been sleeping well, you will want to carve out some extra time for yourself for naps or to get to bed early. Look at your evening routine and see what changes you can make to facilitate getting to sleep easier. Things like darkening the room, having a white noise machine, or getting a better mattress can help a lot.

On September 20, there's a full moon and a great deal of your focus centers around your routines and habits. This is a great time to let go of a habit that is not beneficial to you. Changes in your diet or exercise can really stick right now. Additionally, you are highly intuitive at the moment. If you feel something going on with your body, trust what you feel, and make the effort to establish shifts in what you eat or how you take care of yourself. It's easy for you to pick up the energy of others right now, so make a point of hanging around positive people—at least for the next few weeks.

On September 22, the energy shifts, and Horse natives come into the limelight. Now the work you're doing behind the scenes is easily seen and recognized. You may be asked to do a presentation or to stand up to lead the meeting. If you're interested in a promotion or advancement at work, you will still have to ask, but once you do, you're likely to receive a favorable response.

On September 26, Mercury goes retrograde, and you might have to redo something you thought was done. Check with teammates to ensure that they are on track and that the retrograde Mercury hasn't disrupted their process or caused them to lose data.

October 2021: *October 6 brings the new moon, and Pluto goes direct. On October 11, Saturn goes direct. October 18 has Mercury going direct and Jupiter going direct. October 20 is the full moon. Your High-Energy Days are 4, 10, 16, 22, and 28.*

October brings a lot of good luck for Horse natives as you enter another high energy period. Partnership energy is elevated, and this could include business connections, helpful mentors, or people who wish to collaborate with you. This could bring some attractive financial opportunities. But be aware of your time limits before signing on to your friend's business, or a new marketing plan. You do best when there's balance in your life, some time for work, some time for play.

October 6 brings the new moon, and the seeds you planted earlier in the year ow show healthy sprouts. The resume you posted a while back now seems to show some activity. If you own a business, clients are now finding you. Money flows in nicely, though you'll feel a desire to spend it! Spending money to make more money can be beneficial, but watch out for over-spending; a spending spree won't help your budget in the long run. On October 18, Mercury goes direct, and energy begins to flow much more easily.

The full moon is on October 20; there's a great deal of communication with an intimate relationship or a very close friend. There's also a lot of activity in your area of siblings. Maybe people in your life are not getting along, and you need to step in to help sort things out. Overall this energy is positive, but it will take a little bit of managing on your part. Horse natives are natural leaders, and so you can step up to show others the way.

On October 22, the energy shifts, and your focus moves towards finances for the next few weeks. There is a potential opportunity to bring a stream of income, or your income source becomes stronger. You may receive a windfall from the sale of a large ticket item. But most of the energies indicate a long-term source of money is becoming available to you.

November 2021: *November 4 is the new moon. November 19 is a partial lunar eclipse. Your High-Energy Days are 3, 9, 15, 21, and 27.*

November is one of the most vital money months you have all year. Lots of activities you've done over the previous months are now leading to financial benefit. This may be connected to your job; or your side business beginning to take off. It's good to pay attention to your spending and plug up any holes. You may decide you want to get out of debt or save for something important, like a big trip or buying a home. Now you can get family members on board. You might have met someone who inspired you and now has you enthusiastic about saving and making more money.

November 4 brings the new moon. Look at self-worth and self-confidence issues concerning how much money you make. You may be placing artificial limits on your revenue because you do not feel confident. Horse natives feel best when others support them, but if difficult people surround you, you may find your confidence waning.

November 19 brings a partial lunar eclipse, affecting your area of resources received from others. This is tricky energy; you may talk to a bank or financial institution to arrange a loan or discuss refinancing an existing loan. But with the eclipse energy, you'll likely run into delays. It's necessary to be patient, to fill out paperwork thoroughly, and to see if you can establish a relationship with a banking official.

On November 21, the energy shifts, and there's a great deal of focus on paperwork and communication in general. So whatever didn't happen over the last couple of days now comes to the forefront of your mind. Quickly return phone calls and check email regularly, so nothing is missed. This way, you can come out ahead.

December 2021: *On December 1, Neptune goes direct. December 4 is a total solar eclipse. December 19 brings the full moon, and Venus goes retrograde. (Venus retrograde can cause you to question what you want and inspire you to look for something new that delights you. Venus will be retrograde until January.) December 21 is the first day of winter. Your High-Energy Days are 3, 9, 15, 21, and 27.*

Not surprisingly, for social Horse natives, December brings an emphasis on home and family. It may seem a little overwhelming with people set to arrive for a visit, or your house being designated as this year's venue for holiday activities at the beginning of the month. But within a few days, you have everything well in hand. For some Horse natives, there are still school projects to complete and turn in, so overall, December is a pretty busy month.

December 4 brings the solar eclipse in your area of communications, contracts and agreements. If you plan to sign any contracts in the context of a large purchase or employment, it's wise to read over the terms carefully, or even run the agreement past a lawyer. There can be last-minute changes at this time, allowing you to make some modifications to the agreement before you sign it.

Around this time, communication is also essential. Horse natives are known for their frank and honest talk, but sometimes a little diplomacy is appropriate. This is especially true in relation to conversations around neighbors and siblings.

On December 19, there's a full moon, and the energy slows down considerably. Now, in the last third of the month, you have some time to focus on family and the holidays. You can get some rest. This doesn't mean that the world has stopped banging on your door; in fact, work obligations may bang louder than ever, but take a break. On December 19, Venus goes retrograde, causing you to change your mind about something you want. This goes for everyone in your life. Keep this in mind if you're buying holiday gifts and make sure the things you buy are returnable.

On December 21, a new season arrives and changes the energy. It is an apt time to look at the upcoming year concerning your dwelling. What changes do you want to make in 2022? Some Horse natives will be able to decide to move or to carry out renovations on their current house. You may receive an indication that a move will happen in the next year.

January 2022: *January 2 is the new moon. January 14 has Mercury going retrograde. January 17 is the full moon. On January 18, Uranus goes direct. On January 29, Venus goes direct. Your High-Energy Days are 2, 8, 14, 20, and 26.*

While the calendar year begins, there is still Metal Ox energy to contend with. Many Horse natives are ready to charge forward, but you can feel held back. This is the perfect time to finish things up. Look at what was left incomplete at the end of 2021 and see if you can put any final touches on it. This mainly includes creative projects like screenplays, home renovations, or website creation.

The new moon falls on January 2, and for Horse natives, the emphasis is on home and family, and now to an even greater extent on your extended family. You may help someone move or get settled into a new place. Someone may travel to you to stay for a while. Some Horse natives will send off older children back to college. If the weather permits, clean up around the outside of your house. For those who are homebound because of the weather, consider working on your entryway to make it warm and inviting.

On January 14, Mercury goes retrograde in your area of romance and fun. You may be contacted by a lover from your past, someone who wants to rekindle things. Or you might reach out to someone you knew a long time ago. You can track this person down through Facebook and see how they're doing. Communication with friends or distant relatives you haven't spoken to in a while is also a good idea.

January 17 brings the full moon, and you may find there is a work-at-home opportunity, or the business you run out of the house is expanding. Financially things improve, and while you may have put a lot of money into furnishings or repairs at home, you're also able to put some into your savings account.

The energy shifts on January 19, and there are opportunities for happy relationships for Horse natives looking for love. You can meet someone new through friends, or an online dating app. Over the next few weeks, you could connect with someone who becomes a long-term relationship for you.

February 2022: *February 1 is the new moon and begins the Year of the Water Tiger. February 3 has Mercury going direct. February 16 brings the full moon.*

As the year of the Water Tiger begins, Horse natives start to enjoy the harmonious energy it brings. While others may tremble at the sight of the Tiger, you are up for some excitement and looking forward to the numerous opportunities the Tiger year will bring.

Attract New Love

While Ox years can be challenging for Horse natives, love is an area of your life where you can experience good luck and ease. There are numerous opportunities for you to meet someone new and start a great relationship. There is a little bit of chasing back and forth, some teasing and some intrigue, but that adds to Horse natives' fun. New interesting people are met

through friends or a connection with your children. You also can meet lovers when you are doing things you enjoy, such as sports or art. Be careful in May when some miscommunication can send the other person running away. But you'll most likely reunite in June, and everything will be rosy again.

When you are looking for love, you need to attract someone who helps you feel balanced. A good Feng Shui cure for you this year is the Yin/Yang symbol.

The Yin/Yang symbolism depicts a balance of energies, the talents of one partner support the lack in the other. To successfully attract a new love, you can wear the Yin/Yang symbol (as jewelry, printed on a T-shirt, a patch on a jacket, etc.), or place the symbol in the bedroom.

Enhance Existing Love

2021 is an absolutely electric relationship year for Horse natives. Romance energy is intense, no matter how long you've been together. Together you're having an adventure when you're in the world and having fun behind closed doors. You might explore things together privately, breaking through old barriers, and become more intimate. But most of all, you trust each other, which allows you both to remove blocks and inhibitions. Amid this, there could be a family that throws the rhythm off for a short while. But as you come back together, you seem more bonded than ever.

Not all Feng Shui cures have to be traditionally Chinese in origin. There are many symbols broadly used in many cultures. The wedding ring quilt is such a symbol, in this case, of love and fidelity. To enhance your existing love relationship, place a wedding ring quilt on your bed. You can also hang a small lap quilt or quilted wall hanging in the same design on your bedroom wall to help enhance your partnership's energy.

Looking to Conceive?

In many parts of China, women who want to conceive place a bowl of uncooked rice under their bed. If you would like to test this traditional approach to becoming pregnant, take a decorative bowl made of porcelain or china, and fill it about two-thirds full of uncooked rice (white rice is traditional). Place the bowl in the center, underneath the bed. Do not disturb the bowl until the baby is born.

(From Donna Stellhorn's book, A Path to Pregnancy: Ancient Secrets for the Modern Woman)

Family and Kids

The family unit is strong this year, even though individual members are following their own interests. Everyone comes together for brief but intense times, such as parties, family game nights, or the holidays. There is a lot of attention on you, Horse native, this year. You can lead the family toward more success, whether by taking more risks or being more creative with your choices. Horse natives enjoy a great deal of creative energy this year, this can stimulate fertility energy and help you bring more members into the family. Adult children may also marry and have children. Pets may be added to the household.

The beautiful, hard stony substance formed from certain marine animals symbolizes growth and protection. It comes in a variety of colors and shapes, and it displays beautifully on tables. Place a piece of coral in your dining room or family room. Place it on a shelf or table where it can be seen. You can also find a piece to wear when you feel you need some added protection.

Money

This is an outstanding year for Horse natives to make money if you apply creative thinking and a bit of bravado. Being bold will make profits. This can mean you put your creative work out to the world, perhaps with art, music, or writing.

Money can also be made through investing or by starting a small business. For business, look to partner with people you care about, especially adult children. For your investments, slow and steady wins the race. As the markets gyrate, stick with what you know. Investments in property, luxury goods, and items of value such as coins can do well.

This year, to bring positive career energy, consider burning a metallic gold candle approximately once a month. From a Feng Shui perspective, metallic gold represents large sums of money, and a candle, or anything on fire, focuses our attention. You can find small metallic gold candles in the wedding department of your local party store or online.

You can also write your wish for positive career energy into the wax of the candle. Take a pencil or a sturdy toothpick and write your wish in block letters along the side or the top of the candle. As you write, picture your desires coming true. Burn the candle in your home office or the entryway of your home. If you feel uncomfortable burning candles in the home, you can use a battery or plugin type. Remember, these aren't nearly as powerful, so keep the "candle" on for the entire month.

Job or Career

The energy improves for your career as you receive more recognition for creative ideas. Horse natives work well with others. While the energy is good, don't get too comfortable—there are changes with technology and software platforms you use daily. Embrace these changes and go with the flow rather than set up a blockade against something new. Move towards industries that cater to younger people. You may work with lots of younger people this year. This brings new, exciting energy to your career. You're in your harvest period, and now your considerable skills can bring you better money. There will be opportunities to negotiate for a raise, especially in November.

When you want to attract money in abundance, hang or display a pair of fish by the front door. The fish may be crafted out of fabric, glass, wood, or metal. The symbol of the two fish represents the saying, "May you have so much money, you have left-over money!" In Feng Shui, fish are used to attract wealth because the Chinese word for fish sounds like the word for "abundance." Displaying a couple of fish this year will help the money flow in effortlessly.

Education

You may complete school or be in the final years of a more extended program. You may itch for a change. If you are looking to shift schools this year, or go on to some advanced program, there are some funding opportunities if you look for them. Search places connected to your church or community, as well as looking online. You find school the most joyful part of your day for most of the year, interacting with many friends and connections. Others help you throughout this year, and you help them. This is a perfect time to push yourself outside your comfort zone by taking on more significant projects or doing many presentations. May and December show decisions need to be made about school. Don't rush decisions during these months. Instead, talk things through with your family before making your choice.

Legal Matters

This year you have a lot of luck and positive energy for contracts and agreements. This is true for contracts for your creative work, or involving investments. Read terms carefully and negotiate any points to your satisfaction. Your timing is right in this matter this year. It's possible to get what you want through a formal agreement.

When it comes to lawsuits, you also have luck this year concerning copyright or patent issues, child custody, child care, and child education cases. You have a little bit more luck in class action suits than individual suits. However, there is more positive energy for you this year than you've had in several years.

Health and Well-Being

The good habits you put into place and the additional exercise you have been doing are paying off. Even if you've only taken small steps now, you can pick up speed from a walk to a trot to a canter. Emotionally, there is some stress when you become overly empathetic to others' situations, especially when the stories are on social media. Remember to have some boundaries in relation to other people's issues. It's good to burn sage when you come home at the end of the day, or to add a little salt to your bath to clear any difficult energies. You show a change in eating habits as cooking could become a fun hobby or something you do with friends.

The fragrant herb, rosemary, does more than just flavor your dinner. Rosemary is a powerful herb for protecting health. It's been used for centuries for medicinal and spiritual purposes. It's been used for guarding people and activating the energy of longevity.

If possible, and when it's the right season, grow a rosemary plant on your front porch. Otherwise, place a small rosemary plant in your kitchen window. Whenever you need a boost, you can snip off a small leaf or two to add to your meal.

Sheep/Goat/Ram

February 13, 2007–February 1, 2008:
Yin Fire Sheep/Goat/Ram
February 1, 1919–February 19, 1920:
Yin Earth Sheep/Goat/Ram
February 17, 1931–February 5, 1932:
Yin Metal Sheep/Goat/Ram
February 5, 1943–January 24, 1944:
Yin Water Sheep/Goat/Ram
January 24, 1955–February 11, 1956:
Yin Wood Sheep/Goat/Ram
February 9, 1967–January 29, 1968:
Yin Fire Sheep/Goat/Ram
January 28, 1979–February 15, 1980:
Yin Earth Sheep/Goat/Ram
February 15, 1991–February 3, 1992:
Yin Metal Sheep/Goat/Ram
February 1, 2003–January 21, 2004:
Yin Water Sheep/Goat/Ram
February 19, 2015–February 7, 2016:
Yin Wood Sheep/Goat/Ram
February 6, 2027–January 25, 2028,
Yin Fire Sheep/Goat/Ram

Sheep/Goat/Ram Personality

When considering a Chinese Zodiac animal's qualities, examine its traits, behaviors, and personality. For this sign, we need to consider several animals—Sheep, Goat, and Ram. They have distinctive qualities. We'll start with Sheep.

There are many traditions and stories about Sheep. (A ram is a male sheep, and a ewe is a female sheep, and lambs are both the male and female young.) Sheep are gregarious creatures who enjoy living in a flock. They can become stressed when separated from others in their flock. They have a natural inclination to follow a leader. Sheep are not territorial, but they do like to stay in familiar spaces. They flee from danger, but when cornered, they will charge and "ram" you.

Even though the traits of Ram represent the masculine expression of the sheep family energy, people born under the sign of Sheep appreciate the more "feminine" expression of their essence. By this, I mean qualities such as shyness, sensitivity, tolerance, and compassion. Sheep natives represent these attributes.

While Sheep can come across as thin-skinned, they will willingly forgive when they sense the honesty in an apology. Sheep dislike getting hemmed in, preferring not to be under someone else's rule or schedule. Neither do they care to rule—often opting for the supporting role.

Sheep is a generous sign; known for their kind heart. Despite their generosity—or perhaps because of it—they always have a pleasant home, plenty of food, and money in the bank. Sheep spends their life helping others and are generously reciprocated.

When Sheep make a list of their material goals and share it with others, people step up to help Sheep make these goals a reality. Sheep often receive legacies from people not related to them.

The only time a Sheep is straightforward in word and deed is when they are angry. Most of the time, they will take a circuitous route to tell you what they want or think. They may tell you their story in the most expressive and creative terms, yet never come right out to say what they need or expect of you.

Sheep are devoted to their families and their friends. They remember birthdays, celebrate occasions, and are quick to send help when they sense trouble for the people they care about. Often not reciprocated, their birthdays or special events are often forgotten by those around them, which profoundly hurts the kindly Sheep.

Sheep natives show a tendency to worry and perceive future events as being dark and potentially disastrous. They can spend many hours—even days—stuck in a dark depression. They benefit greatly by talking over their difficulties with others, but many Sheep try to hold everything inside, causing physical issues such as fatigue and low energy.

Sheep can receive money, but they often spread it around quickly, leaving themselves with just the minimum to meet their needs. They often attract money in the first place because of someone else—someone they love needs it. It's imperative that Sheep plan for their future financial security, although they rarely do so.

Sheep are astute in business and are masters of the soft sell. They're able to get beyond objections and help others decide.

People born under the sign of the Sheep wait for the right moment to take action on their goals. They can wait for quite a while to get what they want. Committed to doing things the "right way," things seldom get done at all.

Sheep are hypercritical of their own actions (and sometimes the actions of others.) This leaves them feeling vulnerable and causing them a great deal of suffering. They need to take chances more often—they are more sure-footed than they realize.

In some parts of the world, the creature symbolizing this section of the Chinese Zodiac is the Goat—not Sheep or Ram. While many of the qualities ascribed to Goat are similar to those of Sheep or Ram, the energy of Goat has some unique attributes overall. A person born in the year of the Sheep/Goat can access the attributes of the Goat and also the Sheep.

While Goat is a different animal than a Sheep, goats are a subfamily of sheep. A simple way to tell the difference is by noting a goat's tail points to heaven, and a sheep's tail points to earth. When you act more goat-like, you can focus on climbing to new heights; you seek to get to the top and see the view below. When you are more Sheep-like, you want to stay home and stay in your comfort zone, your routine.

Goat forages for its meal; sheep graze on grass. People born in Sheep/Goat years may find they investigate lots of new things, new foods, new places, and new people. They might then spend months doing the opposite—sticking to a routine and the places and people they know well.

One of the valuable qualities of Goat we see in people born in Sheep/Goat years is curiosity. This quality allows you to explore and examine various opportunities and determine whether they may be viable for you to pursue. Curiosity keeps you interested in the motivations of the people around you. Your life is enriched as you find yourself entranced by new topics and ideas. This keeps life very interesting.

For clarity in this book, we will refer to Sheep, Goat, or Ram as Sheep.

Sheep/Goat/Ram: Predictions for 2021

How to use your High-Energy Days: On these days, plan to take action for your significant goals, make vital phone calls, send critical emails. Your high-energy days are when your energy and luck are the strongest for the month.

January 2021: *Uranus goes direct on January 14. Mercury goes retrograde from January 30 to February 20. Your Lucky Days are 2, 8, 14, 20, and 26. [How to use your Lucky Days: On these days, plan to take significant actions, make vital phone calls, send emails. These are days when your energy and luck are high.]*

Income opportunities are around you, and you can collect money from several sources this month. You may also sell some property or other large ticket items, bringing you some cash.

A neighbor or sibling is communicating with you—a welcomed connection. You can receive useful advice or assistance now from this person.

There is a lot of activity around relationships for Sheep natives already in a love connection. You may move in together or otherwise making the partnership official. This calls for a party.

There are some changes in management or a shift in supervisors at work. This is not the first managerial change you've been through, and it's not the last. Things will settle down again in a few weeks. Just take a wait-and-see attitude—no reason to plan any notable changes for yourself now.

The energy of the new year, Metal Ox, is almost here. Ox is the opposing sign to your own. The world will turn away from all things Sheep to put their attention on Ox. Sheep natives prefer company rather than feel alone. As the energy shifts, you must reach out to friends and family. Looking forward into the next year, you must be the one who initiates contact, suggests the get-togethers, picks the restaurant, etc. It's more work for you, but it will gather to you the people you enjoy.

February 2021: *Lunar New Year begins on February 12. Happy Year of the Metal Ox. February 20 has Mercury going direct. February 27 is the full moon. Your High-Energy Days are 1, 7, 13, 19, and 25.*

February begins, still in Metal Rat energy, putting the focus on relationships for Sheep natives. There may have been changes in a special relationship over the past few weeks. This could mean your sweetheart moves in, or perhaps the two of you begin to look for a house to buy together. If you're looking for love, now you is the perfect time to meet new people by focusing on activities that interest you. You may soon connect with someone interested in music, cooking, hiking, or another of your favorite hobbies.

February 12 brings the new lunar year of the Metal Ox. Now the eyes of the world look away from Sheep towards the sign of Ox. You don't like to draw a lot of attention to yourself, but this year you may be downright ignored. To avoid being passed over, you may have to speak a little louder as you point out your accomplishments.

This month, Sheep natives focus a great deal on your home life. You may be doing some renovations or moving furniture around the house. Some Sheep natives will be looking for a new place to live. You may want to build a house, or perhaps you may even be considering such a big step as moving out of the country. This is the time for decisions; most of the action will happen later this year.

The energy shifts on February 18, and you see an opportunity to achieve a longtime goal. Over the next few weeks, things fall into place, allowing you to take decisive action. One of the gifts Sheep natives possess is the ability to take action that aligns with your goals. If you're not sure what you want, this is an excellent time to sit quietly and meditate on possibilities. Free your mind to think of what could be.

The full moon is on February 27, and there is a lot of activity around family, especially children or younger relatives. The younger generation wants to do things differently, maybe even break some traditions. But before you get too stressed, consider your rebellious earlier years. Be ready to make changes when changes seem practical, logical, and beneficial. Now is not a time to be stubborn.

March 2021: *March 13 brings the new moon, March 20 marks the first day of spring, March 28 is the full moon. Your High-Energy Days are 3, 9, 15, 21, and 27.*

March comes in, and Sheep natives focus a great deal on relationships. You may feel stuck in a situation, feel neglected or taken advantage of. While you don't necessarily like to make waves and you prefer to give the other person the benefit of the doubt, this month, you may need to give voice to your concerns. Fortunately, with a few words from you, you can see a change in their behavior.

The new moon comes in on March 13 with better energy. You have access to some resources from other people. These could be financial resources, but these can also be expertise, manpower, or a helping hand in some area where you need it.

Romance energy is also strong this month, and you may happen to connect with someone through a friend. This link could start with a mutual interest in a hobby or an intellectual pursuit, and grow into a great friendship and even an intimate relationship.

The energy shifts on March 20, and a new season begins. There's a lot of focus on work now, as your office may be short-handed for the next few weeks. It's possible that someone is out on leave, or there could be a hiring freeze. Now your desk is overloaded with things to do. It's a good idea to take frequent breaks as you plow through the tasks.

The full moon lights up the sky on March 28, and the focus is around taking care of yourself, eating well, and getting a good night's sleep. Your job shows to be still busy, and the list of tasks at home is as long as ever. But it's essential to prioritize your to-do list, to put self-care on top. You may benefit from a "pajama day" (when you spend an entire day relaxing in your pajamas). Or find another way to take the pressure off of yourself.

April 2021: *April 12 brings the new moon. April 27 is the full moon, and Pluto goes retrograde. (Pluto moving backward can cause you to review your basic assumptions of life and to eliminate what is unnecessary, bringing you back to what is essential. Pluto will be retrograde until October.) Your High-Energy Days are 2, 8, 14, 20, and 26.*

Your intimate life is the focus in April. Those Sheep natives already in a love relationship may find you're getting along better with your significant other. If you're dating, this is a great time to move the relationship forward, perhaps taking it from a friendship to a romance. If you have children from another relationship, you may be introducing them to your sweetheart. Additionally, there's a lot of fertility energy around you. This is a good month for making plans to add to the family.

The new moon arrives on April 12, and the emphasis is on investments, debt, and banking. Over the next couple of weeks, it's a good idea to look at where you bank and how you approach your investments. You may want to make changes. You can also start a personal program of debt repayment with positive energy towards success. You could consider doing a written budget, keeping track of your money and spending—as Sheep natives can be prone to overspending. Writing everything down keeps your outgo in the forefront of your mind.

The energy shifts on April 19, and over the next few weeks, you may get an employment contract. Or you may agree on a large purchase such as a car or dwelling. Negotiations can go favorably during this time.

The full moon comes in on April 27, and others see that you are more confident and self-assured. You can put yourself forward as a team leader and connect with potential mentors. It's easier now to find people to collaborate with. This can help you expand your business or change jobs. This is possibly one of the best times of the year to reach out to someone of influence and begin a dialogue.

May 2021: *May 11 brings the new moon. On May 23, Saturn goes retrograde. (Saturn retrograde can cause you to review your career choices and make adjustments. Saturn will be retrograde until October). May 26 is a total lunar eclipse. May 29 has Mercury going retrograde. Your High-Energy Days are 2, 8, 14, 20, and 26.*

In May, Sheep natives may think about education as school finishes up, reports come due, or there are final exams for you or your children. You may consider taking shorter courses over the next few months. Online courses related to technology or creative arts could be beneficial. Some Sheep natives will prepare for professional exams during this time. Carve out hours for study and preparation.

The new moon is on May 11, and you may feel adjustments are needed at home or with some aspect of your housing circumstances. This may indicate you are moving, but it's more likely you're carrying out renovations, or someone is moving in or moving out of the home. This also could be a time when you are discussing a major move with your family. You could even be considering a complete lifestyle change, such as moving into a much smaller house, a tiny-house or an RV. This move would couple with a deep decluttering, where you go to the top of the of the attic and into the depths of the basement getting rid of unneeded stuff.

The energy shifts on May 20 and Sheep natives could receive a small windfall. This can be in the form of a sum of money, or you may receive an object of value as a gift. But even more importantly, the person you receive it from is showing how much they care.

On May 26, the energy shifts again, and there is a lunar eclipse shaking up the part of your chart that rules your money. This is the Universe's way of calling attention to your finances. It's an opportunity to be reminded that when you feel you deserve abundance, money flows in. When you feel confident, and you understand your value, you're more likely to ask for the raise; or if you are ready to believe in yourself enough to start your business, you'll know this is the right time.. As this lunar eclipse lights up your money area, consider how to build your sense of self-confidence. This proves to be the key to bringing in more money over the next months and even years.

On May 29, Mercury goes retrograde, and a lot of the plans launched just a few days ago seem to get overturned. This is not a sign you're going in the wrong direction. This is just Mercury retrograde causing you to look at your plans and make adjustments where necessary.

June 2021: *June 10 is the annular solar eclipse. June 20 is the first day of summer, and Jupiter goes retrograde. (Jupiter retrograde can indicate a need to relearn things or review your beliefs. Jupiter will be retrograde until October). June 22 has Mercury going direct. June 24 is the full moon. On June 25, Neptune goes retrograde. (Neptune retrograde can draw you back towards habits and addictions from your past. It can also trigger a return to spiritual practices. Neptune will be retrograde until December). Your High-Energy Days are 1, 7, 13, 19, and 25.*

The month of June brings a reminder to Sheep natives to let your voice be heard. Because this is the year of the Metal Ox and the Zodiac sign of Ox is in opposition to your own sign, the world's attention is turned away from you. You can remedy this by standing up for yourself, clearly stating what you want, and allowing others to help you or offer their support. During June, resources will become available to you. Don't miss this opportunity by not speaking up.

June 10 brings the solar eclipse, and for Sheep natives who own a business, this could bring an opportunity to gain territory, obtain a low-interest loan, or to collaborate with a company in a compatible industry. If you work for someone else, gather the company's perks to make sure you are capitalizing on all that's available. Make sure you've set up your 401(k), so you can receive any matching funds; check if you can purchase company stock at a reduced price, or even see what kind of discounts they have for local shopping.

The energy shifts on June 20 into your area of spirituality. You may feel a desire to take more time for meditation or prayer. You may go back to a church or temple to attend weekly services. You may add spiritual rituals into your daily life, such as lighting candles or reading sacred texts. During the next few weeks, you could feel more connected to God and the Universe. You may receive inspiration and messages.

On June 22, Mercury goes direct, and communication becomes much easier. Emails or texts you have been expecting now flow into your inbox. People are easier to reach, and issues with your phone seem to disappear.

On June 24, there is a full moon and powerful career energy. If you are working for someone else, you may receive some recognition or even an offer of future promotion. Sheep natives looking for a job are likely to get an interview and even an offer over the next couple of weeks.

July 2021: *July 10 brings the new moon. July 24 is the full moon. Your High-Energy Days are 1, 7, 13, 19, and 25.*

Now July arrives, bringing with it the desire and the energy for fun and romance. During this month, your charisma is exceptionally high, and you are attracting several potential love interests. If you're already in a relationship, this could make things complicated in your life. But for Sheep natives looking for love, this is an excellent opportunity to connect with someone where there's good chemistry and lots of shared interests. If you have been looking for love for some time, recognize the blocks you have put up to meeting new people and see if you can break through them.

On July 10, there's a new moon, and for Sheep natives, this can bring an opportunity to travel. You may not have traveled for quite a long time, and there may still be concerns—as there were in 2020—about going to new places. You may plan trips for 2022 or even 2023 now. If you already have plans, the next few weeks is a good time to can confirm plans, put down deposits, or arrange for accommodations.

The energy shifts on July 22 as you become increasingly aware of changes happening with your career over the next few weeks. If your company is financially stable, this could mean it has found a buyer, and there will be changes in upper management. But if your company is not doing well, you may see some signs that it's time for you to leave. Consider updating your resume, and reach out to colleagues who have moved on to other companies (even other industries). This is a time to be proactive.

On July 24, there's a full moon and strong indicators confirm that networking is helpful. This can be good for your career as you search for a new position. This proactivity signals it may also be time to increase or build out your social circle. More friends and connections mean your quality of life improves. This is a great time to be involved with social organizations or charities. Doing work to help the planet or people you care about is very beneficial.

August 2021: *August 8 brings the new moon. On August 20, Uranus goes retrograde. August 22 is the full moon. Your High-Energy Days are 6, 12, 18, 24, and 30.*

August brings some new technology into your life. Maybe you get a new phone or laptop,. or you might make some changes in how you watch television or play video games. You may spend more time with friends because of the new technology coming into your life. You may have more reasons to reach out to them or a better means to get connected.

The new moon falls on August 8, and some of the seeds you planted last month for career opportunities now come through. A friend or colleague of yours may open the door into some new moneymaking venture. This is also a time where you could consider starting a side business. Those Sheep natives who already have a business could see an increase in the work-load now, and feel the need to hire more people. You may even consider hiring a manager to oversee some operations you no longer have time to handle.

The energy shifts on August 22, and the full moon lights up your area of adventure and risk-taking. While Sheep natives are known for being more cautious than other signs, you are also wildly lucky at times. Everything seems to line up, and you can connect with people who open big doors for you. Sheep natives might find an influencer who falls in love with your product line. You may submit a resume at the very moment the position opens up, even before it's posted online. During the next couple of weeks, synchronicity will play a major role in your life, and you will see things line up positively.

The last few days of the month are also interesting from the perspective of love and romance. For those Sheep natives who want to have a little fun, this is a great time to be open with your sweetheart about what you want and need in the relationship. If you're looking for love, there is no better time this year to post your profile to an online dating site or to upload new pictures to your existing profile. Put yourself out in the world, and you will get noticed.

September 2021: *September 7 brings the new moon. September 20 is the full moon. September 22 is the first day of autumn. September 26 has Mercury going retrograde. Your High-Energy Days are 5, 11, 17, 23, and 29.*

In September, Sheep natives become more creative and expansive. Boundaries and limitations are dissolving before your eyes. This month is the time for you to invent, compose, or connect with your muse. If you have been working on a novel, wanting to produce your songs, or maybe paint a mural in your kid's room, there is a lot of positive energy to support creative work. You can also be creative in your everyday life in small ways. You may add a new spice blend to your cooking or reupholster the sofa. Sheep natives are known for being practical, but this is a time you can be absolutely whimsical.

September 7 brings the new moon, and it's a good idea to meditate on your future during this period. You might consider creating a vision board with pictures of things you'd like to have or enjoy. Or perhaps meditate about where you would like to live five years from now. Sit down with your sweetheart to discuss wedding plans or to talk with your high school-aged kids about where they might apply to college next year. Look at where you are now and where you would like to set your trajectory for the future to be sure things are moving in the right direction.

On September 20, there's a full moon, and you become the love interest of someone you know. Someone is expressing their admiration for you. Gratitude comes from friends. People seem to line up to tell you how wonderful you are. It's okay to agree with them.

The energy shifts on September 22, and Sheep natives, it is time for a mini-vacation or a long weekend. Focus on how you can get more sleep and how to create a better work/life balance. Getting rest and spending some time rejuvenating yourself is necessary at this time.

On September 27, Mercury goes retrograde. During retrograde periods, things repeat. There is a long list of things to avoid doing during a retrograde period, such as buying a laptop computer, getting a root canal, or filing for divorce. Fortunately, there are some great things to do during Mercury retrograde because you can use the repetition energy to benefit you—things like starting an exercise program, traveling to a vacation destination, or studying a language. Every time Mercury goes retrograde in the future, you will felt a desire to repeat what you did during this period.

October 2021: *October 6 brings the new moon, and Pluto goes direct. On October 11, Saturn goes direct. October 18 has Mercury going direct and Jupiter going direct. October 20 is the full moon. Your High-Energy Days are 5, 11, 17, 23, and 29.*

The month of October brings Sheep natives heightened intuition and a deeper connection spiritually. This is saying a lot as Sheep natives are one of the most intuitive Chinese zodiac signs. The priority now is that you surround yourself with positive people—as you can be a total psychic sponge during a time like this, absorbing the energies of others. Spend time in nature now, and you can pick up a lot of positive energy simply by being outside. Take walks in the park, hike local trails, or simply sit and watch the squirrels in your backyard; are all beneficial to you.

October 6 brings the new moon. It's a busy time for Sheep natives as you're working behind the scenes on large projects, either for your work or for your current studies. There may be a lot going on at home as you help family members, or even extended relatives. Your tight schedule is wearing you a little thin, so it's imperative you get quality sleep every night. Consider going to bed early or changing up your bedtime routine to help you wind down and fell asleep quickly.

On October 18, Mercury goes direct, and a contract or agreement you've been waiting for can now show up. Give Mercury a few days to get up to speed, and you should see some signs of this important paperwork arriving.

October 20 has the full moon offering robust relationship energy for Sheep natives. If you are dating at this time, you may seek to take your relationship to the next level, perhaps introducing your sweetheart to family and friends, letting people close to you know how important your sweetheart is to you.. Perhaps you discuss moving in together. You may meet their family members and your future in-laws.

On October 22, the energy shifts, and you become more noticeable, possibly for the first time this year. In Metal Ox years, the energy flows the other direction, away from you. It's challenging to get people to listen. But for the next few weeks, you are surrounded by positive energy. There's a lucky angel on your shoulder, so it's a good idea to take risks you have been waiting to take.

November 2021: *November 4 is the new moon. November 19 is a partial lunar eclipse. Your High-Energy Days are 4, 10, 16, 22, and 28.*

The month of November brings some luck to already lucky Sheep natives. You are more able to take direct action towards your goals during this month. Things that held you back now seem to melt away, and your hesitations seem to vanish. You recognize you have every reason to be confident. You're in the flow of the energy now.

On November 4, there's a new moon, and you find help and support coming from a surprising source. Someone you didn't know was your friend steps up and perhaps even makes a sacrifice so you have something you need. This is most likely a "pay it forward" situation, and you will find someone you can help.

There's a lot of energy around home and family. You may offer a relative a place to stay, or you may get some pieces of furniture from someone you know well.

On November 19, there's a lunar eclipse in your area of relationships. Eclipses create change, yet this is an eclipse where something rooted feels like it must be transplanted. A close relationship of yours may move some distance away or because of circumstances in their life, can't spend as much quality time with you. While you may feel momentarily sad, this change is beneficial to both of you as it brings growth and expansion. There might be the desire to keep things the same, but something must change with an eclipse.

On November 21, the energy shifts, and a financial opportunity comes your way. This could be related to something in your job. You might receive an increased commission percentage, land a big sale, or your annual review results in a salary increase. Because this is an opposition year, you may have to talk to your supervisor in order to secure this opportunity. It's a little more difficult to attract opportunities when all the energy turns away from you.

December 2021: *December 1 has Neptune going direct. December 4 is a total solar eclipse. December 19 brings the full moon, and Venus goes retrograde. (Venus retrograde can cause you to question what you want and inspire you to look for something new that delights you. Venus will be retrograde until January.) December 21 is the first day of winter. Your High-Energy Days are 4, 10, 16, 22, and 28.*

December is when Sheep natives can explore hidden talents. You may start a new hobby or be inspired by a friend or family member. You have an aptitude for this new activity. At the same time, you may be more involved with the community this month. It's possible you are doing something charitable or connecting with your spiritual family. This is all on top of what you're already doing with your own family. So it's shaping up to be a busy yet enjoyable month.

On December 4, there's a solar eclipse with a financial focus for Sheep natives. This could signal a bonus is coming in from your job. Perhaps you are negotiating for a salary increase to start after the first of the year. This is also a time to look back over the closing calendar year and analyze spending habits and trends. You may notice you are spending money on different things than you used to, and become aware of the new priorities in your life. Some Sheep natives will look to simplify things and sell off excess stuff. As you free yourself from the objects you no longer need, you find you have more money, more time, and more space in your dwelling.

On December 19, there's a full moon bringing you a confident feeling, especially in the areas of communication and work projects. If you work at home, you may find some distractions because there are extra people at home—such as older children or visiting relatives. But overall, you find time for socializing in addition to getting your work done.

The energy shifts on December 21, bringing more emphasis now on communication. You may have zoom conferences with relatives who are far away, sending out holiday cards, or just spending more time on the phone. If you have some time away from your job over the next week or so, you could consider meditating in preparation for the coming year(where the 2022 energies will be much more favorable to Sheep natives).

January 2022: *January 2 is the new moon. January 14 has Mercury going retrograde. January 17 is the full moon. On January 18, Uranus goes direct. On January 29, Venus goes direct. Your High-Energy Days are 3, 9, 15, 21, and 27.*

Our familiar calendar year begins in January, but there is still a full month of Metal Ox energy remaining. You may have a desire to travel, but there are some limitations at this time due to work obligations or the family schedule. However, short trips are highlighted, and you may consider a drive to the next town, an opportunity to expore local theater, or check out new restaurants.

The new moon comes in on January 2, and energy highlights your area of education. You may be in school, or your children could be ready to go back to school, so it's time to crack the books and get to work. Some Sheep natives will benefit by creating a designated study area, clearing off the workspace, and getting all the necessary tools ready to go. If you're not in a traditional school, you may take online courses. Carving out a little time each day, even if it's just 10 minutes, can help you feel you're making progress.

On January 17, there's a full moon, and in these last couple of weeks of the Metal Ox energy, put yourself forward and make sure you're getting recognition where it's due. This may even mean letting your manager know how much you are contributing to the team's efforts. Maybe you need to standing up at your local PTA meeting and reminding people of what you bring to the table. This is the lesson Sheep natives have been been working for the last 11 1/2 months! So by focusing on this lesson now in the final two weeks of the Metal Ox year, you are letting the Universe know you have learned your lesson, and you're ready to move on.

There is a shift in energy on January 19. Now, with just days left of the old energy, you can finish up any leftover projects from last year, do a little decluttering, and get rid of things you no longer need.

February 2022: *February 1 is the new moon and begins the Year of the Water Tiger. February 3 has Mercury going direct. February 16 brings the full moon.*

February 1 brings the year of the Water Tiger. While this may not be the most harmonious energy for Sheep natives, it's a significant improvement over the year you've just been through!

Tiger energy moves quickly, and so opportunities will come in fast. Sheep natives are known for their networking ability. You will hear about opportunities through the grapevine and get help when you need it.

Attract New Love

This is an excellent year for Sheep natives to meet someone new. Your intuition is strong and can guide you towards a great relationship. You also have friends and family members anxious to fix you up with someone special. It's most likely you will change your living arrangements to welcome in this new person. You can meet this person while doing home-oriented things, such as renovating the house or going to real estate seminars. If you have not met this new person by November, you may want to look at what or who is blocking you. Holding on to someone from the past may stop you from moving forward. Let go and embrace a new relationship.

To attract the right person into your life, use a treasure bowl—this is a covered bowl made from a natural material such as metal, wood, or stone. Write three wishes for your new relationship on a piece of paper. Make the wishes specific, describing something you could easily see in the other person. For example, "He cares for my well-being and shows me by taking my hand when we're going down steep stairs," or,

"When she sees me, she lights up with a smile.." Then place your wishes in your treasure bowl and set the bowl on a table or shelf by the front door. This will call the person's energy to you, attracting qualities you want to find in a partner.

Enhance Existing Love

There is intense relationship energy for you this year as you come together with your sweetheart to achieve a significant goal. This may be buying a house or starting a business. You may decide to become debt-free and go on an extreme budget. You may lose weight together by eating healthy meals and exercising, encouraging each other to go farther than either of you would on your own. This intensity can create some stress, but you are there for each other and have a shoulder to lean on. Some difficulties around family could cause a brief separation, but the distance is not important as long as you're communicating. November could be challenging when others ask you to take sides in a family argument.

A pair of Chinese characters represent double Happiness. The single character translates as "joy." When two of these characters are written together, it is associated with love unions and weddings. It's called "Double Happiness." This motif dates back to the Song dynasty (960-1279 AD). We can find this pair of symbols in artwork, on vases, rugs, or brass sculptures like the one shown here.

Hang a Double Happiness symbol in your bedroom to attract a love relationship. If you prefer to drift into a new relationship such as meeting a friend who, over time, grows into a romantic relationship, then hang this symbol in your living room. Hang it where it is visible from the door. This will attract the energy of someone like you, who desires to unite with you.

Looking to Conceive?

What could be a sweeter fertility symbol than honey? The ancient Egyptians associated honey with love, happy marriage, and fertility. Honey was considered a gift from the divine.

To enhance fertility this year, place a jar of honey in your bedroom near the entrance (on a dresser or shelf), and pair it with a silver spoon. Give your partner a taste of honey to set the mood and attract conception energy.

(From Donna Stellhorn's book, A Path to Pregnancy: Ancient Secrets for the Modern Woman)

Family and Kids

There is significant energy around home and family this year for Sheep natives, including the possibility of a residential move or major renovations on the house. This year the house never seems quiet. People are coming in and going out, perhaps staying for days and then leaving again. There could be parties. You and your partner may work at home, doing business at home, or homeschooling the kids. Fertility energy increases towards the end of the year. There may be a birth or adoption started this year and manifesting in 2022. On the other hand, there could be a significant increase in the number of pets you have, including horses, goats, or chickens.

A pagoda is a many-tiered sacred building popular in the far East. They are often religious or spiritual structures, some dating back to BCE times. Often the very top pinnacle comes to a point and was made of metal to channel lightning strikes. In Feng Shui, the pagoda symbolizes peace and harmony. You might display a small replica pagoda or have a picture of a pagoda. Place this in your living room or family room to attract positive, healthy energy. You can also find stone pagodas to place in the garden for the same purpose.

Money

This is certainly a good year for financially conservative Sheep natives. You could make money through real estate, commercial or residential property, or things related to home and home-building. There are investment opportunities with business partners and/or spouses. If you actively look for opportunities and they can be found. Your biggest challenge this year is to not fall into old spending habits, especially in May and December. As your income increases, you may be tempted to take trips or to invest heavily in education. But look for creative ways of getting what you want and save yourself some money.

A good Feng Shui cure for attracting new prosperity energy (and attracting more money in general) is to get yourself a golden piggy bank. Choose a style that appeals to you, perhaps a classic western-style piggy bank in metallic gold, or the traditional Feng Shui piggy bank decorated with Chinese characters for wealth and good fortune.

Place your bank near your front door or in the home office, and feed it coins at least once a week (no pennies, please). Place a list of your money wishes inside the bank along with the coins to bring in opportunities and positive career energy.

Job or Career

There is compelling energy for your career this year as you have opportunities to move into a new field. You may feel a little uncertain about all the change, but this is a way to capitalize on your skillset. If you take your abilities and move them to a different company, you could gain a significant increase in salary, and people will appreciate you more. Those Sheep natives who want to stay in their current position will need to weather some company changes. You will work with new people, or perhaps with a new system. If management becomes too rule-oriented, you may need to do some networking to find a new team to work with, or to transfer to another office. Sheep natives in real estate or construction do exceptionally well. Those who are in the profession of caring for others will be in high demand.

Gold Flakes remind us of accumulating wealth and abundance through seemingly small actions. You can attract positive money energy by placing a vial of real gold flakes on a table near your front door. (Gold flakes are available in gem and mineral shops and online.)

Write out your money goals and place them under the vial of gold flakes. Every few days, as you pass the table, pick up the vial and shake it. Watch the gold flakes sparkle in the light and think about your goals for a moment. This will increase the positive money energy.

Education

The energy in the area of your life related to education is somewhat intense this year; you may be finishing up a highly difficult program, residency, or dissertation. In a lot of ways, your education is wrapping up. You may find additional classes are unnecessary for what you want to do. Studying at home online is possible this year and can fit nicely into your schedule. You also have good energy for studying anything having to do with the home, such as acquiring a contractor's license, inspector's license, or learning about real estate. The funding sources you have used in the past are available to you again. However, there is some work you need to do to secure it (especially if you're doing this in June). If you are looking at starting a program this year, make sure it's not more than you bargained for. Taking on or becoming very involved in difficult subjects can result in you having cold feet later on.

Legal Matters

There's a lot of activity around legal matters this year with Sheep natives potentially signing several types of agreements, including real estate deals; caring for relatives;, business matters including employment; or work-at-home arrangements. There is positive energy when you don't rush. Take your time negotiating the points you want. If you feel you have no option other than to accept their terms, consider walking away from the agreement, and checking if another opportunity is possible. Don't get married to an outcome, and you will do well in negotiations. Avoid lawsuits this year, especially ones involving family members.

Health and Well-Being

Sheep natives potentially enjoy an excellent year for health in 2021. You may spend time this year taking care of others more than yourself. You may help relatives or close friends with their diet or exercise plans. For you, exercise can be a little challenging this year. Your schedule pulls you in several directions; however, if you focus on something like swimming or hiking where you're out in nature, you're more likely to make time for it. Be aware November could be difficult, when other people's issues cause you to break your own focus. However, if (or when) you fall into some bad habits, this year you can quickly realign yourself and get back on track.

Burn a white candle about once a month this year to clear away negative health energy. Sometimes negative energy can build up in the house when we are stressed about difficulties in the neighborhood, or feel distressed when watching the news. Burn a white candle to remove negativity. You can burn the candle in your living room or family room. Choose a candle style you like—perhaps a tea light or votive.

Monkey

February 2, 1908–January 21, 1909: Yang Earth Monkey
February 20, 1920–February 7, 1921: Yang Metal Monkey
February 6, 1932–January 25, 1933: Yang Water Monkey
January 25, 1944–February 12, 1945: Yang Wood Monkey
February 12, 1956–January 30, 1957: Yang Fire Monkey
January 30, 1968–February 16, 1969: Yang Earth Monkey
February 16, 1980–February 4, 1981: Yang Metal Monkey
February 4, 1992–January 22, 1993: Yang Water Monkey
January 22, 2004–February 8, 2005: Yang Wood Monkey
February 8, 2016–January 27, 2017: Yang Fire Monkey
January 26, 2028–February 12, 2029: Yang Earth Monkey

Monkey Personality

When considering the qualities of a Chinese Zodiac animal, examine the animal's traits, behaviors, and personality. Of all the Chinese Zodiac animals, the most agile and adaptable is the Monkey. Monkeys can live on the ground or in the trees..

The Chinese Zodiac sign of Monkey is the sign of intelligence. This Zodiac animal rules the inventor—intelligent and innovative enough to solve complex problems with ease. Monkeys have an excellent memory and proficiency in communication. They can give you an inspirational speech that motivates you, or a dressing down which leaves you feeling about two inches tall. Monkey is a problem solver. He or she will not offer you sympathy, but will offer you a solution instead.

Monkeys do well in business because they are connectors. They find people who can help them achieve their goals. They know how to play the system, trading favors as part of a strategy for success.

Monkey always has a plan, often several. Monkey wants to do more than merely survive; he or she wants to prosper! The Monkey native will avoid confrontation if you might be of assistance later. Once wronged, they will exact revenge, but only when the time is right.

A Monkey is susceptible to incentives and bribes. To get them on your side, you need to offer something they want. You can criticize the Monkey, but they pay no attention. They are incredibly confident in their talents and abilities.

Monkey can justify their actions to achieve or obtain what they want; thus others can find it hard to trust Monkey. This can affect Monkey's career and personal life. However, On the plus side, Monkey is rarely discouraged by failure, nor envious of the success of others.

Monkeys love a bargain. They're good with money, but would rather save it than spend it. They prefer to find their own solution to spending cash. This choice shows up in their home, where innovative decorating ideas and creative uses for cast-offs abound. They love a party at home (BYOB); if you're invited, you can expect an evening (or night) of stimulating conversation and lively music.

Monkeys are into self-preservation. This can show up as nervousness or hyperactivity, and it causes them to leap out of any situation they don't feel right about. They can get themselves into trouble by trying to avoid what they perceive as "trouble".

But no matter what mistakes they may make, they are quick to rebound. Overall, the Monkey native gets what they want without too much effort or struggle. If there's no apparent benefit, they simply lose interest.

Monkeys are at one moment a passionate lover; the next moment it seems as if they've forgotten you entirely. When in a long-term, committed relationship, they can be a devoted partner; however, they love a good time, and lots of attention, and they tend to get caught up in the moment. Monkey won't notice a partner's jealousy, and before you know, he or she will be back at your side as if nothing ever happened.

Monkey's love projects and can renovate their home continuously. They love to create new things and improve old ones. Sometimes they just like to move the furniture around for a different look. It's not unusual for the combination of half-finished projects and a love of new stuff can make for a very messy house.

Monkey: Predictions for 2021

How to use your High-Energy Days: On these days, plan to take action for your most important goals, make vital phone calls, send important emails. Your high-energy days are when your energy and luck are the strongest for the month.

January 2021: *Uranus goes direct on January 14. Mercury goes retrograde from January 30 to February 20. Your Lucky Days are 3, 9, 15, 21, 27.*

January brings the end of the Metal Rat year, and you can look back on the amount of progress you've made. You'll soon feel the energy of the Metal Ox year. This is more challenging energy for Monkey natives, though you love a challenge. You can feel the energy slowing down and becoming more practiced and methodical. Monkey energy rarely moves so slowly, and you can swing through the crowd as everyone else is plodding along.

Finances are sound this month. You can also see how there have been consistent gains throughout the year. Look at budgets and see if there are any easy adjustments you can make.

There is positive energy around education. If you're in school, you may find renewed interest in getting through your classes, projects, and tests. Consider looking into how to improve study habits or find a new study partner. If you're considering going back to school, there may be some resources to help you pay for the education. Or, if a degree isn't crucial, check into free online schools.

Dating energy abounds this month. If you're looking for love, it's looking for you now. Don't hide at home or bury yourself in your job. It's now time to meet new people, especially in gyms, yoga studios, spiritual retreats, and business conferences. When you're out in the world, show people your positive, witty energy. Don't hide with your head buried in your phone. Lift your eyes and smile at the world. The world will be dazzled.

February 2021: *Lunar New Year begins on February 12. Happy Year of the Metal Ox. February 20 has Mercury going direct. February 27 is the full moon. Your High-Energy Days are 2, 8, 14, 20, and 26.*

February arrives, bringing the final two weeks of the harmonious Metal Rat energy. Monkey natives can take advantage of this by finishing up some projects and clearing off your desk. To be ready for the new energy, focus on sorting and filing accumulated paperwork, filing only what you need to keep, and shredding the rest.

The new moon on February 12 ushers in the Lunar New Year of the Metal Ox. Ox energy is considerably slower and more deliberate energy. As a fast-moving Monkey native, you must switch gears to allow others to keep up with you. The first two weeks of this new energy involves paying a great deal of attention to either communication and transportation. You may negotiate for a new vehicle. Motorcycles and bicycles are also highlighted, though in some areas, the weather may not be conducive to this form of transportation just now.

This year you may find yourself spending more time at home. Connections with neighbors can be helpful, so whenever possible, avoid conflicts with the people who live near you. If this isn't possible, use Feng Shui cures to bring more harmony to your property or apartment.

Mercury goes direct on February 20, and now energy flows more easily, especially in the context of agreements and contracts. If you have a contract to renew, you can now feel confident about signing on the dotted line. (This could be for a dwelling or a new job)

The full moon on February 27 brings increased energy connected to family, extended family, and family traditions. An older relative may relate the family history, or share traditional family recipes. You may exchange furniture or pass down heirlooms. Consider your family's patterns and see which are good to maintain and which need to fade away.

March 2021: *March 13 brings the new moon, March 20 marks the first day of spring, March 28 is the full moon. Your High-Energy Days are 4, 10, 16, 22, and 28.*

March brings lots of work for Monkey natives. Your office may be shorthanded, or an increase in sales has you hopping from one task to the next. While some recognition trickles in from management, you may consider updating your resume and checking what's going on in your field. You have a strong business sense, and you can see future trends. If your company is under-performing, it's wise to take your considerable talents elsewhere.

The New Moon on March 13 brings some new energy into your home life. One of your older children may get married or have a child. You may bring an addition into the home through birth or adoption. Some Monkey natives will add a pet to the family. This could bring considerable joy and lots of activity to your home.

The energy shifts on March 20, with the beginning of a new season. Time for some adventure! An opportunity arrives, perhaps through a friend or relative. It may sound risky at first, but there's also the possibility of success. If this is a business, look to bootstrap it rather than borrowing money at this time. Find creative funding sources. In fact, trust your creativity to serve you well throughout the entire business start-up process.

The full moon on March 28 lights up your area of romance and enjoyment. If you're looking for love, the next two weeks are some of the best for finding a great connection. Get on social media or online dating sites and let the world know you're looking for love. If you're already in a relationship, spend more time together, laughing and enjoying each other's company.

The full moon energy is also excellent for taking risks in business. If you've thought about starting your own business or pursuing a side hustle, use the energy of the next two weeks to take bold action. Focus on connecting with helpful people.

April 2021: *April 12 brings the new moon. April 27 is the full moon, and Pluto goes retrograde. (Pluto moving backward can cause you to review your basic assumptions of life and eliminate what is unnecessary, bringing you back to what is essential. Pluto will be retrograde until October.) Your High-Energy Days are 3, 9, 15, 21, and 27.*

In April your intuition is stronger than usual. Explore your spiritual education, by considering taking classes in mediumship, past life regression, astrology, or palmistry. Monkey natives love to learn, and now you can find an excellent teacher. This is also a good time to study meditation or yoga. Immerse yourself in what you want to learn.

The new moon on April 12 brings a lot of energy around creativity, fertility, and children. If you've wanted to add to the family, now is the time. This can also be a great time to explore your creative side through music, painting, or dance. Monkey natives often make outstanding actors, and if this is something you're interested in, consider going on a casting call. The current energy indicates if you begin something new, this effort can grow into something viable. Focus on doing and trying new things.

The energy shifts on April 19, bringing rather intense times at your job. There may be significant changes among co-workers, or how you do your job. Shifts in the company could mean a merger. Your company could be bought out, and now there is a new organization with new orders trickling down from on high. There could be changes in government regulations or new products coming out, causing a shift in how you do things. This can be an exciting time for Monkey natives.

April 27 brings the full moon, and the busyness continues. Now you're handling the long list of tasks with ease. If you can step off the sales floor for a little while, take a quick break. All of this activity can lead to a bigger paycheck in a few weeks, along with recognition from your supervisors.

May 2021: *May 11 brings the new moon. May 23, Saturn goes retrograde. (Saturn retrograde can cause you to review your career choices and make adjustments. Saturn will be retrograde until October). May 26 is a total lunar eclipse. May 29 has Mercury going retrograde. Your High-Energy Days are 3, 9, 15, 21, and 27.*

In May your thoughts turn to health and exercise. The weather may turn pleasant, and you feel a great pull to the outdoors—hiking, biking, or even a walk in the park. Monkey natives are often healthy because you are almost always active. Your diet, however, sometimes tends towards convenience foods. It's beneficial now recommitting to a natural, simple diet. See if you can take care of your physical self during the next few weeks.

Starting May 11, Monkey native, your charisma reaches new heights and this continues over the next couple of weeks. Opportunities abound to meet new people for friendship and fun, or you want to meet a special someone, you could meet him or her now. Your area of intimacy is lit up. Now you can go from a date to some sexy fun pretty quickly.

The energy shifts on May 20 and Monkey natives can find useful business connections. You can connect with an influencer or potential mentor, someone willing to promote you even as they teach you. Perhaps you initially met this person months ago when you planted some seeds by sending out direct messages. If you're just getting started now, it's a good idea to send emails or texts to many a lot of individuals. To grow a great forest, you need to plant many seeds.

On May 26, there is a total lunar eclipse. There's likely at least one essential aspect of your life you want to change. A door will be closing in your life, something ends, but, but a new opportunity arrives. With so much of your world turned upside down and while others may feel their head spinning—not Monkey native! You know you can trust yourself to handle what's coming. When the dust settles, you find you've landed on your feet yet again and have better prospects than ever before.

On May 29, Mercury goes retrograde. The disruptive power Mercury can cause communications to be delayed. If you're waiting for contracts or doing some negotiations for a loan, be patient. Some paperwork may have been lost, or someone was out on vacation, but they will get around to your request.

June 2021: *June 10 is the annular solar eclipse. June 20 is the first day of summer, and Jupiter goes retrograde. (Jupiter retrograde can indicate a need to relearn things or review your beliefs. Jupiter will be retrograde until October). June 22 has Mercury going direct. June 24 is the full moon. On June 25, Neptune goes retrograde. (Neptune retrograde can draw you back towards habits and addictions from your past. It can also encourage a return to spiritual practices. Neptune will be retrograde until December). Your High-Energy Days are 2, 8, 14, 20, and 26.*

The month of June can bring quite a few changes, not just in your life but for some of your family members as well. These are long-awaited changes, perhaps a result of prayers or affirmations. Even so, as these changes happen, things can feel quite disruptive. You can help your friends and family; you have a knack for finding clever solutions to difficult problems.

On June 10, a solar eclipse can bring significant change to a notable person in your life. This can mean a new job opportunity, perhaps in a new city. This won't be the only person seeking your support. Your phone may ring nonstop as the people you care about need your shoulder to lean on and your resourceful ideas. It's essential to be patient during this time. Allow others to express how they feel. Once they stop talking, they'll be open to listening to your advice.

The energy shifts on June 20 and some significant resources become available to you. If you own a business, you may receive a large amount of funding, or you could get help from a professional networking group. Now is when you want to lean in. Make sure you let others know what you're looking for, and a windfall can happen.

On June 22, Mercury goes direct, moving forward again. If you have been waiting to sign a contract or start a new position, now is an excellent time to take action. This can also bring the return of something that has been delayed over the last few weeks. A flood of opportunities can come in now that the retrograde Mercury no longer blocks them.

The full moon on June 24 highlights your area of finances. Monkey natives are good at handling money, and because you know where to look in your own finances, it's easy for you to spot opportunities. Even though you may feel no money flows in at the beginning of this two-week period, in actuality, a moneymaking opportunity is within your grasp. If you don't see it right away, do some evening meditations to allow the information to come to you.

July 2021: *July 10 brings the new moon. July 24 is the full moon. Your High-Energy Days are 2, 8, 14, 20, and 26.*

July brings some opportunities for love and romance. Monkey natives show improved relations with your sweetheart. If you are in a new relationship, you may move in together or introduce your honey to your friends and family. If you're looking for love, sign up for classes on spirituality, your church, or in groups related to education. Be aware of blocks you have in place, shielding you from finding love. Being single is a state of being, and a relationship is just another state of being. During July, you can transition from single to dating.

On July 10, the new moon brings your attention to investments, debt repayment, and credit. Now the energy is lined up to help you reduce your debt and create passive income sources. New information comes in to assist you in this matter. You may be speaking to a broker or banker about options. If you're new to investing, this is the time to connect with your wealthier friends and see what they suggest you do.

The energy shifts on July 22, and Monkey natives may feel a great desire to travel (not that you don't have that desire all the time). If you're able to go somewhere, consider grabbing the opportunity even if the trip will be relatively short. If obligations or restrictions keep you at home, consider taking a drive to a new part of town or, better still, into the mountains where you can breathe fresh air and see nature.

The July 24 full moon brings a strong emphasis on siblings and extended family, especially younger family members. Someone may visit you, or a special celebration is scheduled. You can now heal some old family issues. You've spent some time reflecting, examining events from the past from different perspectives. This is something Monkey natives can do well. Someone may come to you with an apology, bringing about smiles and hugs.

There is increased energy around your career. You may step up to a leadership role. A chance to transfer to another department or to get a new supervisor may also cross your desk. If you're looking for work, you have some great opportunities in the business world now.

August 2021: *August 8 brings the new moon. On August 20, Uranus goes retrograde. August 22 is the full moon. Your High-Energy Days are 1, 7, 13, 19, 25, and 31.*

August is a month of endings. Monkey natives have a unique understanding of endings and beginnings. As you leap from one thing to another, you see how one thing ends as you jump in the next. But because of your ability to make quick transitions, you may not be clear about when it's time to finish something. It's good to be mindful of what is ending and what still remains undone this month. In the excitement of jumping into something new, you may have to let go of something uncompleted.

The new moon on August 8 triggers focus on communication, contracts, and agreements. You may negotiate a contract for employment yourself, or engage outside service providers for your business. Redo your website, find a videographer, or get some social media marketing help. Let go of current employees, associates, even volunteers if they are no longer needed. Time to change out equipment, get a new phone, or upgrade a computer.

The full moon on August 22 brings energy shifts as it lights up your area of transitions. As you make changes within your career, this energy may ripple into changes at home. You may be setting up a home office, perhaps even changing your residence entirely. There's a lot of activity around close family, especially siblings or cousins. You may be helping others or getting help as needed with all this moving energy. You can't help but smile as others are amazed by your ability to juggle many tasks; for you, it's an adventure.

September 2021: *September 7 brings the new moon. September 20 is the full moon. September 22 is the first day of autumn. September 26 has Mercury going retrograde. Your High-Energy Days are 6, 12, 18, 24, and 30.*

September arrives, and the energy settles down considerably. You have a bit more time to unpack, declutter, or reorganize as the dust settles. While there may not be time for a vacation, you may have your evenings and even part of your weekend back for some relaxation. People around you are busy, especially children—probably with school. Their activity actually gives you a break some "Me-time"..

With the new moon on September 7, you enter a period of adjustments leading to positive results. There's a difference now between what people want you to do, and your usual skillset. While this can create uncertainty, it does makes life interesting. A supervisor may ask you to take the lead on a project you're not entirely sure about. Your sweetheart may ask you to get along with a member of his or her family. Monkey native, you can push back on this request and bring about a struggle, or you can be a leaf on the wind and go in the direction it blows.

The full moon on September 20 focuses the energy and activity around transportation over the next two weeks. You may need car repairs, find a new route to work, or perhaps even buy a new car. If you're thinking about the latter, you may want to hurry, as Mercury will be going retrograde soon. (It's not beneficial to try to do vehicle negotiations during Mercury retrograde.)

The energy shifts on September 22, and you're likely having more fun with friends. You might have a get-together or be celebrating more than one birthday. You may be reconnecting with other parents at your child's school now that it's back in session. If weather permits, consider backyard barbecues or organizing a game night.

Mercury goes retrograde on September 26, and for Monkey natives, you may receive a message from a potential lover. A person you had a relationship with in the past could be reach out to you through social media, or you might bump into them at the grocery store. There are still sparks, although one or both of you may not be available for a relationship. Don't move forward on this without considering the ramifications.

October 2021: *October 6 brings the new moon, and Pluto goes direct. On October 11, Saturn goes direct. October 18 has Mercury* *going direct and Jupiter going direct. October 20 is the full moon. Your High-Energy Days are 6, 12, 18, 24, and 30.*

Travel is highlighted in October. Friends or family members may want to visit, or perhaps you want to get on the road. Right now your busy schedule doesn't allow you a lot of time off. However, it would be a morale booster if you can take an afternoon to drive to the mountains, or down to the ocean. Prepare your guest room so you can welcome a visitor. On an unrelated note, towards the end of the month, expect an important message. (This could be test results or a professional license.)

The new moon is on October 6. Monkey native, your charisma is high, and you connect easily with others. If you belong to a professional or charitable organization, you may be tapped to take on a leadership role or organize the next fundraiser. You may connect with more people through your job and enjoy your now expanding circle of friends. People line up to tell you how happy they are to have met you. You're building a support coalition.

On October 18, Mercury (and Jupiter) stop and turn, then start to to move forward again. Start a new job or sign a contract you've been waiting on. You will have several weeks when negotiations are facilitated; you can even seal a couple of deals now. It is also an excellent time to update your technology by getting a new laptop or downloading some helpful apps. Consider getting car repairs or car registration updated now that Mercury is moving forward.

The full moon on October 20 brings a couple of weeks highlighted by you feeling both more productive and energetic than usual, Projects are exciting, and you get help when you need it. Help is available to you at work, and you find helpful people in the neighborhood. This means there's someone around to help you move a sofa, give you investment advice, or to socialize with.

The energy shifts on October 22, and you enter a four week period when your spiritual connection to the Universe is stronger than usual. You may be more intuitive and interested in things like meditation, chanting, or reading sacred texts. And this time, it's good to take classes on subjects like palmistry or psychic self-defense. You're tapping into your natural aptitude. During this period, it is more likely you will grasp and retain this valuable information.

November 2021: *November 4 is the new moon. November 19 is a partial lunar eclipse. Your High-Energy Days are 5, 11, 17, 23, and 29.*

This November, Monkey native, you have more energy but less desire to do some of the things you've been doing up until now. You are hitting your boredom wall, and unless you change things up a bit, you're going to find yourself procrastinating a lot. Add challenges to your everyday tasks by instituting a deadline, or finding a new way to do them. Evaluate situations where you feel stuck, or where life just feels stale. See where you can turn things upside down to do something entirely different. The spiritual work you started last month can help. Tap into your expanding network of friends as they can have some interesting ideas.

The new moon on November 4 can bring some interesting dreams. You may be picking up impressions from other people, even psychically absorbing emotions from others. This can leave you feeling negative or fearful, even though that's not a natural state for Monkey natives. Find positive people to hang out with. Also, consider doing a space clearing by burning sage or sprinkling holy water around the house.

On November 19, the lunar eclipse brings the most likely time for feeling bored. This may even extend to your personal relationship. You need to tread softly now so as not to damage this relationship. Sometimes, Monkey Native, you're too clever for your own good, and if an argument ensues, you need to ask yourself whether you rather be right or happy.

This is a challenging time for Monkey natives looking for a love connection. It's better to use the next couple of weeks to determine why you have protected yourself from a love relationship. Work on the internal reasons for your current state of singlehood before you go out into the world looking for a match.

On November 21, the energy shifts, and you feel a sense of confidence and general self-assuredness. The best use of these good feelings is to connect others in your business or career. Choose influencers, celebrities, or people who could become mentors and write a compelling message to them, something that piques their interest. This is the best way now to connect and materially change your life.

December 2021: *December 1 has Neptune going direct. December 4 is a total solar eclipse. December 19 brings the full moon, and Venus goes retrograde. (Venus retrograde can cause you to question what you want and inspire you to look for something new that delights you. Venus will be retrograde until January.) December 21 is the first day of winter. Your High-Energy Days are 5, 11, 17, 23, and 29.*

December arrives, and your certainty and cool-headedness continue. Now you can impress at work; and you have more support than usual. Seeds you planted all year long now bring you an abundant harvest. In a Metal Ox year, there is the energy of rebuilding. As more money flows into your pocket and more resources become available, it's a good idea to set some aside to reestablish accounts or to build up security. Look at your 401(k) or IRA to see what can be funded and what other tax planning can be done.

On December 4, there is a solar eclipse, and changes you've been planning or wishing for now start to happen. For those Monkey natives in a new relationship, you may want to take things to the next level, discussing moving in together or getting engaged. At the same time, business ventures are expanding as you reach a wider audience with your marketing posts. This can translate into more money for your bank account. Still, it's a good idea to set aside most of this profit for opportunities ahead.

On December 19, the full moon ushers in a couple of weeks when you find opportunities to bring in more money. Discuss a raise or promotion with your boss. You may receive an end-of-year bonus or some other windfall. You feel a strong desire to spend, since Venus goes retrograde on the same day, and something you've wanted for some time might now be available at a very tempting price. It is good to invest in yourself, but avoid frivolous spending. Monkey natives are adept at handling money, so this should be easy for you.

December 21 brings a new season and a shift of energies. Look at the skills and experience you bring to the table. This is not a time for modesty, instead make an accurate assessment of how valuable you are. A little introspection now will directly affect what you receive going forward, including money and others' help.

January 2022: *January 2 is the new moon. January 14 has Mercury going retrograde. January 17 is the full moon. On January 18, Uranus goes direct. On January 29, Venus goes direct. Your High-Energy Days are 4, 10, 16, 22, and 28.*

January, and the new calendar year arrives, though we are still in the Metal Ox energy for the next four weeks. Monkey native, you are finishing up your three-year seed tending period. This has been a time to nurture your business prospects as well as your personal relationships. Pretty soon, you'll enter your three-year harvest time. You'll be able to capitalize on all of your experience and connections.

You need to focus on finishing rather than starting. Look at which projects need your attention and see what can be completed (even though the desire to create something new will be extreme right now). Any new projects this month will probably need re-doing later in the year. Skip this frustrating step and focus on getting current issues finished up and off your desk.

The new moon on January 2 may bring trouble at home. Perhaps some relatives are taking advantage of you; or you may have been in a struggle with a landlord or neighbor. You may want to withdraw and not engage. However, the best course of action is to give some deep thought to what you want and what is reasonable to expect of others. Avoid arguing during this time. It's about more than winning a debate this time, it's time to be strategic.

On January 14, Mercury goes retrograde, and things begun over the last two weeks can now unravel. You feel the new energy for change approaching, but it's better to visualize, affirm, or even create a vision board with pictures of things you want to attract. Vision Boards are an especially useful tool for creating a complete life change, such as leaving a job and working for yourself, or moving into a yurt in the middle of a forest.

On January 17, the full moon brings several people seeking advice and help. People around you may be struggling and need your advice or even material assistance. Keep your goals in mind as you assist others. There will be situations where helping is entirely in line with your success strategy. But it's good to maintain your boundaries, especially when it comes to people with whom you've had difficulties in the past.

The energy shifts on January 19, and you may be waiting for specific paperwork or an agreement. But Mercury is still retrograde, so it's better not to push this. Even though you know different ways to move forward, it would be better to use the last bit of the Metal Ox energy to step back and allow this to happen in its own time.

February 2022: *February 1 is the new moon and begins the Year of the Water Tiger. February 3 has Mercury going direct. February 16 brings the full moon.*

The February 1, 2022 new moon ushers in the Water Tiger. Now, the world turns away from Monkey natives and becomes mesmerized by the Tiger. But you Monkey native have a trick or two up your sleeve. The solution to this lack of energy and support is to draw some attention to yourself. Because of your skill and showmanship, you will have no trouble doing this—time to bang your own drum and toot your own horn.

Attract New Love

The energy sizzles as you magnetically attract interesting people to you. You have several opportunities for love this year, and you can take your pick. You can meet new people in your daily life, at coffee shops, the post office, or the grocery store. Online dating will also bring you some possibilities. You're naturally a good communicator, so consider striking up a conversation with a new person. You also have friends and siblings trying to fix you up with matches they think would be right for you. Your charisma is exceptionally high in May and December. But be careful in June, as miscommunication can send your new relationship into a brief tailspin and have you backtracking to put things back together.

If you want a serious relationship with a partner to settle down with, consider using the Wedding Ring cure. Find a replica wedding ring (you can often find these at party stores in the bridal section), and place the ring under the mattress on the unoccupied side of the bed. Just lift the mattress and slide the ring underneath.

If you're not ready to settle down, but you still want a romantic new love in your life, instead of the ring, place a copy of your house key under the mattress. Put it under the side of the mattress where your new lover will rest their head. If you decide later you want to make the relationship more permanent and official, change the house key for the replica wedding ring.

Enhance Existing Love

Positive relationship energy happens pretty much throughout the year. There is good communication, and for the most part, you enjoy each other's company daily. You may be having parties or making some quick overnight trips, which add to the fun. You become stronger as a couple when you study or do a side business together. Do something involving technology or social media, with each of you contributing your own unique talents. Monkey natives have a playful nature, and there is much banter back and forth. It's good to keep an eye out, to make sure there are no hurt feelings from all the joking around. Outsiders may not understand you as well as you know each other. But as long as you support each other, you will have no serious issues this year.

You can enhance relationship energy and bring a bit of art and beauty into your home. Place a figurine or statue of a couple in love in your living room, family room, or bedroom. Place this figurine in a prominent place, so it is easily seen. This will help pull the love energy into your space and your life all year long.

One additional tip is to hang a small bag of cardamom seeds from the love figurine. Cardamom has been used in passion/lust potions for centuries.

To make a bag, take a small piece of cotton cloth about four inches square and lay it out on the table. In the center, place about a teaspoon of cardamom seeds. Gather the corners of the fabric and tie it together with thread or embroidery floss, leaving a bit of extra string for hanging the bag. Adding this touch of spice will help bring in the romance.

Rabbits are a universal symbol of procreation, so using a rabbit image will help bring fertility energy. Choose a figurine, hanging artwork of rabbits, or place a couple of little stuffed bunnies on the bed. But remember, you need two rabbits to make things happen, so make sure there's more than one hare depicted in the bedroom.

What would be even better than a figurine of a pair of rabbits? Chocolate bunnies, of course. Chocolate has long been known for its aphrodisiac qualities. These delicious rabbits will put you both in the mood.

(From Donna Stellhorn's book, A Path to Pregnancy: Ancient Secrets for the Modern Woman)

Family and Kids

In general, there is harmony and happiness at home in 2021. At times during the year, it will be a full house with people visiting or going in and out. There's a lot of activity related to siblings or cousins. Monkey natives don't mind a little bit of excitement. Additionally, there is a good deal of energy around fertility for the extended family. You may gain some relatives this year.

Due to noise or property boundaries, difficulties from neighbors could be a problem around May or June. It's unwise to let these problems escalate, rather try to see them as small annoyances.

Children are active this year, working hard in school and playing hard at home. More than one household item gets broken. There could be increased activity around looking for colleges or finding new schools to attend for older children. Friendships are very strong and important this year for your kids, and their families will help expand your circle of friends.

To help you feel more safe and secure for wherever you land, use the representation of the turtle to bring protection energy to you. Three turtles would be even better. Find a figurine of three turtles stacked one on top of another. This represents protection, friendships, and security through community. Each turtle has everything they need with them to protect them, no matter what comes. Place the figurine on your nightstand or in your family room.

Money

This is quite a good financial year for Monkey natives, especially for generating income. If you're in a communication field or working on your communication skills, such as negotiating contracts or learning to sell, you can do very well. Also, working in banking, construction, and creative fields can be beneficial. The challenge for Monkey natives is patience is needed to see the big rewards. There could be delays in May and December. But 2021 can be profitable for the persistence seeker. There are opportunities to work with someone you know well, a close friend or sibling, on a new venture. This could bring you another stream of income.

This year consider displaying an abacus. This device was used for thousands of years to calculate money and do accounting. Displaying a beautiful abacus helps you attract so much money, you'll need help to count it.

Place the abacus in your home office or where you pay bills and work on your finances. You can display it on the wall or place it on a desk or table. You can also learn how to use it. People adept at using an abacus can calculate sums as quickly as a person with a state-of-the-art calculator.

Job or Career

There is quite a bit of excitement in your career this year as you could receive several opportunities. Headhunters may be knocking at your door, and you can get many responses when you post your resume. If you want to make a change this year, you are in harmony with the energy, especially if you want to shift your efforts to a different field. The strongest opportunities for change will be in May, or at the end of the year in November (or December). Brush up on your selling skills, interviewing, and communication technology. Consider writing or speaking opportunities to enhance your career and resume. An increase in income is connected to a bonus or sales commission. There are also opportunities for creating a profitable side hustle.

In choosing a Feng Shui cure, remember the universal rule: "Like attracts like." This concept allows us to use representations of things to attract the real thing. For example, as you are looking for your new job, visualize that you will be showered with money when they make you the offer.

To complete the picture, find a wind chime made of Chinese coins. Choose a chime with many coins—This is to represent a shower of money.

Hang the wind chime outside your front door or if you're in an apartment, hang it from your balcony/patio. As you hear the coins tinkle and chime in the breeze, imagine the sound of raindrops showering money on your roof and your windows. While it's best to hang the chime outside your front door, if this isn't a viable option where you live, hang your wind chime on your back porch or balcony.

Education

There is quite an emphasis on education for you this year. And since Monkey natives love to learn, this can be a very happy period in your life. If you are looking to start school, you will identify several options. You can also pursue more unconventional methods of study through self-guided programs, tutoring, or mentorships. Online learning is also highlighted.

If you study engineering or tech, make sure this is something you genuinely want to do, not just you following the herd. That said, having two majors, especially ones that seem disconnected, can give you an advantage in the career world. Focus on classes to improve creative thinking, artistic ability, or anything about marketing. Stay flexible in your choices as you may change your mind about the direction you are heading in December.

Legal Matters

Monkey natives can find contracts and agreements to be somewhat tricky this year. If you rush through an agreement, you could miss an important point, or lose an opportunity to negotiate for something you want. Be careful about taking an agreement at face value, instead of reading the fine print. Don't let yourself be hurried, especially with agreements involving employment, construction, or the purchase of a vehicle.

When it comes to lawsuits, you can do well by organizing all of your pertinent information or evidence. If a situation arises and you do not, consider postponing court dates until you have things together. Class action suits are likely to do better for you than individual claims in the Metal Ox year. June can be a difficult month to start a lawsuit. Consider waiting until later in the year if you need to initiate one.

Health and Well-Being

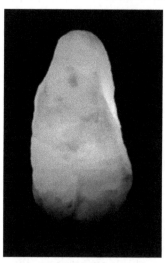

There's a lot of harmony in your health area this year, but expect some changes. Fortunately, adaptable Monkey natives like the challenge of change—it sure beats being bored! You may have been on a diet or exercise program for the last couple of years. Now is the time for a change. Consider getting together with friends for martial arts, ballroom dancing, bicycling, or if you're daring, parkour. May and December can be challenging as other obligations cause your schedule to go a little wacky. But put self-care first, and you will do well all year.

Consider adding a salt lamp to the home to bring in good health energy. Salt lamps are made from solid pieces of Himalayan rock salt. A hole is carved into the bottom of the block of salt, and a small light bulb is placed inside. When lit, the lamp glows with a soft peach-colored light. The heated salt emits negative ions into the air, like a miniature version of the ocean's air.

The combination of the heavy object (the rock salt) and the negative ions it produces will bring stability and peace to an environment. Place the salt lamp in the living room or bedroom and keep the light on for long periods during the evening hours. You can also display several salt lamps since they come in many interesting shapes and sizes.

Rooster

January 22, 1909–February 9, 1910: Yin Earth Rooster
February 8, 1921–January 27, 1922: Yin Metal Rooster
January 26, 1933–February 13, 1934: Yin Water Rooster
February 13, 1945–February 1, 1946: Yin Wood Rooster
January 31, 1957–February 17, 1958: Yin Fire Rooster
February 17, 1969–February 5, 1970: Yin Earth Rooster
February 5, 1981–January 24, 1982: Yin Metal Rooster
January 23, 1993–February 9, 1994: Yin Water Rooster
February 9, 2005–January 28, 2006: Yin Wood Rooster
January 28, 2017–February 15, 2018: Yin Fire Rooster
February 13, 2029–February 02, 2030, Yin Earth Rooster

Rooster Personality

When considering a Chinese Zodiac animal's qualities, it's a good idea to examine the traits, behaviors, and personality of the mythic creature we are discussing. While most Chinese Zodiac animals do not differentiate between male and female, the Chinese sign of the Rooster is the male. (No one ever says they're born under the sign of the hen or the chicken.)

When we look at this creature's personality, we think of Rooster as the boss of the hen-house. Roosters are polygamists; they can have many 'hens' under their care. He also will guard and protect all he sees as his from any interlopers. He will oversee from a high perch, keeping a sharp lookout, sounding his distinctive alarm if predators approach.

Because of the substantial duties a Rooster always seems to have (particularly that of keeping an eye out for others,) the Rooster personality is to be a perfectionist, someone with a sharp eye for detail and the ability to keep an accounting of everything (and everyone). In matters of money, Rooster excels. Roosters are adept at handling finances, protecting assets, and making sound investments.

As perfectionists, Roosters are intolerant of even the smallest error. They will aggressively go after what belongs to them, from a small overcharge at the bank to a raise or bonus they believe is owed them at work. (It's best not to owe a Rooster money unless you can pay them back.)

Roosters like to look good and equate looking good with respect from others. Roosters open their pocketbooks to add things to their lives to make others take notice. Money is well spent on a flashy car, a nice suit, or a piece of sparkling jewelry.

Roosters prefer routine over surprises. Surprises are seen as a danger warning and perceived on a range from merely irritating to stressful. Those born under the sign of the Rooster like to be prepared. They will keep extra things in their home or their handbag just in case—everything from change for the parking meter, to remedies for headaches, to extra pens.

Rooster natives like to be seen as the person who has it all together. Because of this, they can be convinced to take part in projects which prove to be impossible tasks.

Rooster natives are very inquisitive. They end up taking on more and more and still find the energy to do it all. They give parties, volunteer for groups, and make their own bread, possibly all in one day. Overall, they keep a calm demeanor—unless things go very wrong. Then you will witness their extreme distress and hurt, erupting from out of nowhere.

If we can find fault with Rooster, it would be their sense of entitlement. It's true, Roosters do a lot, but then they also want a lot of praise and compliments for their actions. Roosters can be prone to jealousy when others seem to be in the limelight, causing the Rooster to take actions that don't benefit him like being insensitive or even vengeful.

When a Rooster falls in love, it's serious business. He follows his practical manner in his approach. This can lead to great disappointments in Rooster's love life, as it's hard to categorize and schedule emotions.

Many Roosters find that being in a relationship is preferable to being alone. It's not that they need the romance, it's more their life, and the house just seems to run better when there's two. Rooster loves an orderly house. To romance a Rooster, share kitchen duties, and he'll pronounce it, "true love."

Rooster: Predictions for 2021

How to use your High-Energy Days: On these days, plan to take action for your most important goals, make vital phone calls, send important emails. Your high-energy days are when your energy and luck are the strongest for the month.

January 2021: *Uranus goes direct on January 14. Mercury goes retrograde from January 30 to February 20. Your Lucky Days are 4, 10, 16, 22, 28.*

The Lunar year comes to an end, and the new year begins. You may start to feel the energy of the Metal Ox year throughout this month. This will be very harmonious energy for Rooster natives. But it's not time to move forward yet. There are still loose ends to tidy up. Try to get as much of your old life cleared out or cleaned up as possible.

To clear clutter, get rid of debts or past obligations, answer emails, and clear out your inbox. Mercury goes retrograde at the end of the month, and will bring any missed items back to you. February will be much less stressful if you are mindful of what needs to be completed in January.

Finances improve, and you find opportunities for additional sources of income. You may see only small amounts come in now at the beginning, but it's a sign of better times ahead. You can be optimistic even while those around you are wallowing in doom and gloom.

Something is changing at home. Someone may move out, or you may clear out some extra space. This shift in energy is positive. It opens up good prospects in the home. There is more peace (not that this person was so disruptive—but now there is one less voice in the house).

Romantic energy continues. There can be fun behind closed doors. If you're already in a love relationship, allot some time to spend with your honey. Sit by the fire together and talk. Play a game and share a laugh. Spoon together in front of the TV and cherish each other.

February 2021: *Lunar New Year begins on February 12. Happy Year of the Metal Ox. February 20 has Mercury going direct. February 27 is the full moon. Your High-Energy Days are 3, 9, 15, 21, and 27.*

The month of February begins with the last two weeks of Metal Rat energy. This is a good time to focus on completing projects and letting go of what is no longer beneficial to you. Review your finances and move money into investments or to pay down debt. Look at items you no longer need and sell them. During February, organize your resources, decide what's important and what's worth storing, and let go of the rest.

On February 12, a new moon begins the Lunar New Year of the Metal Ox. This is very harmonious energy for Rooster natives, as you have an innate understanding of the Ox energy. Ox and rooster coexist on the farm without competing for food or space. During this year, you will find you're in sync with the times. Rooster natives are naturally hard-working, frugal, and driven to succeed—all respected qualities in the Metal Ox year.

On February 18, there's a shift in the energy and a contract you've been hoping for comes through, however Mercury is still retrograde. Delay signing while you review the finer points and do some negotiating.

On February 20, Mercury goes direct, and now things move forward again. Give Mercury a couple of days to get up to speed, and then it's a good time for starting a new job, making a large purchase, or upgrading electronics.

On February 27, there is a full moon, and Rooster natives may be irritated regarding a money matter. You could find your risk tolerance and spending habits differ from your partner's. If you are involved in a business, put the details in writing to preserve the relationship, so there is a clear understanding. That said, there can be an opportunity for the Rooster native willing to take a risk. A marketing collaboration or some favorable press from an influencer could be available to you.

March 2021: *March 13 brings the new moon, March 20 marks the first day of spring, March 28 is the full moon. Your High-Energy Days are 5, 11, 17, 23, and 29.*

As March begins and you settle into the Metal Ox energy, finding a focus on transportation. You may consider a new vehicle, either something for getting around town or a vehicle to ride around in for pleasure—perhaps even your dream car.

You're busier than usual, especially with emails and reports. Some Rooster natives will have the chance to speak at a big meeting or do some teaching.

March 13 brings the new moon and a lot of activity in your neighborhood. Street construction may be going on, or new neighbors moving in. New alliances and friendships can be made, including with your children's friends and their families. You can expand your circle of friends now. Consider hosting a party to get to know some more of the people who live nearby.

On March 20, the energy shifts, and a new season begins. Now your thoughts turn towards home and some of the renovations you've been considering for some time. If you own your home, you may build a granny flat for extra income, or renovate your home office to make it a more efficient workspace. If you rent, you'd still like to make some changes. You may move furniture around or add some renter-friendly décor. If you're looking to move, you'll have opportunities to find a new place over the next four weeks.

There's a full moon on March 28, and if you're in a new relationship, you may decide to start living together. It's also possible you are assisting relatives with their living arrangements, helping them move or get settled into a new place. All of this activity is based in joy and helpfulness. You're great at keeping everything organized and helping your family and others.

April 2021: *April 12 brings the new moon. April 27 is the full moon, and Pluto goes retrograde. (Pluto moving backward can cause you to review your basic assumptions of life and eliminate what is unnecessary, bringing you back to what is essential. Pluto will be retrograde until October.) Your High-Energy Days are 4, 10, 16, 22, and 28.*

Now, with the arrival of April, you may consider the very foundations upon which you build your life. You may examine beliefs you have carried with you since childhood and how events in your younger days affect your current life. This could be a cathartic exploration where you release negative ideas and replace them with a narrative more in line with your current, confident self.

April 12 brings the new moon, and there's a possibility of an additional income source for Rooster natives. A new job, promotion including a raise, or a new stream of income is flowing into your life. Rooster natives are naturally good with money, so you will probably direct this flow into accounts to generate passive income or pay down debt (like student loans). Real estate investing is also a possibility. If you've thought about making money through flipping houses, getting into a career in mortgage lending, or doing construction, you now have a lot of support.

On April 19, there's a shift in the energy, and romance comes to the forefront. You may have just started dating someone new, and now you introduce this person to your friends and family with great success. If you're looking for love, this is a good time to enlist the help of those who care about you to help you find a good match. Rooster natives are very particular and discerning, but you will want to trust your friends in this case. Go on a first date, even though you're doubtful about who they've chosen for you.

The full moon comes in on April 27, and cautious Rooster natives may feel encouraged to take a risk. It's possible a close friend or family member has a business idea and is trying to enlist your support. They may want financial backing, but you also have talents and skills which can be useful in building a business. At the same time, it's a good idea to get involved in something so different from your regular job it gives your creative brain something really interesting to work on.

May 2021: *May 11 brings the new moon. On May 23, Saturn goes retrograde. (Saturn retrograde can cause you to review your career choices and make adjustments. Saturn will be retrograde until October). May 26 is a total lunar eclipse. May 29 has Mercury going retrograde. Your High-Energy Days are 4, 10, 16, 22, and 28.*

In May, you can expect an enormous amount of activity. This extends way beyond just being busy at work. There may be some travel, visits from friends and family, as well as complex creative projects. If you have kids, they will pull you in multiple directions as well. Most of these activities are enjoyable; however, when they are stacked one on top of the next, it can feel like you're constantly rushing to keep up. Rooster native, you may notice your usually good boundaries are not in place and that everyone relies on you these days. It's time to re-balance this energy, to give yourself time for personal pursuits.

May 11 brings the new moon, and you have a strong desire to reorganize and take control of your personal environment. You may do a big declutter, or put up shelves and baskets to organize stuff. A stream of money could now come to an end. You likely knew this was coming; it signals a time when you have to make some changes. As this door closes, another will open in the next few weeks.

May 20 shows an energy shift, and your thoughts turn to health and well-being. You may get annual physicals out-of-the-way, switch your diet for some healthier fare, or try a new exciting exercise program. Friends and family may join you in this move towards a healthier lifestyle. Lead the way and all who join you feel better.

On May 26, there is a lunar eclipse bringing some changes at work. A person you've worked with for a long time may move on to another position, or even another company. There could be new rules in your company which almost completely change your daily duties. This all happens while you are assessing whether or not you should stay in your current job. Consider whether the industry you work in is growing or in decline. Rooster natives have a knack for finding success no matter what the circumstances; however, it's easier if you're involved in a growing enterprise.

On May 29, Mercury goes retrograde, and this puts some of your plans on hold. You may have to redo some things you started over the last week. Try to have patience and allow yourself the time to go back and make changes.

June 2021: *June 10 is the annular solar eclipse. June 20 is the first day of summer, and Jupiter goes retrograde (Jupiter retrograde can indicate a need to relearn things or review your beliefs. Jupiter will be retrograde until October). June 22 has Mercury going direct. June 24 is the full moon. On June 25, Neptune goes retrograde. (Neptune retrograde can draw you back towards habits and addictions from your past. It can also encourage a return to spiritual practices. Neptune will be retrograde until December). Your High-Energy Days are 3, 9, 15, 21, and 27.*

The month of June begins with harmonious energy for Rooster natives. Much of the work you've been doing over the last six will months is now coming to fruition. Seeds you have planted are now bearing fruit. The business networking and connections you've made in the community now all bring you benefit. It's wise to continue making these connections, remembering people's birthdays, and reaching out to them when things happen in their lives. People appreciate how much you care.

On June 10, there's a solar eclipse. For some Rooster natives, this will mean starting a new job either within your current company or with a new company. If you own a business, you may receive your latest marketing campaign results and scramble to keep up with the orders. It's appropriate now to do some creative work to market your business or your personal brand. Rooster native, you are known for your confidence and courage. This helps in a world that is continually shifting.

On June 20, the energy shifts towards relationships, both the casual and the intimate ones. You may say goodbye to a friend as they pack up to move back to another city. If you have been dating, now you might get engaged or announce a wedding date. If you're looking for love, Rooster native, this is probably one of the best times of the year to engage in online dating activities. This energy will last for about four weeks. Let the Universe know what you're looking for in a match.

On June 22, Mercury goes direct, and the energy clears. A problem at work seems to vanish on its own. A dispute in the neighborhood disappears as well. Everyone seems to be more understanding and reasonable now.

On June 24, the new moon lights up your area of partnerships, relationships, and connections. This is a great time to expand your circle by meeting the friends of your friends. You might also connect with people through networking groups or professional organizations. This is an excellent time to get an internship or to find a mentor.

July 2021: *July 10 brings the new moon. July 24 is the full moon. Your High-Energy Days are 3, 9, 15, 21, and 27.*

The month of July brings spontaneous romance opportunities for Rooster natives. If you're already in a committed relationship, you only need to put some time to spend with your partner into your schedule. Mark the date with a big heart and allow what happens to happen. This is also a good month to have deep, meaningful conversations with your partner about the future, children, and goals (like, "Where would you like to live in 10 years?"). At these moments, let the world go by and focus only on each other. Single Rooster natives looking for love will have ample opportunities this month for meeting someone and starting out on a great connection. Don't procrastinate and miss this energy!

July 10 brings the new moon and doors open for all kinds of partnerships; romantic, business, friendship, acquaintance, etc. There is a lot of emphasis on balance—make sure there is give and take in your relationships. You may feel a need for change. Now you can bring it up with the person. You will find a very willing listener at the other end.

The energy shifts on July 22, and for the next four weeks, there's a greater emphasis on finances. Opportunities arise, bringing material gain if you focus your attention on completing applications, talking to bankers, or investigating your spending habits. You may want to gather the family to get them on board with your budget plan; however, tread lightly here and talk more about what you are doing rather than what they should do.

The full moon is on July 24, and the energy around finances increases. A windfall is possible, but it will take a concerted effort to make it happen. You may have to ask for a raise more directly than you usually would like. When selling items, you may need to stand firm to get the full price. Ultimately, this will help your bottom line.

August 2021: *August 8 brings the new moon. On August 20, Uranus goes retrograde. August 22 is the full moon. Your High-Energy Days are 2, 8, 14, 20, and 26.*

Welcome, August, the month that brings you the most resources and help from other people. This may come in the form of financial help, such as loans for your business, bill consolidation, or assistance with student loan modification. You can access all kinds of resources during this month, including information, technical help, and general support for what you're doing. You may even find it useful to ask someone else to play devil's advocate and challenge your ideas. Practice improves your skill—and Rooster natives are excellent debaters. As you lay out your points, you come to understand your position better.

The new moon is on August 8 and brings intimate romantic energy. You and your sweetheart may spend more time than usual behind closed doors. You may want to explore some things you've wanted to do (with your partner's consent, of course). This is even better energy for those Rooster natives looking for love. The Universe is bringing potentially suitable matches to your door. Let friends and family know you're looking and fully utilize all the options available through online dating websites.

On August 22, there is a full moon, and the energy makes a shift. For most Rooster natives, the emphasis will be on education as you and/or your kids go back to school. There's a flurry of activity getting school supplies, books, or clearing out space at home for online learning. This is a good time to meet with teachers. Rooster natives love being efficient. Consider looking at study guides and how to do effective learning.

September 2021: *September 7 brings the new moon. September 20 is the full moon. September 22 is the first day of autumn. September 26 has Mercury going retrograde. Your High-Energy Days are 1, 7, 13, 19, and 25.*

September begins, and energy is elevated for Rooster natives. Recognition comes your way. You stand out in the crowd and are noticed by people of influence and importance. You may teach or lead a team meeting. Your name is on something others value. If you do social media, recognize your posts can now reach further than ever before, so plan your content accordingly. Rooster natives don't mind making some waves as long as it benefits your reputation.

September 7 brings the new moon, and over the next two weeks, there may be doing a number of applications, and dealing with a great deal of paperwork. You may be studying to gain a professional license or to renew a certification. Your job may send you to a conference or offer an accelerated learning program for a new technique. Rooster natives enjoy diving deep into a topic. Look for classes where you go beyond the surface and beginning content.

There is a full moon on September 20, and now the spotlight is entirely on you. You may be the host or a facilitator for meetings. All eyes are on you, Rooster native, and you have an opportunity to shine. If you are looking for a new job, this is a great time to be reaching out to people through professional websites like LinkedIn. As you send out your resume, it's more likely to land on the top of the pile, because your energy is so noticeable right now.

On September 26, Mercury goes retrograde. Since you are still in the spotlight, this retrograde Mercury is not so debilitating as most retrogrades. That said, think twice about rushing into a new agreement for employment or a large purchase. Draw out negotiations to until you are past this Mercury retrograde period. However, if the contract offered is one you plan to renew again in the future, it is fine to sign and get started during the next few weeks.

October 2021: *October 6 brings the new moon, and Pluto goes direct. On October 11, Saturn goes direct. October 18 has Mercury going direct and Jupiter going direct. October 20 is the full moon. Your High-Energy Days are 1, 7, 13, 19, 25, and 31.*

October finds you feeling more confident and proficient. This is a great time to start a new job or a new project, anything involving brainpower. Perhaps you're creating an outdoor room with a fire pit, designing and constructing it yourself. Maybe you're organizing the family history and digitizing the photographs all in date order. You may tackle building your own website. Your ability to concentrate and to get things done is strong now. Don't waste this energy by doing everyday things.

October 6 brings the new moon, and people notice something different about you. This can signal a change of status; single Rooster natives may get married or at least move in together. But status changes can also be related to your career. You may take a different position or accept a promotion. If you move to a new location, you'll be updating social media profiles and becoming more noticeable that way. It's also possible the inner work you have been doing is now apparent to others, and people are commenting on how different you've become.

On October 18, Mercury moves forward again. If you have been waiting to take a new job, now is the time to schedule your start date. Contracts and agreements can now be signed with more confidence (still taking care to read the fine print). Rooster natives are known for their decisiveness, and now that Mercury is moving forward again, it's time for you to shine.

On October 20, there is a full moon, and your attention is on your dwelling and the people who live with you. If you have roommates, there can be a change with someone moving out, or someone moving in. If you rent out part of your property, there's also the possibility of a change of tenants. Keep an eye out for any problems with heat-producing equipment in the house, such as the furnace, fireplace, or the stove. But most of the energy here is about bringing the family together for dinner, game night, or watching a movie together.

On October 22, there's a shift of energy, and your thoughts turn to the future. Over the next few weeks, it's good to review your vision board or your goal board, and sit down with your family to discuss plans for the next few years. The universe will bring you opportunities. By having a goal board, you'll more easily see when a door opens bringing new opportunities, and whether or not they are in harmony with you plans for the future.

November 2021: *November 4 is the new moon. November 19 is a partial lunar eclipse. Your High-Energy Days are 6, 12, 18, 24, and 30.*

November arrives, bringing a hectic month. There's a great deal of focus on work projects, sales to boost numbers. Those Rooster natives who own a business may want to offer some paid marketing plans online, or increase the number of posts you're putting out. This energy may indicate you're launching a new product or service, and now is a really good time to let the world know what you have to offer. Rooster natives are the most organized and efficient of all the signs of the Chinese zodiac. Once everything is in your schedule or your calendar, you'll do just fine.

November 4 brings the new moon and a surprise. A friend may make an unexpected announcement, possibly about you. Rooster native, you may find someone you know pursuing you romantically. You can fall head over heels in love in an instant! If you're already in a love relationship, this surprise announcement could be that a friend wants to date your sister or your cousin.

On November 19, there is a lunar eclipse. Most eclipses bring changes you have been looking for, but this eclipse is different. You may not see the benefits of the coming changes (which may affect a meaningful relationship in your life) but know that you will see why this change happened, and how necessary it was after the dust settles.

This eclipse energy may also influence your children and affect changes in their lives. There could be changes at school; or for older children, changes in a significant relationship. They may run to you for solace and advice. Instead of giving them a list of tasks to do, listen to what they have to say, and let them express their feelings. When they've done speaking, they will be ready to hear what you have to say.

December 2021: *December 1 has Neptune going direct. December 4 is a total solar eclipse. December 19 brings the full moon, and Venus goes retrograde. (Venus retrograde can cause you to question what you want and inspire you to look for something new that delights you. Venus will be retrograde until January.) December 21 is the first day of winter. Your High-Energy Days are 6, 12, 18, 24, and 30.*

The month of December brings powerful opportunities for Rooster natives, especially in the areas of finance and business. You often keep your eyes open for ways and means to move forward, and now you will see not one, but several directions you can choose between, each leading to their own special pot of gold. There may be job openings within your company, but it's just as likely a colleague or former supervisor has moved on to another company and is now pulling you in with an offer of a job.

If you own a business, you may get some traction on all the social media work you've been doing and all the direct messages you've been sending out. A person of influence may want to connect with you, put you on their podcast, or promote your product. The entire month brings opportunities for you, but it certainly feels like you're riding a bucking bronco! The ups and downs could leave you feeling a little dizzy. Take it slow, keep your goals in mind, and you'll do just fine.

December 4 is a solar eclipse falling in your area of synchronicity and intuition. The Universe is speaking loudly to you, sending signs and symbols. You may see pairs of numbers like 11, which tells you to do planning, 22 which tells you to build something, or 33, which reminds you of synergy, that cooperation gives you an outcome greater than the sum of the parts. You can be in the flow now.

You may temporarily feel overwhelmed by all the feelings and information coming in. But this is a time to push forward, to follow your heart, and move boldly forward on your goals.

On December 19, there's a new moon and a busy time ensues for the next couple of weeks. This is really the time to streamline your finances, or tasks at the office. You may have been considering hiring a personal assistant or using a service for cleaning and meal prep at home. It's a good idea to look into these things now, even if they're just on a temporary basis while you get you through the holidays. Rooster natives are excellent managers, and you can find some good, reliable at help at this time.

January 2022: *January 2 is the new moon. January 14 has Mercury going retrograde. January 17 is the full moon. On January 18, Uranus goes direct. On January 29, Venus goes direct. Your High-Energy Days are 3, 9, 15, 21, and 27.*

It is January; however, the energy remains under the influence of Metal Ox year the entire month. This is good news for Rooster natives, as Metal Ox is harmonious energy for you. The new calendar year has energized you. Others notice that you are filled with confidence and have the ability to get a lot done. This is a great time to do things at work, and to put your name on them! Don't settle for being a cog in the wheel, take the lead. You may feel some irritation with your financial circumstances. There may be a few delays in receiving money later this month. Plan ahead so you don't get caught unaware.

On January 2, a new moon brings increased relationship energy for Rooster natives. You and your sweetheart are of one mind. You may finish each other's sentences and are intuitively aware of each other's needs. If this is a new relationship, you may move forward by discussing the topic of living together, even of getting engaged. If you're interested in meeting someone new, you have an excellent chance of finding a person who is a great match. Enlist the Universe's help with romance by adding (or refreshing) your Feng Shui cures for love and romance.

On January 14, Mercury goes retrograde in your area of finances. You may discover an error in your banking statement, or there might be some suspicious activity on a credit card. It's wise to monitor things closely over the next few weeks. A payment you were expecting may be delayed. Be very proactive about this and make calls as soon as you notice. On the plus side, a financial source you had before could come back to give you a little more money.

January 17 brings the full moon and the last two weeks of the Metal Ox energy. Consider completing things which have been in the works during the previous 12 months or so. If you are procrastinating over home renovation projects, maybe it's time to give up the project or hire a professional? Now is also the time to declutter, especially your wardrobe. Rooster natives are known for having style, but it's not helpful to keep so many items you no longer wear, ones that don't fit or need repairs.

The energy shifts on January 19, bringing some positive flow to your finances. This is tempered somewhat due to Mercury being retrograde; however, there are indications a new source of money can be found. Of course, with Mercury retrograde, you want to be cautious about signing agreements. It's better to be in planning-mode, rather than doing right now.

February 2022: *February 1 is the new moon and begins the Year of the Water Tiger. February 3 has Mercury going direct. February 16 brings the full moon.*

February 1 brings the new moon and the beginning of the Year of the Water Tiger. This is challenging energy for Rooster natives, as no rooster would like to find herself or himself in a room with a hungry tiger. This means that you will need to pivot more often, be flexible, and adaptable. When opportunities arise (and they will), you'll be ready to receive them with open arms.

Attract New Love

Love is available for you this year if you slow down long enough to look. Your focus on business and other activities can cause you to miss opportunities. Rooster natives looking for love should start the day with an affirmation. Affirm that love is available to you, and this will help you see when the right person is standing right in front of you. Good places to meet new potential relationships are at investment seminars, real estate Meetup groups, and inventor's workshops. Changing activities in June could cause you to run into someone you met in the past and start things up once again. There's a lot of fertility energy for you in November. Take precautions this month if you don't want to add to the family.

Burn a red candle in your bedroom about once a month to stimulate the energy for bringing a love relationship into being. You can use a tea light or votive candle for this purpose, or you can choose a large pillar candle to burn over a series of days.

Burn the candle for an hour or two each night until the candle burns out. So, a large pillar candle or a jar candle could take all month to finish. But that's okay, the act of burning the candle over many days strengthens the energy. As you light the candle, visualize happy times together for the two of you in your new relationship.

If you don't feel comfortable burning candles in your home, you can use a battery-operated or electric candle. Choose one that has a red base. Because this type of candle is not as powerful a cure as a real candle, it's helpful to "light" this candle each day. You don't need it on at night, as that might disturb sleep. Instead, keep it on during the day.

Enhance Existing Love

While there is the occasional disconnect this year between you and your partner, Rooster natives can feel assured that when you have a common goal, you will be dancing together to the same tune in perfect step. Support each other on financial decisions as well as what to keep and what to get rid of in the house. Your relationship may reach a milestone or some other reason to celebrate. Don't skip this celebration. Gather others to share the joy, and you will deepen your current love relationship.

This year, consider getting a moonstone to increase love energy. It can be in a piece of jewelry or a loose, polished stone.

Reasonably priced moonstones are available in mineral shops and online. If you light a red candle on the night of the full moon and place the moonstone by the candle, the moonstone will gather the moon's energy and bring you luck with love.

There are also stories of how the energy of moonstone can smooth out trouble in a relationship. Give a moonstone piece of jewelry or a tumbled stone to your beloved and let the moonstone's loving vibrations bring peace to the relationship.

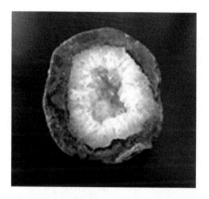

Looking to Conceive?

One gemstone associated with pregnancy is the geode. A geode is a hollow mineral mass with gemstones growing inside the shell. Outdoors, a geode often looks like an egg, and when it is cracked open, the inside reveals the sparkling gemstones.

Geodes range from a couple of inches in size to several feet in diameter. When you find a geode you like, place it in your bedroom to enhance the pregnancy energy.

(From Donna Stellhorn's book, A Path to Pregnancy: Ancient Secrets for the Modern Woman)

Family and Kids

In some years, things like finances or career can take center stage, while other areas of your life recede into the background. This is the case with home life this year. Things are going well at home but are not a major focus because there is so much going on in other areas. Home becomes a refuge, a place to rest and recuperate. But there is little energy for making changes within the home or for moving this year. If you want to do these things, it will take extra effort. There is positive energy around children. If you'd like to add to the family, it is possible—though it may come as a surprise. Younger children will do well in school, and older children have opportunities to increase income or gain a promotion this year in their chosen profession.

For a little extra protection energy for the family this year, plant lilac in your garden, or get some dried lilac blossoms and mix with some potpourri in a bowl. Place the bowl by your front door (inside or out). Ancient stories tell of lilac driving away evil. It helps attract positive energy and keeps negativity away. In winter, you can sprinkle a little dried lilac on your doorstep. When spring comes, plant this beautiful flower.

Money

Rooster natives focus on making money this year. A plethora of opportunities are coming your way. Sources of income include creative endeavors, working in an office, partnerships, passive income sources, and various methods of promoting yourself. In other words, you can make money doing just about anything this year! You do well because you are so focused on money and looking for new income sources. The challenge is not to get stuck in just one way of making money, or to allow yourself to be limited to familiar ways. Be creative and ask yourself whether this opportunity looks like you could make twice the money in half the time.

A good Feng Shui cure to attract wealth/money is to have a representation of flowing water in the house. A fountain is a good representation of flowing water, for example, and you can find small tabletop fountains just about everywhere. Place a tabletop fountain in your entryway or home office to attract prosperity energy to the house. Run the fountain at least a few times a week for the best results.

Job or Career

There's harmony for you in your career this year. While new things are happening within your industry, you keep up and show supervisors you can handle the responsibility. There are new opportunities for you within your current company in June, as it may go through a merger or a renovation from within. But if you find you would like to do something new, it's possible to step outside your usual career path to make more money. Keep in mind the work you do needs to be something where you feel respected, and you enjoy the process or the tasks. Look for work you're passionate about, rather than a job that just brings you a paycheck. It's possible this year to find work-at-home options and to work remotely. Or, you may find work in a remote office of a larger company.

In the West, when we think of gold, we think of a gold bar, but in the East, a gold ingot is shaped like a little boat called the *yuan bao*. These ingots were used as a form of currency. Now you can find replica gold ingots in painted metal to use as a symbol of wealth. They often have embossed Chinese characters of "wealth" and "fortune." Place your ingot on your desk or in your family room on a shelf near a picture of your family to attract a great job opportunity or a raise from your current employer.

Education

This year, Rooster natives in school may question why you're there. This can happen if you take classes outside your area of interest, or the school doesn't have up-to-date equipment. You may find the information being taught is out of date or not applicable to what you want to do. The best courses of study for Rooster natives this year are subjects which help boost your creativity, such as art, entertainment, or technical skills such as video game design.

College could take a big chunk of your finances. Rooster natives may find it challenging to juggle a job and full-time school. To get back in balance, do some spiritual things to help you re-energize. Burn orange candles when you study, or wear an elephant pendant to improve memory.

Legal Matters

This year, you can do well with contracts as long as you take the time to negotiate the finer points. Don't let yourself be rushed by others. You will probably have agreements to consider in the context of your employment, perhaps from more than one party. Take the time and negotiate for increases in income, more vacation time, or a work-at-home option. Taking your time to review the points and state your case can cause even a seemingly intractable employer to agree with you.

It's okay to enter class-action lawsuits this year. But individual court cases could cost you far more than you could win in the suit. See if you can find solutions outside of the courts this year.

Health and Well-Being

Rooster natives have positive energy around health this year. You may have made it your mission to improve your health through positive thinking and good nutrition. These are some of the best building blocks of a healthy, joyful life. Consider walking through national parks, jogging, or working out at home. You can encounter some challenges in June when you find you are no longer eating as healthily as you used to. This will be the time to get back on track. You may look into growing your own food this year, starting a kitchen garden or getting fresh veggies right from the farm through a farm co-op.

The Feng Shui gourd is a symbol related to health, longevity, and well-being. The gourd can be made of wood, metal, glass, or stone. It can also be a natural gourd that's painted or otherwise decorated. You can find gourds like these in Asian markets and art & crafts festivals.

Place the gourd in the bedroom or family room. You can tie a red ribbon around the center of the gourd to increase the energy. But do this only if no one living in the house is ill. If someone in the house is recovering from illness, place the gourd in the family room and not a bedroom.

Dog

February 10, 1910–January 29, 1911: Yang Metal Dog
January 28, 1922–February 15, 1923: Yang Water Dog
February 14, 1934–February 3, 1935: Yang Wood Dog
February 2, 1946–January 21, 1947: Yang Fire Dog
February 18, 1958–February 7, 1959: Yang Earth Dog
February 6, 1970–January 26, 1971: Yang Metal Dog
January 25, 1982–February 12, 1983: Yang Water Dog
February 10, 1994–January 30, 1995: Yang Wood Dog
January 29, 2006–February 17, 2007: Yang Fire Dog
February 16, 2018–February 4, 2019: Yang Earth Dog

Dog Personality

When looking at a Chinese Zodiac creature's qualities, it's a good idea to consider the animal's traits, behaviors, and personality. When considering the Dog's qualities, many of us have some idea about dog personalities and behavior.

Dogs came to live with humans around 100,000 years ago. Humans found dogs to be valuable—helping to hunt and herd, pull loads, and even protect their people from wild animals.

Sometimes we confuse Dogs' overall personality with the characteristics of specific dog breeds (most of which are only a few hundred years old). We want to consider the energy of a dog as we think about the personality traits of natives born under the Chinese Zodiac sign of the Dog.

The animal dog is known for companionship; similarly, individuals born during the Year of the Dog are usually very well-liked and friendly. They have a deep sense of loyalty and fair play. They are happier around people than on their own. They go with the flow, being less demanding, always meeting others halfway, so everyone gets something of what they want.

Early humans brought dogs into their lives to increase their chances of survival. The dogs would help them find food, keep them warm at night, and protect them from dangers. Those born under the Chinese Zodiac sign of Dog are protective of their friends. They watch over them and will fight for them. Dogs are eager to take up a cause, whether on behalf of an individual, a group, or an organization.

Because they take loyalty so seriously, Dog natives choose their friendships carefully. Accepting a new person into their circle takes time. At the same time, many people want to be their friends. Dogs are often in positions of influence and connected with people of power. Dogs are rarely selfish, and when they crave power or money, there is usually a person or cause who will benefit from everything Dog creates.

Dog natives are known to work hard and to play hard. They have to be cautious to avoid overindulgence in food or over-spending. They often like competitive sports, and they often love a good hard workout. They don't mind a night out dancing, followed by an early morning yoga session. They like a stylish home, but their home may not be neat—it doesn't matter to them since they're not at home that often.

Dogs make good lawyers, always looking for justice and fairness. These characteristics also make them excellent employees. They're particularly good at managing several projects simultaneously. They won't gossip at the water cooler, nor will they speak ill of others. Dog prefers to be a team player, and if you're part of the team, you can count on them.

Dogs alternate between aggressive spending and aggressive saving. Regarding investments, they are better at investing in property, precious metals or stones, or other tangible things rather than intangible derivatives.

Most in life, Dog wants loyal, honest, intelligent friends, who will share a dinner or attend the theater, or join them on an impromptu trip to the Bahamas for the weekend. They love to be treated fairly, and they honestly don't like to be questioned too deeply about their reasoning and thinking processes. They'd love to have enough money—in fact, so much money they never have to think about what things cost!

Even when Dog seems happy, they are pessimists by nature, capable of worrying a great deal, including the small things. They can count the times when they were overconfident, and it led to disaster, and they use this information as a tool to confirm their need to worry.

They are resourceful and resilient and overcome any difficulty. However, Dog spends a great deal of time visualizing potential problems, and they look for the storm clouds and never the silver lining.

Dog: Predictions for 2021

How to use your High-Energy Days: On these days, plan to take action for your most important goals, make vital phone calls, send important emails. Your high-energy days are when your energy and luck are the strongest for the month.

January 2021: *Uranus goes direct on January 14. Mercury goes retrograde from January 30 to February 20. Your Lucky Days are 5, 11, 17, 23, 29. [How to use your Lucky Days: On these days, plan to take significant actions, make vital phone calls, send emails. These are days when your energy and luck are high.]*

You feel more determined and disciplined now. It's easier to get up on time, get your exercise done, even eat a healthy breakfast. You are more productive than you have been in a long time. This is a great time to work on a pet-project. Perhaps this is a side business or a hobby you want to turn into a business.

If you're in school, use this highly motivating time to finish school projects or prep for exams. Find a study partner and hit the books. Schedule tests outside of the Mercury retrograde period if possible, so you don't have any unforeseen difficulties or delays. Mercury will go retrograde at the end of this month.

Friendships abound. People want to see you, and you may receive several invitations to parties and events. A new friend feels very familiar—maybe because of a deeper spiritual connection with this person. Possibly this is a new best friend.

There is movement at home. You may consider changing residences, but there also may be people moving around you. Neighbors may change houses, renovate, or carry out major construction. You may also shift rooms and furniture around. As the Metal Rat year ends, you can get rid of what you don't need and bring in some fresh updates for the home.

You enjoy a great deal of positive interaction with children or younger relatives. One or more ask to spend time with you. You can consider a day trip or a gathering for a special occasion.

February 2021: *Lunar New Year begins on February 12. Happy Year of the Metal Ox! February 20 has Mercury going direct. February 27 is the full moon. Your High-Energy Days are 4, 10, 16, 22, and 28.*

February begins with the final two weeks of Metal Rat energy bringing a busy month for Dog natives. You may complete a big project at home while juggling your usual duties at your job. The last 11-1/2 months have been a wild ride, and intuitively you can already sense the changing energy on its way.

On February 12, the Lunar New Year begins, and the world welcomes in Metal Ox energy. Your mind turns to practicality as people around you slow down to a steady pace. On the farm, the dog's role is to keep the cows and oxen heading in the right direction. In this case, the right direction represents your goals, and the herd represents those who will help you on your quest. It's a good idea to refresh your vision board or to post a list of your goals where you can see it every day. You'll have quite a bit of support this year. Though you need a lot of activity, you can make a lot of headway if you keep your goals in mind.

On February 20, Mercury goes direct. The energy picks up speed; however, this is still Metal Ox energy, so there is an emphasis on getting things organized and having an inventory of the available resources. You and your partner may wait for vital information, but now that you have outlined your goals, decisions are easier.

On February 27, there is a full moon and a great deal of emphasis on your finances. You may weigh some choices. The planets are lining up to bring you a potential windfall, but they balance the sweet with the sour. This opportunity comes with some responsibilities as well, hence the choices.

March 2021: *March 13 brings the new moon, March 20 marks the first day of spring, March 28 is the full moon. Your High-Energy Days are 6, 12, 18, 24, and 30.*

March begins and a reminder to be kind to yourself. No one can be in motion 24/7. It's important to schedule breaks and downtime. You may feel you've done some backsliding on a goal, or something is taking longer than you thought it would. The best way forward is to treat yourself with understanding and kindness. Dog natives have excellent instincts when looking outward, but you can be self-critical. When you need a break, take a break. This will help you prioritize your energy at other times for intense work and essential projects.

March 13 brings the new moon, and there's a possibility of financial gain as well as a sizable expenditure: money coming in, money going out. There is positive energy around buying real estate or setting down a large deposit for a future vacation. If you want to save money, it's wise to put funds into an account that's hard to reach. You could consider investing in an annuity or buying commodities. Ask some of your investment-savvy friends to help you choose the best financial instrument for you.

On March 20, the energy shifts, and there is a great deal of emphasis for Dog natives on communication. You could do some marketing for your business or your brand. This is a favorable time to send out your resume or interview for a new position. There's a lot of movement around you. You could apply for a transfer to a new team within your company, or get a new office.

March 28 brings the full moon, and there's a possibility of a favorable outcome for a legal matter, contract, or professional license. While you may have to make some minor concessions, you get most of what you want, and better still, the process can be completed. It's one more thing you can check off your to-do list.

April 2021: *April 12 brings the new moon. April 27 is the full moon. Pluto goes retrograde. (Pluto moving backward can cause you to review your basic assumptions of life and eliminate what is unnecessary, bringing you back to what is essential. Pluto will be retrograde until October.) Your High-Energy Days are 5, 11, 17, 23, and 29.*

April brings in harmonious communication energy with neighbors, siblings, and your family in general. As the weather brightens up, there could be a neighborhood garage sale or opportunities to meet new neighbors. A sibling or younger relative may come to you for advice and encouragement. A nearby relative could move and need your help in finding a new place or moving a sofa.

April 12 brings the new moon, and over the next two weeks, there's a great deal of activity putting you on the front line. You may lead meetings, or your team's project is coming due. If you own a business, marketing and design work is needed. This is an appropriate time to look at rebuilding your website or increasing your social media following.

There's a lot of energy around transportation, and some Dog natives will consider getting a new vehicle. This doesn't necessarily have to for practical purposes, you might even acquire a motorcycle or mountain bike.

On April 19, the energy shifts. There may be a delightful get-together at home to celebrate a milestone birthday or anniversary. Dog natives rarely miss a special occasion. Enlist help, so you don't end up doing all the preparations yourself.

On April 27, there is a full moon and good partnership energy for the next couple of weeks. No matter how long you've been together with your sweetheart, it feels fresh and new right now. Dog natives do well in long-term relationships, and your connection with your partner grows better with time. If, on the other hand, you're looking for love, stick to familiar places to meet new people. You might connect with someone through your church, a professional organization, or in your neighborhood.

May 2021: *May 11 brings the new moon. On May 23, Saturn goes retrograde. (Saturn retrograde can cause you to review your career choices and make adjustments. Saturn will be retrograde until October). May 26 is a total lunar eclipse. May 29 has Mercury going retrograde. Your High-Energy Days are 5, 11, 17, 23, and 29.*

In May, you pay a lot of attention to your dwelling. Dog natives love to be at home and collect a great deal of stuff to make their home feel comfortable. Every once in a while, it's good to take a look around and see which objects no longer bring you joy. Then it's time to declutter. This is also a good time for renovations, purchasing rental property, or getting together with an architect to discuss plans for building your dream home.

May 11 brings the new moon and could bring an addition to the family through a birth, adoption, or an older child may enter a long-term relationship. Joyful celebrations are happening under your roof.

This new moon also brings positive energy when you connect with your ancestral line. It's good to collect photos in scrapbooks, or to digitize old family records. If you are not the archivist of the family history, find the person who is and tell them your story and what you know of family traditions.

On May 20, the energy shifts, and there is exceptionally positive relationship energy for Dog natives. You feel more in harmony and in sync with your partner. You support each other and work as a team. For those Dog natives looking for a love relationship, you can make an intriguing connection through friends. Allow others to fix you up with someone new. You can also do well meeting new prospects through a matchmaker.

May 26 is the lunar eclipse which occurs for you personally in your area of risk-taking and adventure. Dog natives can be cautious until action is needed, and then you're absolutely fearless. This could be one of those times when you do something well outside your comfort zone. You might jump out of an airplane, do comedy in front of an audience, or launch your own podcast. By doing something completely different, you're likely to feel exhilarated.

May 29 has Mercury going retrograde, and this could indicate a slight setback. You've taken a couple of steps forward and one slide back. This allows you to take a deep breath and check your bearings. Allow obstacles in your road to give you a chance to pause, especially if this involves waiting for someone else's response. Work on something else while you wait.

June 2021: *June 10 is the annular solar eclipse. June 20 is the first day of summer. Jupiter goes retrograde. (Jupiter retrograde can indicate a need to relearn things or review your beliefs. Jupiter will be retrograde until October). June 22 has Mercury going direct. June 24 is the full moon. On June 25, Neptune goes retrograde. (Neptune retrograde can draw you back towards habits and addictions from your past. It can also encourage a return to spiritual practices. Neptune will be retrograde until December). Your High-Energy Days are 4, 10, 16, 22, and 28.*

June can be a month filled with laughter, fun, and excitement. You may spend a lot of time with children or younger relatives. Some Dog natives may be expecting at this time, planning for the new addition to the household. Or, you may adopt a pet and bring that bundle of joy into your home.

This month is marked by endings as well. Think about what you can let go of in your life now, including bad habits or too much stuff. As you take steps to simplify your life, you will have more space in your schedule and more bandwidth in your brain to take on significant things.

June 10 is the solar eclipse, and you may take a big step in your new love relationship. You may talk about getting engaged or moving in together. You might introduce your sweetheart to your family and friends. There's a possibility of blending two families together. While this is an exciting time, it all takes a little bit of finesse. Be patient and understanding.

The energy shifts on June 20, and work is heating up. Your office may be shorthanded, or recent changes have created new procedures for you. You may feel pulled in two directions between home and your career. Trying to balance these two energies can feel difficult, but Dog natives can turn on a dime. Permit yourself to move seamlessly from one task to the next.

On June 22, Mercury goes direct. It will take a few days for Mercury to get up to speed, but in the course of this, you'll find things are already a little easier at work. Your recent objections or concerns have been heard.

The full moon is on June 24, and Dog natives have an opportunity for some recognition in the office. Coworkers are complimenting you and showing their support. You may be noticed by some of the higher-ups. You can be recognized for your achievements or meeting a big sales goal. These accolades can be parlayed into something more tangible later in the year, such as a promotion.

July 2021: *July 10 brings the new moon. July 24 is the full moon. Your High-Energy Days are 4, 10, 16, 22, and 28.*

July is marked by changes at home. Someone may move in or move out. There could be changes in the neighborhood where longtime residents are going on to a new place. There may be construction in the area, bringing some noise, dust, or a longer commute. There's a lot of motion around you, but you're in the eye of the storm where life is pretty calm. You can become involved if you like, and take a step into the storm, or you can hang back and just observe.

July 10 brings the new moon, and you may be enthusiastic about a new exercise program or a novel way of eating. You pay a lot of attention to your personal well-being. You may have started yoga, meditation, or tai chi. Scheduling mental health breaks is quite useful now. To relax, try walking in nature rather than playing a first-person shooter game. Look for how you can simplify your life to bring yourself more peace. When things get complicated, see what can be eliminated to bring back the balance.

The energy shifts on July 22, and now Dog natives experience positive relationship energy. If you are in a long-term relationship, there's more harmony now. Some past disagreements have been settled, and there are good feelings on both sides. If you're looking for a love relationship, you have powerful charisma now for attracting an exciting match. Look at how you can update your profile on social media or dating websites. But more importantly, reach out to connect with somebody, even if you just talk on the phone for a while.

On July 24, there's a full moon, and the positive love relationship energy continues. If you're in a new relationship, it may get serious now. You may discuss the possibility of seeing each other exclusively, or even going so far as to set a wedding date. At the same time, some Dog natives want a lot of freedom. However, there's more than one road to autonomy. You can find inner peace by recognizing you are more confident, self-assured, and certainly more capable than you've ever been in your life.

August 2021: *August 8 brings the new moon. On August 20, Uranus goes retrograde. August 22 is the full moon. Your High-Energy Days are 3, 9, 15, 21, and 27.*

The month of August has some ups and downs in the context of family and extended family members. You might be shocked at something a family member does, and since Dog natives can be very family-oriented, many people are looking to you to see your reaction. There may be potential disagreements, as the family takes sides. You, ever the peacemaker, will help bring things back together.

At the same time, there could be a flurry of activity at home with children going back to school. Now it's back to a set schedule, and early mornings with everybody moving in a different direction. As you start to embrace your new routine, think about what you do some other time in order to give yourself more time—especially in the mornings.

The new moon is on August 8, and there could be a significant change in life with your sweetheart. He or she may have received a job offer, one that takes them to another state (or even to work in another country). Or perhaps there's a surprise pregnancy announcement. Your honey may want to leave their job and start a business. Recognize that whatever this is, it's been brewing for some time. You probably at some level knew it was coming, since Dog natives are very perceptive and watchful. You're also resourceful, and the changes happening will bring new opportunities if you're willing to look.

The full moon is on August 22, and the next two weeks are marked by a period of endings. It's important to finish projects. Let go of things that have reached the end of their usefulness. Release friendships that are not bringing you joy. Even let go of the house if it's no longer the best place to live. Endings signal a new beginning is coming. Just as you can't reach for something when your arms are full, procrastinating to avoid an ending will keep what you want just out of your reach.

September 2021: *September 7 brings the new moon. September 20 is the full moon. September 22 is the first day of autumn. September 26 has Mercury going retrograde. Your High-Energy Days are 2, 8, 14, 20, and 26.*

For the most part, September brings harmonious energy even though there's a lot of activity around you, especially with school. You are adjusting to new circumstances for sure. Not everything is exactly the way you want it to be. You recognize you can handle even big changes, and change makes life more exciting.

On September 7, the new moon brings light and energy to your area of resources provided by others. Now you can connect with investment managers, bankers, or the HR department of your company. You may lower your insurances or find a new investment with better payouts. Consolidate loans or apply for more credit, especially if you are building your business.

On September 20, the full moon reveals how the seeds you planted earlier in the month are coming to fruition. You may sign an agreement or put the final touches on a new financial plan. While this positive energy lasts for a few weeks, you may want to move with alacrity as Mercury will go retrograde soon. Consider expanding passive income sources, including dividends, income from business, or royalties.

The energy shifts on September 22, and your thoughts turn to education. You may have scheduled a test you need to qualify for a professional license or for school. Your children may take SATs or work on projects at home.

On September 26, Mercury goes retrograde, and you can feel very hesitant to complete paperwork. You may procrastinate because the paperwork is boring or because your intuition says, "Don't move forward." Tread lightly here for a few days until you can get more information. Then, at the very end of the month, look at this issue again and see if you're ready to complete the project.

October 2021: *October 6 brings the new moon, and Pluto goes direct. On October 11, Saturn goes direct. October 18 has Mercury going direct and Jupiter going direct. October 20 is the full moon. Your High-Energy Days are 2, 8, 14, 20, and 26.*

October arrives, bringing some course corrections, something Dog natives are excellent at. Who besides yourself can change directions so quickly? There could be a spontaneous trip, an overnight stay with friends or family. But during the same month, there could be a work or school project where you need to pull an all-nighter to get it done. The thing to remember about October is to remain flexible. If something needs to change, remember you can handle it.

The new moon comes in on October 6, and the focus on education continues. You may look at doing a standardized test. For those Dog natives not in formal education, there can be paperwork, licensing, or some education related to your career coming up in the next two weeks.

Also, during the next two weeks, you may receive a contract or agreement to sign. It's good to take your time and read all the details and negotiate any points you want to change. This may be a continuation of a previous agreement, like an annual lease or an extended work contract.

Mercury goes direct on October 18, and now things get a little easier. People respond to your requests. This is especially true if you're looking for a new job and have been waiting for a background check to come through or an interview to be scheduled. You may have to remind people with a phone call or quick email over the next couple of days, but you should get some suitable responses.

On October 20, there's a full moon and is a great deal of attention on you. This may be because of a milestone celebration. Some Dog natives are getting engaged. Or you may be in the process of moving. You are noticed on a lot of levels, not just in the physical world, but also in the spiritual world. Many people from your past may reach out to you—people you haven't heard from in years. You can capitalize on this energy now by marketing your business or sending out posts on social media. What you send could be seen by many, many people, so make sure what you post is in line with your values.

November 2021: *November 4 is the new moon. November 19 is a partial lunar eclipse. Your High-Energy Days are 1, 7, 13, 19, and 25.*

A great deal of activity highlights the month of November. During the month, everything seems to flow, falling quickly into place. But there will be a moment or two this month when you feel you're trudging uphill carrying a bag of rocks. Be mindful of what you do during times like these to make sure your actions align with your goals. When you need a break, take one. But otherwise, commit to your course of action. Recognize that others are going through their own difficulties. Even if they promised to help, they might not be available when you need them. This month, rely on yourself first.

The new moon on November 4 focusing positive energy in the area of your career. A supervisor recognizes your efforts, and you can possibly be offered a promoted. If you are due for a performance review now, it's the right time to talk about what you want to achieve in the coming year. If you can't muster the enthusiasm for this conversation with your manager, you might not be in the right job. Take some of this positive energy of this time and use it to update your resume.

On November 19, there's a lunar eclipse which can signal changes in the romance area. Those Dog natives looking for love now have a chance to connect with someone who's energy sparkles in your eyes. Let your friends fix you up with someone who may not initially seem like your type, or finally say, "Yes!" to someone who has been asking you out for a while. You may be quite surprised how well things work out.

Eclipses bring change, and lunar eclipses shift the life areas where you have been feeling blocked emotionally. You may work too much, not feeling your hard work is recognized or appreciated. Things may not seem fun in your life right now. This is a time to branch out and explore some new activities. Do some things you haven't done before and discover the joy of doing new things now.

December 2021: *December 1 has Neptune going direct. December 4 is a total solar eclipse. December 19 brings the full moon, and Venus goes retrograde. (Venus retrograde can cause you to question what you want and inspire you to look for something new that delights you. Venus will be retrograde until January.) December 21 is the first day of winter. Your High-Energy Days are 1, 7, 13, 19, 25, and 31.*

The month of December brings friendships and camaraderie right to your door. Maybe you're hosting a holiday get-together, or renting your own place and inviting friends and family to join the fun. Last-minute changes are possible, especially ones caused by bad weather; this keeps Dog natives hopping. If you are making travel plans, make sure everything is refundable or changeable. At home, consider having extra food in the freezer in case more people show up than you were expecting.

December 4 is a solar eclipse; eclipses bring change. There could be some difficulties with computer equipment. Hang on to your phone lest you drop it into the soup you're making. It's a good idea to make sure automatic backups are working, and your photos are going into the cloud. Protect your valuable data.

There's a lot of activity going on at work, related directly to your income. This may mean you're getting more hours or more sales (which are then reflected in your commissions). There's talk about future changes at your job; however, many of these might be rumors rather than actual plans. That said, you should consider discussions about the financial health of the company important. This information helps you decide whether you want to put down roots at this company or move on in 2022.

On December 19, there's a full moon, and life settles down quite a bit. You may have some time off around the holidays and get to spend it traveling with friends. You may see some distant family members either in person or by video conference. Venus is retrograde at this time. While not as disruptive as Mercury retrograde, it can cause you to think twice about a purchase or something you've received. If you're doing holiday shopping after December 19, make sure that you are keeping the receipts.

December 21 shifts the energy, and you may want to become a hermit for a while. Now it's a good idea to stay in bed a little longer, hang out in your slippers and pamper yourself. This is the right time to do some home cooking with quality ingredients to nurture your body.

January 2022: *January 2 is the new moon. January 14 has Mercury going retrograde. January 17 is the full moon. On January 18, Uranus goes direct. On January 29, Venus goes direct. Your High-Energy Days are 6, 12, 18, 24, and 30.*

The calendar year begins, but Metal Ox energy lasts for the entire month. This is an excellent time to plan for the future and see what still needs to be cleaned out, filed away, or tossed out. By focusing on completing things, you open up your life to more expansive opportunities. Because Mercury goes retrograde this month, if you find you are falling behind on your New Year's resolutions, recognize you can start them all over again next month in the New Lunar Year.

There's a new moon on January 2, and your intuition is very strong over the next two weeks. You may be receiving messages and impressions from the world around you. Unusual thoughts are popping into your head. This is a good time to work with tarot cards, Angel cards, or even a pendulum. Allow yourself a few minutes each day to shut off the phone and listen to the Universe. Sit with the cards or the pendulum and ask a single question. Give yourself some time to hear the answer.

On January 14, Mercury goes retrograde. Many things you began in the past two weeks are now interrupted or have to be started over. Mercury retrograde has a purpose besides just disrupting your life—and it is to allow you to go over past decisions to see if you want to rethink your choices. Now you can change your mind. Dog natives are often committed to a course of action, but you must remember you can change, and sometimes change leads you straight to your objective.

The full moon on January 17 highlights relationships. You may have temporarily been separated from your sweetheart because of a work or a family matter. But now you come back together, and things are better than ever. For those Dog natives looking for love, someone from your past may return to your present. This may be someone you only met once before and barely remember. But they remember you.

On January 19, the energy shifts, and you come into the spotlight. You have an opportunity to lead a meeting, or even be on stage. This is a great time to launch your YouTube channel.

February 2022: *February 1 is the new moon and begins the Year of the Water Tiger. February 3 has Mercury going direct. February 16 brings the full moon.*

February 1 brings the new moon and launches the Year of the Water Tiger. Dog natives can now find so many opportunities, options and so many directions to move forward. You may run at full speed the entire year. After the slow, methodical energy of 2021, you can look forward to the chase. Ready. Get set. Go!

Attract New Love

Love comes when you don't expect it this year. Someone has been admiring you for some time, and you may not have noticed. But now the stars have shifted, and suddenly this person's good qualities come into your view. Sparks could be flying. You may feel uncertain at first because this person is very different from anyone you've dated before. You're breaking new ground and perhaps some of your rules, but it's the connection you've wanted all along. The best way to meet someone is to be yourself and do things you enjoy. Communicate often with those around you. You will attract love like the flame attracts the moths. Love energy is strongest in June. Make sure you get out of the house that month.

You can use little stuffed animals—especially teddy bears—this year, when you want to attract more love into your life. Teddy bears have long been associated with comforting love.

When you're ready to enhance love in your life, take a sheet of paper and write down the three qualities you find important in your partnership. You may have more on your mind but start with three. A quality would be something like "they show me kindness," or "they do the dishes without me asking," or "they ask me how my day went." Do not list vague qualities like "open-hearted," or "generous," or "loving" because these are too hard to quantify.

Take the sheet, roll it up, and use a ribbon to tie it to the paw (or the waist) of a soft teddy bear. Get a second bear and place them both, either sitting on your bed or nightstand, in an embrace or side by side.

Enhance Existing Love

Your love relationship is tested this year by changes at home, pulling both you and your partner in different directions; and then squishing you together in a tiny space. The underlying basis of your relationship is strong, but external details can wear on both of you. There can be some irritations, but the make-up sex could be glorious. It's essential to treat each other fairly, with consideration and patience. The friendship that started your relationship can be rekindled as you find new interests to enjoy together. Look for physical activities such as dancing, hiking, or biking as well as intellectual pursuits involving technology.

This year enhancing love-energy is easy—just add a big splash of red to the bedroom. Consider getting a red bedspread. Red is the color of excitement and passion. Choose a shade of red that appeals to you. The spread can include other colors in a pattern, stripes, or floral design.

Looking to Conceive?

Find a necklace made of cowrie shells. Cowrie shells have long been associated with pregnancy because of their uterus-like shape. Small, usually white cowrie shells are made into necklaces and bracelets.

You can also find larger cowrie shells; these may be striped or spotted brown and white. Place one or more of these larger shells on your bedside table. Cowrie shells are reputed to be fertility cures and also have been used as currency in some cultures. The shell will attract good money energy, too.

(From Donna Stellhorn's book, A Path to Pregnancy: Ancient Secrets for the Modern Woman)

Family and Kids

There's a great deal of activity this year for Dog natives in home and family. There is a likely move, or at least changes in the residence. Someone could move in or move out. This may even occur several times during the year. Home is very active, and you try to make it more comfortable (which may cost you some money purchasing furnishings, or pulling things out of storage). Since self-care is so important this year, it's helpful for you to enlist your family's support.

There is some energy around fertility, especially in the middle of the year. If you want to add to the family, luck is on your side, and you can find the medical support you need. For those Dog natives who have children, communication is excellent. Older children are busy, not spending as much time with you as in previous years. However, phone calls and videoconferencing help you stay in touch with them.

Chamomile is a beneficial herb in Feng Shui. Sprinkle dried chamomile flowers around your property to clear it of negative energy. Place a bowl of chamomile flowers in your bedroom to help you get restful sleep. Make a tea from chamomile, let it cool, and pour it into a spray bottle. Spray it around the house to attract prosperity and peace. (You can store the unused portion in the refrigerator for up to a week.)

Money

It can be a challenging year from a financial perspective for Dog natives, but you are now more focused on the big picture. Money is flowing out for large projects or education. If this were a poker game, you'd be "all in." This year's challenge will be to have boundaries on spending and not let your vision of what you want cloud the creative opportunities to do things less expensively.

There are energy connections to home and family. You may make money through real estate, or partnering with an investment-savvy relative. Income flows when you're in line spiritually. Visualization, affirmations, and a little magic can go a long way to helping you create money opportunities.

When you wish to find or bring additional money into your life, imagine you are unlocking a magic door. Behind this door are all the opportunities for money you could imagine. What better symbol could there be than a key to unlock the magic door? Indeed, the perfect Feng Shui cure to attract more money into your life this year will be a symbolic key!

Job or Career

There can be changes in your career this year as you follow your passion. As you move from the seed planting year last year (2020) into your first-year seed tending year, you begin to see the results of the hard work you've done over the previous three years. Now you can take the bull by the horns and focus your creative energy on building the career you love.

There may be a slight setback in November; however, the lessons from this can help you considerably in the future. From the beginning of the year to the end, your career may transform a lot, even if you stay with the same company. Your title may change; you may change teams or take on much more responsibility. This year, you look for more freedom in your work, and so you may have your own business and to supervise yourself.

An excellent Feng Shui cure to give you the power and energy to hunt down and capture the job you want is to hang a picture of a lion in your home office or kitchen. You can choose a picture of either a male or female lion (though remember, the female does most of the hunting).

Write out a job description you want and tape it to the back of the picture. Or, if you don't want to hang a picture of a lion, you can display a figurine or even a little stuffed lion.

Education

Dog natives like the social aspect of school but prefer to do something hands-on and practical rather than sitting in a classroom. Examine your study habits to find more effective ways of processing information and taking tests. If procrastination or poor memory has plagued you, solutions are coming this year.

Dog natives who are studying business can apply what they've learned almost immediately. Dog natives who are studying medicine or construction also do well. But the ideal scenario for you this year would be short, interesting classes where you can immediately apply what you've learned.

Legal Matters

There's a lot of energy and activity surrounding agreements and contracts this year. You may be given a contract for employment or to continue your current work with a specific company. Dog natives who are in business may receive contracts from companies to be an influencer or spokesperson. If you're just starting out, the job may not pay well, but this income source can grow over time. There could be a lot of activity around contracts concerning the care of relatives, or working with relatives.

When considering lawsuits, you will do better in individual suits rather than class-action suits. Either way, it is essential to have a very strong case before entering into something serious because it could end up being expensive.

Health and Well-Being

There's a lot of harmony in your area of health this year. You are very active, finding new and fun exercises to do. You may be involved in sports. You're likely taking care of yourself at home by making healthy food, experimenting with recipes, and making food based on your heritage. When you have the occasional health issue, it's easy to find reliable sources for information and treatments this year. Look into alternative healthcare modalities such as acupuncture, massage, and aromatherapy.

Turquoise, a beautiful blue-green stone, is often made into jewelry. Its long been known for its healing qualities. Find either a piece of turquoise jewelry or a tumbled stone you can carry with you. The turquoise will remind you to stick with positive health changes. Once you establish these new habits, you can keep the stone in your kitchen or the bedroom on your bedside table.

Pig/Boar

January 30, 1911–February 17, 1912: Yin Metal Pig/Boar
February 16, 1923–February 4, 1924: Yin Water Pig/Boar
February 4, 1935–January 23, 1936: Yin Wood Pig/Boar
January 22, 1947–February 9, 1948: Yin Fire Pig/Boar
February 8, 1959–January 27, 1960: Yin Earth Pig/Boar
January 27, 1971–January 15, 1972: Yin Metal Pig/Boar
February 13, 1983–February 1, 1984: Yin Water Pig/Boar
January 31, 1995–February 18, 1996: Yin Wood Pig/Boar
February 18, 2007–February 6, 2008: Yin Fire Pig/Boar
February 5, 2019–January 24, 2020: Yin Earth Pig/Boar

Pig Personality

There are two signs of the Chinese Zodiac that nobody ever wants to be, and one of them is Pig (or Boar) (in case you haven't guessed it already, the other is Rat). You should understand Pig is one of the best signs to be! Pig is the symbol of the prosperity and good fortune of the family.

When considering a Chinese Zodiac creature's qualities, it's a good idea to examine the animal's traits, behaviors, and personality and associate our traditional knowledge about the animal with the metaphorical creature who is part of the zodiac. Throughout history and in many cultures, there are traditions and stories about the pig.

The ancestor of the domesticated pig is the wild boar. While the male wild boar is solitary, the females and piglets live in groups and welcome the males at breeding season. The Chinese zodiac sign of Pig (or Boar), therefore, represents one of the most sociable signs, known for being community-minded and gregarious.

The animal pig is an omnivore, consuming both plants and animals. Pig/Boar natives are known for their culinary abilities (or at least their love of great food). They are delightful hosts who provide their guests with lots of comforts and splendid meals.

The animal pig is renowned for his acute sense of smell. People born under this sign are very discerning and able to suss out what's going on. Scientists tell us that in social situations, when we are connecting with others whom we may not know (or not know well), we often use our sense of smell to determine friend or foe. People born in the Year of the Pig (or Boar) can better access this ability in their daily lives.

At home, Pig loves a social gathering. The kitchen is always filled with ingredients should they be needed for an impromptu party. At the sound of the doorbell, Pig is ready to greet guests. The people who come to the party are lucky; Pig does whatever they can to make their guests feel welcome and comfortable. This doesn't necessarily mean that the house is spotless. Some Pig natives keep a very messy house, but they still welcome guests with open arms.

In the business world, Pig is often underestimated. On the outside, they seem "sweet," gullible, and rarely able to say "No!" However, Pig is rather smart and is ready to take on a leadership role whenever called upon to do so.

Pigs do not like confrontation and are always looking for a win-win situation; they dismiss insults and easily shrug off negativity. Should you hire a Pig to work for you in your struggling business, they will devote their time and energy to building your success.

Pigs are generous. They like to see a smile on someone else's face. They love the good things in life: gourmet food, designer clothing, the upscale exotic car. They are looking for a life of luxury, comfort, and ease, and they are willing to put effort into your being comfortable, too.

On the other hand, Pigs can trip themselves up with the excessive rules and limitations they put upon themselves. When others cross them, they can respond very aggressively, which can be quite a shock to the person on the receiving end.

Pig natives are susceptible to lawsuits and can become entangled for years. Because they want to see the best in people, they can be swindled, and need to watch out for con-men. Pig has a warm heart, and when things don't go well in their lives, they can be subject to depression. Their desire for perfection can overwhelm them, resulting in increased stress.

Pig: Predictions for 2021

How to use your High-Energy Days: On these days, plan to take action for your most important goals, make vital phone calls, send important emails. Your high-energy days are when your energy and luck are the strongest for the month.

January 2021: *Uranus goes direct on January 14. Mercury goes retrograde from January 30 to February 20. Your Lucky Days are 6, 12, 18, 24, 30. [How to use your Lucky Days: On these days, plan to take significant actions, make vital phone calls, send emails. These are days when your energy and luck are high.]*

Your popularity is on the rise. At work and in social situations, you are commanding attention and admiration. While Pig natives naturally accept these compliments with grace, you're still in a Metal Rat year for another few weeks, and. Keep your eyes open to see how these contacts and connections may open some doors for you.

You're busy at work, and the office seems a little short-handed. Ask for help and delegate what you can from your long list of things to do. Working overtime and skipping your workout is not a good idea and definitely don't skimp on sleep. Take care of yourself and allow others to step up and help you.

Finances remain strong. A second or additional source of income likely comes through this month. Even small gains are a sign that a larger flow will happen in the future. It's a good idea to reinvest any unexpected gains in the business or pay down debt. You might have been eyeing a new pair of boots, but there are wiser places for your money now.

Expect to spend time and share a lot of activities with friends. You may receive more invitations than usual. You may travel to a wedding or host friends who are visiting your town. This is generally all good, as you love a social occasion.

You may have some difficulty with a device like a phone or small computer towards the end of the month as Mercury slows to go retrograde on January 30. If you need to replace this item, try to do it before then.

February 2021: *Lunar New Year begins on February 12. Happy Year of the Metal Ox. February 20 has Mercury going direct. February 27 is the full moon. Your High-Energy Days are 5, 11, 17, 23, and 29.*

February comes in, bringing with it the last two weeks of the Metal Rat energy. This is an opportune time to focus on completing projects from the previous few months. Pig natives do well to emphasize self-care. Spend some time doing things like yoga or qi gong. Also, review your footwear. Getting new shoes represents finding a new path forward.

February 12 brings the new moon, the new Lunar New Year, and the Metal Ox's energy. This is far more harmonious energy for Pig natives. You'll find it easier to be more mindful and to slow down, to enjoy the simpler things of life. Over the next two weeks, you are more intuitive than usual (which is saying something). Through meditation and quiet times, you can hear the music of the Universe, bringing you the information you need. Use caution when around negative people, as you can absorb their feelings and think those feelings are your own. Burn sage or use sage spray to clear yourself and your home.

The energy shifts on February 18, bringing renewed vitality and a desire to take on loftier projects. It's easier now to find support from others. A business partnership is possible but avoid signing any agreements now as Mercury is still retrograde.

On February 20, Mercury goes direct. The information you need for a project comes through. It's a promising time to reach out to others to coordinate efforts.

On February 27, there is a new moon, and increased relationship energy comes in. More than one person compliments you on your appearance and confidence. (In fact, this is a good time to have publicity pictures taken). You can feel closer to your partner as you agree on an important decision. If you're looking for love, this is a wonderful time to start a conversation with someone you're interested in.

March 2021: *March 13 brings the new moon, March 20 marks the first day of spring, March 28 is the full moon. Your High-Energy Days are 1, 7, 13, 19, 25, and 31.*

The positive energy continues, and you may expand your circle of friends. You have the opportunity to meet several interesting people leading to even more connections. Reach out to knowledgeable others for help.

The new moon is on March 13, and life may seem hectic for the next couple of weeks, possibly working behind the scenes on a large project for work or school. Make sure data backups are working properly and that you have extra printer ink available, just in case. Consider making some slight adjustments to a home office or study area to decrease distractions and make it comfortable.

The energy shifts on March 20, and a potential windfall arrives for Pig natives. You may receive a sum of money from the sale of a big- ticket item, or a bonus/commission check could arrive. This windfall energy continues for several weeks, and you may be offered several items from friends, such as electronics or furniture.

On March 28, there's a full moon, and your focus moves to investments and retirement savings. Speak with your broker to make sure both you and your partner are on the same page. Ask yourself whether you would consider buying the investment you currently own if it were being to you now at its current price. This will let you know whether you should remain in the investment or sell it. During this time, review your insurance. Make sure you have enough coverage, as your circumstances may have changed over the past year. Finally, make a quick review of your credit cards to see if there are any opportunities to lower interest rates or consolidate debt.

April 2021: *April 12 brings the new moon. April 27 is the full moon, and Pluto goes retrograde. (Pluto moving backward can cause you to review your basic assumptions of life and to eliminate what is unnecessary, bringing you back to what is essential. Pluto will be retrograde until October.) Your High-Energy Days are 6, 12, 18, 24, and 30.*

In April, there is an opportunity for gain through your employer. You may be up for a promotion or a raise. Consider having a discussion with your supervisor on this topic. If you're not enthusiastic about staying on, your intuition may be indicating you need to update your resume, and put feelers out into the job market. Reach out to former colleagues on professional websites like LinkedIn and see how they're doing at their new jobs. You now have several financial opportunities, so you may have a chance to move up in your current company, or a door will open for you elsewhere.

The new moon comes in on April 12, and now it's almost as if you you have a guardian angel on your shoulder. You can take more risks, especially when it comes to relationships. Review what you want in a love relationship and send this message to your guardian angel. Then all you need to do is watch magical things happen!

The energy shifts on April 19, and an agreement you've been waiting for arrives. It's now a matter of going through the details and possibly negotiating a couple of points. This agreement could be for the sale of a house, purchasing a vehicle, or continuing a contract position with your company.

There's a full moon on April 27 and a lot is going on in your community. There could be some road construction happening outside your door, a new neighbor moving in, or a house in the neighborhood is going through some major renovations. All of this brings more value to the neighborhood, though, in the interim, it could be inconvenient for you, Pig native. Try to be patient with all that is going on.

May 2021: *May 11 brings the new moon. On May 23, Saturn goes retrograde. (Saturn retrograde can cause you to review your career choices and make adjustments. Saturn will be retrograde until October). May 26 is a total lunar eclipse. May 29 has Mercury going retrograde. Your High-Energy Days are 6, 12, 18, 24, and 30.*

In May, you can expect the opportunity for a brief trip. This could be an overnight stay or a weekend away. This trip may be travel for your work, but it's more likely a family outing. Since travel is highlighted all month, you may receive visitors—friends or family who have been on the road. You may explore ideas of getting an RV eventually or talk about finding a vacation home.

The new moon is on May 11, arriving with the energy for letting go of something. New opportunities are coming, but it's hard to add tea to a cup that is already full. Consider letting go of clutter and things you no longer need. You may even make some extra money by selling some of the antiques or vintage items you have in your home. Now is also a really good time to let go of emotional issues. Release anger and resentment, and recognize how strong you become. Updating your vision board or your goal list is ideal now.

The energy shifts on May 20, making it a time to consider some smaller home improvements. Avoid getting into anything involved, as Mercury will go retrograde at the end of the month. During the next couple of weeks, you may find someone is moving back into the house. Significant changes could be on the horizon; you may even begin to make plans to change residences later this year.

On May 26, there's a lunar eclipse with an emphasis on the family. You may blend the family together when an adult child once again moves back your roof. There's the opportunity to pull together to reach a greater goal, everyone chipping in and focusing on how they can help the family as a whole. This can be a very harmonious time for the family, even if you can feel storm clouds growing outside in the world.

On May 29, Mercury goes retrograde, and some of your plans at home get disrupted. If you are looking for a new apartment or in the process of buying a home, you could encounter some challenges with paperwork. Be patient, and you can work through them. Don't allow others to rush you into signing an agreement before you are ready to do so.

June 2021: *June 10 is the annular solar eclipse. June 20 is the first day of summer, and Jupiter goes retrograde. (Jupiter retrograde can indicate a need to relearn things or review your beliefs. Jupiter will be retrograde until October). June 22 has Mercury going direct. June 24 is the full moon. On June 25, Neptune goes retrograde. (Neptune retrograde can draw you back towards habits and addictions from your past. It can also encourage a return to spiritual practices. Neptune will be retrograde until December). Your High-Energy Days are 5, 11, 17, 23, and 29.*

June is here, and it's time to finish up some things up. A school graduation or a project at work comes to completion. As you finish something, you're able to move towards new opportunities. In a Metal Ox year, taking even a small action causes doors to open. Metal Ox energy is patient energy and waits for something to rouse it. Thus, making a phone call or sending an email proposal makes all the difference.

On June 10, there's a solar eclipse. Solar eclipses bring change, but as one door closes, another one opens. The more you let go during this time, the more space you have for new opportunities. Have a family meeting to let go of disagreements, resentments, and start working together as a family towards a bigger goal. Now you can get real support.

On June 20, the energy shifts, and now Pig Natives find abundant opportunities for love and romance. If you're already in a love relationship, plan some time for romance in your schedule. Spend evenings cuddling on the sofa, Sunday mornings in bed together; and schedule a date night for one evening during the week. If you're looking for love, strong possibilities arise as a result of help of a friend of a friend. This may take you a little out of your comfort zone, but now you have an opportunity to meet someone who brings joy to your life.

On June 22, Mercury goes direct, and some Pig natives will move forward on a real estate contract. This could be to purchase a new home, renting a new apartment, or buying rental property. After a few days, communications will flow more easily. You could use this time to get government paperwork out-of-the-way, perhaps updating your driver's license, passport, or scheduling tests for a professional license.

On June 24, there's a full moon, and some business opportunities become available to you. Now you can take a risk, albeit a calculated one. A friend may have started a business and want to get you involved. Or you may gather some of your talented friends together to launch a new venture. This could be a side hustle or something to build into your primary business. This is exceptional energy for getting outside your comfort zone, and as you do, the Universe takes notice.

July 2021: *July 10 brings the new moon. July 24 is the full moon. Your High-Energy Days are 5, 11, 17, 23, and 29.*

New energy arrives in July. An opportunity you missed a while back now becomes available again. You're older and wiser and much more ready to take on something new. Pig natives are courageous, have stamina, and a thirst for new experiences. You may get to capitalize on some of the changes going on in your company. Perhaps new offices are being opened, and they're looking for a leader. Or there are changes in the org-chart, and you can see a way forward for your career. Now you can see opportunities in other companies, maybe outside your industry, but ones which fits your skill set. Consider enlisting the help of a career coach or resume writer.

There's a new moon on July 10, and you have lots of good fortune, luck and protection surrounding you, especially in the area of love. In fact, this is one of the best two-week periods for finding a great relationship. If you're already dating, consider moving the relationship forward; discuss the possibility of living together, even getting engaged. Fertility energy is also robust. If you want to add to the family, you can find help with your goals. Some Pig natives may add to the family by getting a pet. This can bring a lot of joy to your home.

On July 22, the energy shifts and work becomes exceptionally busy. You may be pulled in multiple directions, not just because of your job but also with the work you do for a charity or your church. It's hard to keep up with all the activities in your schedule. This is where you can enlist the help of family members.

On July 24, there's a full moon, and the exceptional relationship energy continues. You may introduce your sweetheart to friends and family. If you're in an established relationship, it's good to celebrate the relationship is getting better and better. If you're looking for love, this is a great time to put yourself out on dating websites and click "wink" when you see someone who catches your eye.

August 2021: *August 8 brings the new moon. On August 20, Uranus goes retrograde. August 22 is the full moon. Your High-Energy Days are 4, 10, 16, 22, and 28.*

In August, the energy slows down for a bit. Towards the end of the month, things will heat up again as you or your kids go back to school. The overall emphasis of this month is about finding a balance between work and play. Give yourself time to take care of you. Get fresh air, eat right, and find an exercise you enjoy. If you have annual medical visits coming due, this is an excellent month to get those done and out-of-the-way.

The new moon is on August 8, and relationships are highlighted. You and your sweetheart might work together on a project such as refinishing the living room floor or getting an adult child off to college. Relationships with some of your neighbors improve as well. You might be surprised to find you have more in common with a neighbor than you thought. Finally, there are more social activities connected with organizations you belong to. You might be in a professional networking group or a member of a book club. It's good to make time for these as they help you with your work/life balance.

On August 22, there's a full moon. At the same time, the energy shifts. You are in the third year of your three-year seed planting time when it's good to do many new things. You are discovering what you like and don't like. News flash; you don't need to continue doing things you don't want to do! Over the next two weeks, see what you can automate, delegate, or eliminate. This could be anything from washing your car to scrubbing toilets to doing your taxes.

September 2021: *September 7 brings the new moon. September 20 is the full moon. September 22 is the first day of autumn. September 26 has Mercury going retrograde. Your High-Energy Days are 3, 9, 15, 21, and 27.*

September comes in, and you enter a more peaceful time. The harmonious Metal Ox energy helps you to focus more on practical, mindful, and intentional actions. This is something you excel at. Pig natives find great joy in the simple things in life. In keeping with this idea, September is about partnerships of all kinds, especially supporting close friendships and those who can assist you, such as mentors or teachers. This is a good month to reach out to people who are outside your circle. This can include people just a step outside, or people who seem to live in a different universe. The connections you make this month can bring you abundance over the next few months.

There's a new moon on September 7, activating your area of resources from others. You could receive money from a passive income source, such as royalties or commissions. You might have a side business where you do affiliate marketing and see a jump in your monthly check. This is a time where you can connect with knowledgeable others about investing. You might consider attending a real estate seminar or even looking into something like bitcoin. If you work for a large employer, consider talking to the HR department to make sure you are capitalizing on all the benefits company has to offer.

There's a full moon on September 20, and positive energy continues. There are opportunities for you; however, you do need to step out into the spotlight. This may not be the most comfortable place for a Pig native, but you know you can do it—it's just not your first choice. That said, as you step onto the stage (whether it's a literal stage or not), you are drawing opportunities to you.

There's a shift in energy on September 22, bringing romance. For the next few weeks, fun and romance take center stage. You may want to go dancing, have a candlelight dinner at home, or lock yourselves in the bedroom. If you're looking for love, you can certainly find someone at this time with whom you have great chemistry.

On September 26, Mercury goes retrograde, and there's an emphasis on the truth. You may find that someone in your life has not been entirely forthcoming with you. This may shock you, since Pig natives tend to see the very best in people. But you are also fairly intuitive, and when you check with yourself, you will find that you knew long ago something wasn't right. Now you have proof, and you can take steps accordingly.

October 2021: *October 6 brings the new moon, and Pluto goes direct. On October 11, Saturn goes direct. October 18 has Mercury going direct and Jupiter going direct. October 20 is the full moon. Your High-Energy Days are 3, 9, 15, 21, and 27.*

October has arrived, and there's a mix of energies this month. There could be challenges related to education, including tests, preparing children for tests, term papers, or things related to financial aid for future semesters. This all goes well if you're proactive. But Mercury is retrograde for the first half of the month and it can be challenging to get people to return your calls, or to find all the materials you're looking for. Be patient. However, there is positive energy around financial resources, even extending beyond education. You can find a small business loan or refinance your mortgage. Keep in mind that final paperwork is best submitted after Mercury goes direct on October 18.

There's a new moon on October 6, and you're rather intuitive right now. You pick up energies easily anyway, but you could be on overload at this time. For the next two weeks, take care to be around positive people. Be aware of your boundaries. This will help you sail through this period.

On October 18, Mercury goes direct, and a financial matter can move forward. Give Mercury a few days to get up to speed, and use this energy to ask your boss for a raise, or discuss how you can move up in the company. If you're expanding your home business, consider launching a new website or making your podcast debut.

There's a full moon on October 20, and you can receive a lot of support from others if you let them know what you need. Pig natives can be independent, but you do better when you allow others to give to you. People can be helpful right now. Let family and extended family members know you're looking for love, and invite them to make suggestions.

On October 22, the energy shifts to powerful spiritual energy. This may mean you are attending church services or doing meditation at home. It's a good idea to set up a spirit's hearth or altar. This can be a table spread with objects that have spiritual meaning to you, such as sacred texts, crystals, or perhaps a figurine of an angel. This is a reminder that you are an eternal spirit living in a physical world.

November 2021: *November 4 is the new moon. November 19 is a partial lunar eclipse. Your High-Energy Days are 2, 8, 14, 20, and 26.*

With the arrival of November, you enter a special period for Pig natives: the holidays. Decorating for the holidays can put you in the mood. Time to intentionally establish traditions by pulling things from your past that have meaning and value in your life now. Mindfulness is key in a Metal Ox year. You can let go of family traditions no longer suited to your current lifestyle; like sweet potatoes with marshmallows and brown sugar, they may not be to your taste any longer.

On November 4, there's a new moon, bringing an emphasis on education. If you're in school and helping your kids with their lessons,, you may be moving at a fast pace, trying to keep up with everything. It's helpful for you to get yourself in a routine. Search books and videos with tips on retaining information, and how to get through homework more quickly. Also, look at hacks for eliminating procrastination. This can be a wonderful time for you, but it's always a good idea to follow effective work time with relaxing playtime.

On November 19, there's a lunar eclipse. This can be a challenging eclipse for many people, as significant others in your life recognize where they are stuck and unhappy. This energy is more harmonious for Pig natives. It's likely the change energy is happening to your family members, or people close to you rather than to you personally. With all that's happening, be fluid instead of stubbornly clinging to something from the past. Let go, and the Universe will carry you forward.

On November 21, there's a shift in the energy, and you may receive some recognition at work. A customer may send a complementary note which will be added to your personnel file. It's essential to recognize the value you bring to your job. If you find you're not doing your best work, be aware it's a sign it's time to move on.

December 2021: *December 1 has Neptune going direct. December 4 is a total solar eclipse. December 19 brings the full moon, and Venus goes retrograde. (Venus retrograde can cause you to question what you want and inspire you to look for something new that delights you. Venus will be retrograde until January.) December 21 is the first day of winter. Your High-Energy Days are 2, 8, 14, 20, and 26.*

December is here, and there are happy times ahead for Pig natives. Much of the financial work you've been doing over the past few months has now settled down, and you find some streams of income from passive sources (or at least work you enjoy). If you have been looking for a new job, you'll see opportunities opening up. There may be applications to complete, interviews, and background checks. Colleagues you've worked well with in the past may beckon you towards the companies they work for now. It's likely a friend will approach you with a business idea. If you decide to move forward on a business plan, it's a good idea to put all the terms in writing. This will save the friendship in future.

On December 4, there's a solar eclipse, and there could be changes in your company or in the industry itself. Your intuition has been letting you know about this for some time. Maybe you are thinking back and forth, going between loyalty to your old boss and the desire to move on. As long as you're proactive in the situation (having your resume ready and continuing good communication in your current job), you'll do just fine. Pig natives are very good at going with the flow.

December 19 is a full moon, and the next two weeks could be a happy period filled with visits with friends and family. While there is some busyness at work, you are finding time to relax. Older children may come back from school to see you. Younger children could help in the kitchen. Now you can let the world go by. Focus on being aware of the present and what you love about your life.

On December 21, there's a shift in the energy, and your thoughts turn to the future. This is a great time to look at your one-year, two-year, and five-year plans. Do a vision board or update your list of goals. The journey is easier when you have an idea of the destination. While not set in stone, the destination provides boundaries for decisions coming up next year.

January 2022: *January 2 is the new moon. January 14 has Mercury going retrograde. January 17 is the full moon. On January 18, Uranus goes direct. On January 29, Venus goes direct. Your High-Energy Days are 6, 12, 18, 24, and 30.*

The new calendar year begins, but there still is a full month remaining of the harmonious Metal Ox energy. As others rush around trying to start new things, intuitive Pig native realizes beginnings only come after an ending. This is a great month for looking at what you have, paring down to only those things that genuinely bring you joy. It's possible you love everything in your house and about your house. But if there are items stuffed in a closet that haven't seen the light of day in some time, perhaps they need to be with someone else. What's important is to start to plow through the paperwork of the previous year (or years). Scan what's important, shred where you need to protect your privacy, and discard the rest. Your home will feel lighter, and energy will circulate throughout your entire life..

There's a new moon on January 2, and for the next two weeks, there's an emphasis on courageously following your dreams. In the morning, start with spiritually centering yourself. Perhaps the tool you use is yoga or meditation, or perhaps you recite affirmations or your goals. As you go through the day, you'll see the Universe's generous hand in your life. Over the next two weeks, an acquaintance may offer you something quite out of this world.

On January 14, Mercury goes retrograde. Over the next few weeks, you may return to studying a subject you have left in the past. You can be drawn to reread a novel or series. Mercury retrograde allows you to go back and collect some information from your past and bring it forward now because it is needed. Let your intuition guide you. Trust when the feeling pushes you in one direction or the other. You'll notice if any of your friends are moving toward something, and you may be attracted to join in as well.

On January 17, there's a full moon and intense love and romance energy, especially if you're willing to take a few risks. Recognize any blocks you've put on yourself which hold you back from love. You're stronger now and able to handle the ups and downs in life. So why not let a special someone know you are interested? It could be the beginning of a whole new adventure.

On January 19, there's a shift in the energy. You may work behind the scenes on a project at the office. The amount of work ahead may be daunting. Break things down into manageable parts and put them into your schedule. Knock one thing off the list whenever possible. Soon you will celebrate success.

February 2022: *February 1, and the new moon begins the Year of the Water Tiger! February 3 has Mercury going direct. February 16 brings the full moon.*

February 1 and the new moon ushers in the year of the Water Tiger. The challenge for Pig natives in 2022 is an abundance of opportunities will come and go more quickly than may be comfortable for you. You may vacillate in your choices; even become stuck in indecision. Be aware of where you're heading in life, and decisions will be much easier for you. When the opportunity seems right, don't hesitate.

Attract New Love

As you draw a big sigh of relief exiting 2020, you may feel you don't have any energy left to look for love. That's okay; love is on your doorstep. Look around at the people you hang out with daily, people your family knows, friends of people you work with, the people in your book club; love is found among the people around you. June brings an opportunity to move in with somebody; but be cautious about fighting in November, as you may have to eat some crow in order to patch things up.

In Feng Shui, we often use wind chimes to call new energy. The material the wind chimes are made of will tell us what kind of energy a specific one will attract. When looking for new love, choose a silver-tone wind chime. The color silver attracts relationship energy.

Hang your wind chime on the in- or outside of your front door, or outside your bedroom window. (If this is not possible, then hang the wind chime in your bedroom window inside the house.) Remember to touch the chimes manually and listen to the tones every few days.

Enhance Existing Love

While overall, your relationship remains strong, and you are as sensitive as ever to your partner's wants and needs. Sometimes it feels like you need a little bit of space. Circumstances may have thrown the two of you together to work and live together in a small space, however you, Pig native, are very good at making a space comfortable. At times, you may feel you just want a room of your own. Aside from this, your relationship brings you joy this year. You know each other well and can finish each other's sentences. Be sure to ask for space when you need it. Your partner will be ready to welcome you back when you feel ready to join the party.

If you are already in a relationship and want to create more harmonious feelings and happier times, hang a fan in your bedroom. It can be one of those large painted fans, one that depicts a landscape scene (make sure the scene is a prosperous and tranquil one, avoid pictures of people toiling in the fields or of wild animals with sharp teeth). Or it can be a small fan hanging from a hook that you grab and use on hot days. The fan is a symbol of peace and harmony, and this will help attract happy energy.

Looking to Conceive?

The mighty oak tree may provide help for those wanting to conceive. In Feng Shui, an oak tree in your back yard is a symbol of fertility and children's success. In fact, any oak tree on your property is good energy for conception. Hang a small chime or bell from the tree to call in the fertility energy. If you don't have a tree, find and plant an acorn. If you don't have a yard, plant it in a flowerpot, or better still, take a trip to a forest and plant several.

(From Donna Stellhorn's book, A Path to Pregnancy: Ancient Secrets for the Modern Woman)

Family and Kids

Pig natives enjoy harmonious energy for home and family this year. There is the possibility of acquiring a second home, or making a move. Perhaps you're getting a vacation home, time-share, or maybe an RV? There's a strong possibility you could increase income by renting a room through Airbnb or some similar service.

This year, your kids are busy, and it's hard to get them to slow down long enough for conversation. Adult children text but perhaps don't visit or call as often as they are working hard on their chosen paths. They'll come together if you ask. Fertility requires a little bit of concerted effort, but it's quite possible—especially if your goal is to have a child in 2022.

To protect your health this year, consider getting a piece of petrified wood. It can be part of jewelry you wear or a piece of polished stone you display in the home. Petrified wood is from ancient trees and represents a long life filled with joy and peace. It's been used for centuries as a barrier to protect against negative energy.

If you find a piece of petrified wood, you can display it in your kitchen or family room. If it's a small, smooth stone, you can keep it in the dirt of a houseplant. If it's large and flat, you can use it as a coaster. Or you can display it near family photos to protect everyone in the house.

Money

You have a lot of money opportunities this year; they come easily—if you take the first step. A little action on your part will open doors. Communication will be key. You must ask for what you want, then step back and see who answers the call. If you get too focused or fixated on one source of income, you may miss other opportunities. It's good to use your intuition to guide you. But in new areas of investing or making money, it's better to rely on expert help and reliable data. There is challenging energy in November when a miscommunication could end up costing you money. If you're signing contracts during this time, read it over twice before affixing your signature.

You are probably familiar with lucky bamboo, i.e., bamboo sticks growing in water, or small pots with bamboo growing in stones and water. There are about ten species of bamboo grown in China. Some can measure a diameter of 3 feet and a height of 40 feet. Bamboo has many uses. It's been used for food, in the manufacture of paper, for making buckets and furniture. The leaves have been used to thatch roofs; the seeds and sap are used for medicinal purposes.

So this versatile plant is a perfect Feng Shui cure, a symbol of attracting money and benefit of all kinds this year. Place a lucky bamboo plant in your living room—in sight of your front door—to attract easy money opportunities.

Job or Career

Now you're in the last year of your three seed-planting years. This year, you can settle into a new job, or get comfortable in the job you currently have. Check where you need to brush up on skills or make new connections to feel better about your career choices. There can be changes in management at work or in the company itself beginning in May or, if not then, at the end of the year in December. But your position seems stable—if you want to keep it. If you want to change jobs, you can focus the energy by reaching out to colleagues who moved on to better positions, or connecting with hiring managers on professional websites like *LinkedIn*. You can stay on this current path and expand what you started in the last few years as you branch out and go a whole new direction. This is typical during seed planting time.

The Phoenix is a mythical bird, said to live 100 years. When it's life span is over, it bursts into flames, and a new Phoenix is born out of the ashes. The symbol of the Phoenix represents living through challenges, surviving adversity, and reinventing yourself as needed. Hang a picture of the Phoenix in your home office. It's also effective to carry a Phoenix charm on your keychain.

Education

There's education energy this year; however, you may felt less happy with the institution you've chosen or some of the teachers. There may also be changes in your institution, especially a private institution, causing you to rethink your educational future. Self-directed study programs you can do at home can work well for you this year. The best things to study are technology, medicine, and anything to do with entertainment and the arts. It's possible in November to decide you want to make a change in schools or majors. Consult with friends and family before doing anything permanent.

Legal Matters

There's a great deal of harmony this year when it comes to contracts and agreements. You can have easy negotiations, and people seem to go out of their way to give you the terms you want. Don't hesitate to ask for more than you are looking for. Contracts for land, vehicles, or anything to do with creativity and entertainment can be beneficial. There is a possibility of entering into an agreement with a sibling. This could be for a family business or legacy financial arrangements.

While lawsuits are never pleasant, this year, you can enter into lawsuits with some confidence. If you feel you need to bring a suit against someone, this is the year to do it.

Health and Well-Being

Your health remains good this year—when you take the time to get enough sleep and find ways to mitigate stress. Focus on creating a bedtime routine and having your bedroom set up for optimum sleep: blackout curtains are helpful, a white noise machine, or a comfortable bedroom temperature. This year, consider supporting your good health through alternative modalities such as hypnosis and NLP. It's wise to take special care of your feet through massage and good shoes. Exercise involving yoga, aerial acrobatics, and swimming are all good for you.

Gain additional protection energy for your home by placing a pair of Foo Dogs (also spelled Fu Dogs) by your front door. These "guard dogs" come in pairs; one male with his paw on the world and one female with her paw gently on the baby. There are some Foo Dog pairs where all four of their paws are on the ground. This is fine. In this case, there may be no visible male or female dog.

Place one dog on either side of the door. This can be inside or outside the house, depending on the size of the Foo Dogs and the material they are made of. Some pairs are so large they must be outside. Or you can find decorated and painted Foo Dogs of the most delicate porcelain, and these should be placed inside.

Compatibility Between Signs

In this section, I will explain a little about the compatibility between the Chinese Zodiac signs concerning love and friendship. Sometimes there is a lot of harmony, but at other times a pairing of two signs isn't the most promising. We can often improve the energy by placing a Feng Shui Crystal cure to support the relationship energy.

Feng Shui Crystals are round, cut glass crystals which have a prismatic effect. When light hits the crystal, a rainbow of glittering, shiny light prisms twinkle around the ceiling, walls, or floor. Shiny things attract energy, so the sparkling crystal attracts energy to balance the relationship.

Cut glass crystals come in many shapes, but round is the most balanced and harmonious shape, so it's used to balance relationship energy. Whenever a Feng Shui Crystal is called for, you can use a clear one (clear crystals are the easiest to find). Or you can use colored crystals to bring in the energy of one of the five elements.

Use green to represent the Wood element if you want to increase growth and prosperity.

Use blue to represent the Water element to activate excellent communication, flow, and harmony.

Use amber or yellow to represent the Earth element, to bring stability and longevity.

Use red to represent the Fire element to stimulate energy and passion.

Use clear to represent the Metal element to attract resources and business success.

Along with the compatibility listings below, you will find suggestions about where to place the crystal if your relationship needs some help. Choose a green crystal if troubles in the relationship are because of finances. Choose a blue crystal if the problems in the relationship center on communication.

Choose an amber or yellow crystal if there has been infidelity, and you want to heal the relationship. Choose a red crystal if there's been a lack of passion, romance, and sex. Choose a clear crystal to come closer together, and to receive help and support from your partner.

To find the correct direction for placing the crystal, think of your home and the rising sun. The sun always rises in the east. The sun sets in the west. If you know where the sun rises and sets in relation to your home, you can easily identify the other cardinal directions, north and south. (Hint: Google Maps aerial view can make this task very easy, as it always shows north as up, south is down, to the left is west and to the right is east.).

To find the inner directions such as North-by-Northwest, find north and find west. Halfway between these two is Northwest. North by Northwest is halfway between north and Northwest.

Place the diagram on the floor, east pointing towards the rising sun. The diagram will help you find the right direction for placing the appropriate crystal.

If you can place the crystal in a window, it will catch the most light. If there is no window in that direction, hang the crystal on a lamp, a plant, a drawer pull, or from a wall hook.

To see all the different ways to use Feng Shui Crystals and how to hang them, go to WWW.FENGSHUIFORM.COM.

We can divide the 12 animals of the Chinese Zodiac into four groups. Each group has some key personality traits:

Rat, Dragon, Monkey are the action-oriented ones. The Rat takes care of the details; the Dragon has the big ideas, and the Monkey can improve the skills of others.

Ox, Snake, and Rooster are the deep thinkers. The Ox is methodical, thinking things through. The Snake is wise and sees things from various perspectives. The Rooster is alert and aware of everything going on around him.

Tiger, Horse, and Dog are the freedom lovers. The Tiger is impulsive: he sees what he wants and pounces. The Horse runs across the prairies and lands with power and grace. The Dog can work alone or within a group and still keep his independence.

Rabbit, Sheep/Goat, and Pig/Boar are the peace lovers. The Rabbit is diplomatic and can bring opposing forces together. The Sheep/Goat is the humanitarian, wanting to bring peace to the world. The Pig/Boar is the homebody, wishing to create comfort and peace for the family.

Chinese Zodiac Signs and Compatibility

Rat Compatibility

Rat with Rat: Well suited and lots of fun. Always busy, doing things, making deals, and making money. You'll need to respect each others' time and secrets. Occasionally you'll need time apart as much as you need to be together. If you find one of you is too bossy, or you both need to focus a little more on the big picture and the future, hang a Feng Shui Crystal in the North side of the house.

Rat with Ox: A happy and long-lasting relationship. You will benefit from Ox's stability and strength. You are both optimistic and enjoy the little things in life. You can start the job and know that Ox will be there to help you finish it. If you find your partner is stubborn and not open to your ideas, hang a Feng Shui Crystal in the North by Northeast part of the house.

Rat with Tiger: Hot and cold, with lots of energy and excitement in this relationship. Sometimes the Tiger will ignore the little Rat, and sometimes the Tiger will be surprised at how loud a Rat can squeak. If Tiger's unpredictable ways get on your nerves, you can steady this relationship by hanging a Feng Shui Crystal in the East by Northeast part of the house.

Rat with Rabbit: Arguments after the fling is what we have here. You are both clever, but a little too clever. One wants commitment, and the other wants freedom, and neither wants the same thing at the same time. If you find Rabbit too passive and you're looking for more dedication to this relationship, hang a Feng Shui Crystal in the East side of the house.

Rat with Dragon: Happiness abounds when the Rat joins with the powerful Dragon. The relationship can be very intense. But use caution (and flattery) because if you break the spell, there is no putting the broken relationship back together again. If you find Dragon's head in the clouds and need a more grounded partner to help you with the day to day parts of the relationship, hang a Feng Shui Crystal in the East by Southeast side of the house.

Rat with Snake: Volatile pair that sometimes can be a good relationship... at least until the Snake gets hungry. Avoid being on the menu. This is more of a learning experience than a love match. If you find Snake too secretive and a little on the manipulative side, hang a Feng Shui Crystal in the South by Southeast part of the house.

Rat with Horse: Unhappy pair that can't see eye to eye. You find Horse's needs exhausting. If you get into this relationship, keep a life raft handy. You'll be paddling to shore in no time. If you insist that this is the relationship of your dreams and you want Horse to settle down and be not so restless, hang a Feng Shui Crystal in the South part of the house.

Rat with Sheep: Poor match because the sensitivity of the Sheep is no match for your quick tongue. Communication starts well, but there will be problems with words, and that will be the end of the relationship. You would think with horns; he wouldn't have such thin skin. If you only see eye to eye when pampering your Sheep partner and want to have things be a little more equal, hang a Feng Shui Crystal in the South by Southwest part of the house.

Rat with Monkey: Very lively meeting of people from different worlds. Monkey can take Rat on the trip of a lifetime and open new worlds. It's the unlikely pair in love. You will give each other new perspectives on life and living. But if all the excitement and Monkey's high energy starts to wear on you, hang a Feng Shui Crystal in the West by Southwest part of the house.

Rat with Rooster: Need to work hard at this to make it work at all. You are natural barnyard enemies, both hunting for the same big prize—and not just chicken feed. So you're better off avoiding this cage-match. If you find yourself with an overly critical Rooster on your hands, hang a Feng Shui Crystal in the West part of the house.

Rat with Dog: Lots of energy and togetherness; this is good for you, you both enjoy being out and about, enjoying others and each other. However, you may find you have trouble finding personal space. Dog will tag along wherever you go, and keep trying to pull you back home. If you feel your life restricted by Dog's constant bark, hang a Feng Shui Crystal in the West by Northwest part of the house.

Rat with Pig: Picture this charming pair of homebodies, both taking care of the other. There is optimum togetherness when you want it, and alone time when you need it. Pig keeps the house cozy and warm. If you find all this happiness and optimism is maxing out your credit cards, hang a Feng Shui Crystal in the North by Northwest part of the house.

Ox Compatibility

Ox with Rat: You are a happy, practical pair that compliment each other. You have the potential here for a very stable relationship with benefits for both partners. Rat sees the details, and your tireless energy can envision what will become of them. If you find Rat is too picky about the small things and can't get the big picture, hang a Feng Shui Crystal in the North part of the house.

Ox with Ox: A caring pair where each is interested in the comfort and security of the other. Not exciting to others, perhaps, but you can be quite content. You can enjoy decades of holding hands and feeling safe, as the cold winters blow outside. While you can remain content for long periods, should you want to add some fun (or at least a break from the constant work), hang a Feng Shui Crystal in the North by Northeast part of the house.

Ox with Tiger: Your goals in life are entirely different, as are your methods of pursuing outcome. This cat doesn't come when he's called (what cat does). There are quarrels that lead to nowhere. Build a stable home, and Tiger looks for the door. If you want this temperamental kitty with claws to be your lifelong partner, you have some work ahead. Hang a Feng Shui Crystal in the East by Northeast part of the house.

Ox with Rabbit: A so-so match. You want stability and clear rules, and Rabbit wants some pampering and kindness. It takes a while to get this one to work, but when it does, it lasts. He can be your lucky Rabbit in the end. But if you honey-bunny spends his or her time sulking in the corner and being overly sensitive, hang a Feng Shui Crystal in the East part of the house.

Ox with Dragon: Tricky pair; expect battles to start from day one. These are two powerful forces with two different ideas of what a relationship is and should be. Ding goes the bell, and the fight begins. If you can see the strong qualities in each of you, there's hope. Hang a Feng Shui Crystal in the East by Southeast part of the house.

Ox with Snake: Supportive, though there can be some conflicts. This is the strong Yin and Yang: together, opposite sides of the same coin. You need each other, and over time with Snake's clever thinking and your perseverance, you both can prosper. While Snake can make an attractive partner, if they are draining your bank account on clothes and toys, hang a Feng Shui Crystal in the South by Southeast part of the house.

Ox with Horse: Difficult match for you. The Horse is fast and careless, compared to your slow and thoughtful ways. There is little Horse can give you that you really want, and so you're more likely to send him on his way. If you want to stable this pony and try to make this restless soul settle down, hang a Feng Shui Crystal in the South part of the house.

Ox with Sheep: Steer clear, this one is trouble from beginning to end. You will have to be exceptionally patient to ride this one out. After butting heads for a while, heartbreak is the most likely ending. You can make this work if you have deep pockets, but it's more likely he/she will spend the money when they're feeling hurt or insecure. To balance the energy, hang a Feng Shui Crystal in the South by Southwest part of the house.

Ox with Monkey: Love and joy can abound with this combo. Monkey will bring you fun times and surprises every day. That will make your steady life more interesting. Once the Monkey settles down, the match can be good for both. If you find Monkey is only interested in him or herself, and too independent for your peaceful dream of a relationship, hang a Feng Shui Crystal in the West by Southwest part of the house.

Ox with Rooster: Good match for these barnyard pals. You both understand the need for hard work, and Rooster appreciates your patience and understanding. You like having someone around who can mind the details. Together you're the soul of productivity, if you would like to have a bit more romance or at least the occasional cuddle, hang a Feng Shui Crystal in the West part of the house.

Ox with Dog: Possibly good, but too many compromises will be required. This is too much Yin energy together; communication will suffer. Both of you are hesitant to lead. Let the Dog go and see if he comes back of his own accord. If you are tired of coming home and always finding a house full of people, or your partner is always on the phone, you can hang a Feng Shui Crystal in the West by Northwest part of the house.

Ox with Pig: This needs effort and adjustments on both sides. If there is chemistry (and good cooking), the relationship may last. But most likely, the Pig won't respect your goals and effort. You get frustrated with his/her play-all-the-time attitude. There can be harmony if there is an understanding of the work and sacrifice it takes to create a financially stable home. If overspending is a problem, hang a Feng Shui Crystal in the North by Northwest part of the house.

Tiger Compatibility

Tiger with Rat: Hot during the chase, and cold when caught, Rat is not a great match for you. Rat is too cynical to see your splendid qualities, and it will need to be taught how to behave. This is more work than you want to do. If you think this is a mouse you want to keep, but the pettiness and demands are hurting the relationship, hang a Feng Shui Crystal in the North part of the house.

Tiger with Ox: Needs effort to keep from being a boring relationship. You might think that Ox will help you settle down and get serious, but in the end, you are just bitter from having all the fun taken out of your life. But if you long for an established relationship that will withstand a bitter winter or a wild party, hang a Feng Shui Crystal in the North by Northeast part of the house.

Tiger with Tiger: Happiness… with claws. As long as you both retain your thick skins, this will be a happy, fun relationship. But arguments can get nasty, so be ready to forgive each other later—and keep bandages on hand. Of course, making up can be the most fun, and what's life about but having fun? So hang a Feng Shui Crystal in the East by Northeast part of the house.

Tiger with Rabbit: Can be good, but Rabbits are not known for their decisive action. You'll have to be patient with this one and prepared to leap into the fray of this relationship without waiting for the careful Rabbit to make the first move. If this Rabbit keeps sprinting away and you want to lure him/her back, hang a Feng Shui Crystal in the East part of the house.

Tiger with Dragon: The explosive power of you and the Dragon is legendary, making for either the most exciting relationship ever, or you'll both knock the world off its axis. If you want to be looked up to, this is not your match, but if you can work things out and share the leadership roles, giving credit where credit's due, this can work. Hang a Feng Shui Crystal in the East by Southeast part of the house.

Tiger with Snake: Steer clear no matter how attracted you are! You are not going to get the Snake's attention easily, and as soon as your back is turned, he's moved on. You can chase again, but after a while, it just gets tiresome. When you leave, Snake chases you; and when you are available, Snake is off without a care. To get this match together, hang a Feng Shui Crystal in the South by Southeast part of the house.

Tiger with Horse: Good ally out in the world, but there may be a conflict about who has to stay home and do the dishes. If you can accept and be happy with an unstable relationship, then grab an apron and give this one a try. Or, better still, pool your creative minds and social nature and make enough money to hire a maid. Stimulate this energy by hanging a Feng Shui Crystal in the South part of the house.

Tiger with Sheep: Can work it out over time, but the Sheep will be cautious. You will have to follow the rules given to you by the Sheep, and this can bring conflicts into the relationship. Mr./Ms Planner will not appreciate your impetuous nature. If you find Sheep too clingy (which surprises you, you thought you were the one with claws), and you wish he or she had more confidence, hang a Feng Shui Crystal in the South by Southwest part of the house.

Tiger with Monkey: It's very difficult to catch a Monkey who's swinging from tree to tree. You might be attracted to one playing hard to get, but after a while, it's no fun always being the one who has to chase... even for a Tiger. If you want to make this work, but Monkey's loud, know-it-all behavior is grating on your nerves, hang a Feng Shui Crystal in the West by Southwest part of the house.

Tiger with Rooster: You come from different worlds, so once at home, there's not much to talk about. You feel bossed around by the nagging Rooster who's frustrated that you don't seem to fall in line like the other chickens. If you find he or she is always on you about your spending and your inability to do the laundry right, smooth things over by hanging a Feng Shui Crystal in the West part of the house.

Tiger with Dog: Strong ally and a good match for you. The Dog can keep the home fires burning while you prowl the world for wealth to acquire. There are a few differences of opinion, but the good definitely outweighs the bad. Sometimes it's hard to get Dog to agree to a quick vacation or a last-minute party, but you can bring some energy to this partnership by hanging a Feng Shui Crystal in the West by Northwest part of the house.

Tiger with Pig: Good match if you take it slow. Pigs can be a little nervous facing Tiger's mandibles of death (actually that's just your smile). But if you approach Pig with gentle understanding, Pig will comfort and take care of you. You both have a tendency to help others before yourselves. If you find you're giving away too many resources to hapless friends, hang a Feng Shui Crystal in the North by Northwest part of the house.

Rabbit Compatibility

Rabbit with Rat: You may argue and fight, and this doesn't make your peace-loving nature euphoric. Rat will have too many demands on you, so a long-term relationship will be very challenging. You may seem similar, but your differences are huge. If your Rat partner is running you ragged with work and social plans, temper the energy by hanging a Feng Shui Crystal in the North part of the house.

Rabbit with Ox: If you want a long term relationship, this one can work—after you get past the boredom of the stable Ox. However, if you are looking for a fling, look elsewhere. Be in this one for the long haul, or not at all. If you find your Ox partner is not the one to sit down and have a good discussion about feelings and the relationship, hang a Feng Shui Crystal in the North by Northeast part of the house.

Rabbit with Tiger: Can be good if you like being pursued and what Rabbit doesn't? If the Tiger catches you, you can have a happy relationship... after you teach him to behave. Tip: Play hard to get even after you've been got. If you find this energetic Tiger keeps you up all hours discussing life and relationships and you just want a peaceful time to hold hands, hang a Feng Shui Crystal in the East by Northeast part of the house.

Rabbit with Rabbit: The pair of you are truly loving and having endless fun. You will play and laugh and bring each other tokens of your affection. You can cuddle in front of a fire or talk until you fall asleep in each other's arms. If you find, however, your bunny-buddy is not doing his or her share of the home duties, hang a Feng Shui Crystal in the East part of the house.

Rabbit with Dragon: Hard going at first, but things get easier over time. The Dragon is a bit of a show-off and hogs your stage. He may think you're small, but you're packed with power and easily a match for any Dragon. Your Dragon has big ideas for both home and business, and if you want to bring him or her back down to earth, hang a Feng Shui Crystal in the East by Southeast part of the house.

Rabbit with Snake: It'll take hard work to get this to be a happy match. The Snake may want you for a relationship, or just for dinner. Once you're in this relationship, you will be looking for a way out of it. You both have good taste and a desire for a good life, but if you're keeping secrets from each other, trouble is ahead. Hang a Feng Shui Crystal in the South by Southeast part of the house.

Rabbit with Horse: Can work it out as friends, even if it doesn't work out as lovers. There are a few conflicts here and there, but in the long run, there are many possibilities with this match. Just don't try to possess this one. Horse may want to run free, but he'll keep coming back. Trouble can arise when your Horse partner does everything by intuition rather than as a result of a discussion between the two of you. If more sharing is needed, hang a Feng Shui Crystal in the South part of the house.

Rabbit with Sheep: Great fun at times, because you'll always win against a Sheep. The Sheep will love you and keep trying. If you give a little to this relationship, the Sheep will give a lot. This could be the peace and happiness you've been waiting for. Your Sheep partner will be quick to depend on you, and this can make you feel great, but if the dependence becomes a burden, hang a Feng Shui Crystal in the South by Southwest part of the house.

Rabbit with Monkey: You'll need effort to understand the changeable and tricky Monkey. This is not a match that happens easily. You could be in danger of getting your heart broken by bad Monkey if you're not careful. If he or she is not understanding your feelings and is glossing over your anxieties, you may feel this Monkey's mocking you. Balance this relationship by hanging a Feng Shui Crystal in the West by Southwest part of the house.

Rabbit with Rooster: Many conflicts with this noisy bird who's constantly pecking and prodding you. Rabbits are the silent ones, and these Roosters are constantly making noises at you—too much so to make you happy. If your Rooster partner is telling all the friends and neighbors the intimate details of what works and doesn't work in your relationship, you can create a tighter bond between you by hanging a Feng Shui Crystal in the West part of the house.

Rabbit with Dog: More chasing than actually having fun. The Dog will make lots of demands on you, and you may find this relationship quite tiring in the beginning. If it lasts, it can grow into a real loving relationship, but it will take quite a bit of work. The loyalty of this partner can make this match worth it, but if you find the communication just not flowing, hang a Feng Shui Crystal in the West by Northwest part of the house.

Rabbit with Pig: Superb match; both of you can have a lot of fun. But if you get bored, you may try to create a little drama in the relationship just to stir things up. That could backfire big time! Once Pig's feelings are hurt, it will hard to tempt him back. Count your blessings, as your Pig partner can be devoted to you. If you find his or her attention on you is not strong enough, hang a Feng Shui Crystal in the North by Northwest part of the house.

Dragon Compatibility

Dragon with Rat: Suitable match where both feel compatibility and interested in one another. You can explore the world together. You will have secrets, and so will Rat, but the secrets won't hurt the relationship. Learn to trust, and Rat will take your grand ideas and turn them into reality. There is much the two of you can accomplish, although sometimes Rat will keep a tight hold on the purse strings. If you need to balance this energy, hang a Feng Shui Crystal in the North part of the house.

Dragon with Ox: Tricky times with the stubborn Ox will make the relationship rather exhausting. If you hold on, you can smooth things out and have a good long term relationship. This can happen because Dragons are said to live a thousand years. You love to dream up new ideas, but your Ox partner could be unsympathetic if he or she doesn't see immediate results. To temper this energy, hang a Feng Shui Crystal in the North by Northeast part of the house.

Dragon with Tiger: Requires patience and understanding, as together you represent two powerful Yang forces. Those around you might not believe the relationship will work out, but if you don't make too many demands on each other, you have a chance at a happy time with the Tiger. With two leaders and no followers, there can be some fights, even out the "eventful" energy by hanging a Feng Shui Crystal in the East by Northeast part of the house.

Dragon with Rabbit: Hard going at first, but you will soon find the Rabbit admires your good qualities. Rabbit also helps you strengthen some areas where you are weak: like being calm and quiet. You can help Rabbit be more detached and able to deal with the world. If you can let Rabbit have a soft place to land, you two will get along just fine, in the meantime, hang a Feng Shui Crystal in the East part of the house.

Dragon with Dragon: The best or the worst relationship for you. You love to be the center of attention, and so does your partner. This [airing will work if the two of you can share the stage. It can be glorious, or it can be a battle. You could make an enviable couple and rule the social scene. Agree now that you, together, will hang a Feng Shui in the East by Southeast part of the house to make this happen.

Dragon with Snake: Can be good as friends, but as lovers, things tend to break down. Snake wants you to try harder in the relationship, but your attitude is, "It will work if it's meant to be." This causes the Snake to slither away eventually. If you feel that holding on to this relationship is going to benefit you both, you can hang a Feng Shui Crystal in the South by Southeast part of the house.

Dragon with Horse: Lively pair; this combination can bring both fun and fights. You may become irritated that the Horse always thinks you're up to something. There will be more physical compatibility than intellectual or emotional. You both have a lot of energy but no patience for mundane tasks; create enough income to hire help by hanging a Feng Shui Crystal in the South part of the house.

Dragon with Sheep: Sheep thought he was on top of the world until he saw you flying overhead. You may want this relationship to work, but Sheep may get frightened by your power and energy. Coax him in slowly before you reveal all your greatness to him. If you feel strongly about this relationship, you can put in the effort to help temper your Sheep partner's moods by hanging a Feng Shui Crystal in the South by Southwest part of the house.

Dragon with Monkey: Good pair because you admire Monkey's cleverness. You have the inner strength to get Monkey to behave; this can be a good match. Monkey will amuse you every day! Take this act on the road, and you can be stars, or keep it close to home and be the toast of the neighborhood. Adding a Feng Shui Crystal to the West by Southwest part of the house will bring you some exciting opportunities.

Dragon with Rooster: The legendary Dragon and Rooster (okay, Phoenix). This pair feels a lot of attraction to one another. You can have a long term happy relationship as long as the Rooster doesn't look for reasons to be suspicious of all the happiness. If your Rooster partner starts snapping at you, hang a Feng Shui Crystal in the West part of the house.

Dragon with Dog: Not suitable, unless you like putting oil and fire together. This is a battle waiting to happen! Dog doesn't care how powerful you are; he's willing to take you down a notch. If your Dog partner wants to curtail your freedom and put you on a leash, hang a Feng Shui Crystal in the West by Northwest part of the house.

Dragon with Pig: It's hard not to like being at home with your Pig partner, nothing but comfort and good food abounds. But to keep Pig happy, you'll have to pitch in and do your share of the chores. Ever the peacemaker, your Pig partner will support you on your goals. Attract what you both want by hanging a Feng Shui Crystal in the North by Northwest area of the home.

Snake Compatibility

Snake with Rat: Is it love you're feeling? Or, is it just casual amusement? You may feel common interests at first, but unless you want to commit, Rat will flee the first chance he gets. You can have a very profitable relationship if you set the right tone from the beginning. Keep things moving upward by hanging a Feng Shui Crystal in the North part of the house.

Snake with Ox: Can be so supportive of each other, but someone has to make the first move. If you two get together, you are likely to enjoy a long and happy relationship. Set your boundaries and then take a chance. You both have the drive and interest in making this work. To keep the lines of communication open, hang a Feng Shui Crystal in the North by Northeast part of the house.

Snake with Tiger: Steer clear, this is a battle waiting to happen. The Tiger is seductive, and you might be tempted, but it's you who should be doing the tempting. This is a match destined for a breakup. If you're determined to stay together, and yet you're both suspicious of the other's actions and intentions, hang a Feng Shui Crystal in the East by Northeast part of the house.

Snake with Rabbit: It's hard work to find the balance here. Rabbit will bring out your deeper qualities, but his thin skin won't stand up to your assessments. There could be pain on both sides. On the other hand, if you can see the best in the other, you will both benefit from your refined sense and mental acuity. Hang a Feng Shui Crystal in the East part of the house to stimulate this positive energy.

Snake with Dragon: Can make a good couple—from dating to a long term relationship. There is fun to be had by both. Keep your demands light, and you and the Dragon will fare very well. Keep in mind how much you admire the qualities of the other and communicate this often. To bring more harmony, hang a Feng Shui Crystal in the East by Southeast part of the house.

Snake with Snake: Wonderful pair that can balance each other. If you share leadership with your partner, you can expect a long and happy relationship. You can work together to bring yourselves power and success. Hang a Feng Shui Crystal in the South by Southeast part of the house to increase success energy.

Snake with Horse: This combo is difficult. You might be afraid of being stepped on, but you should be more worried about being forgotten or left behind by the popular Horse. Keep your eyes open because Horse may not be all that faithful. If Horse's impulsive nature starts to drive you around the bend, hang a Feng Shui Crystal in the South part of the house to calm that energy.

Snake with Sheep: Needs concentrated effort, but by taking a thoughtful approach, you can find happiness together. Be considerate of the Sheep's feelings, and you will have to tread lightly at times, but you can work this out. This relationship may start out with you both in a constant embrace, but after a while, Sheep's clingy behavior may put you off. To ease this energy, hang a Feng Shui Crystal in the South by Southwest part of the house.

Snake with Monkey: Long-lasting match, once you get past the game-playing. You are both very clever, and you can learn much from each other. There is fun and romance for both here. But if this relationship is punctuated with fights and competition, temper that energy by hanging a Feng Shui Crystal in the West by Southwest part of the house.

Snake with Rooster: What seems impossible at first turns into a wonderful pair. Rooster may be lots of talk and fussy behavior, but deep down, he truly cares for you. Try not to get irritated, don't take things too seriously, and things will work out. Turn your attention to business, and you two will be the dynamic duo. For wealth energy, hang a Feng Shui Crystal in the West part of the house.

Snake with Dog: Quite charming match with you being both friends and lovers. But try not to be too possessive—Dogs need to run and play sometimes. (Know that Dog always comes home afterward.) On the other hand, when Dog is out of sight, you can do some of the things you may not be able to do under Dog's keen nose. Hang a Feng Shui Crystal in the West by Northwest part of the house for harmony in this relationship.

Snake with Pig: Not a good match, as your temperaments are entirely different. You are a deep thinker, and the Pig is looking for a comfortable, non-drama home. You might appreciate all that Pig can do for you, but the conflicts will be challenging. If you find your Pig partner being loving and supportive, not just to you, but the whole neighborhood and every charity they can find, you can bring Pig's attention back to you by hanging a Feng Shui Crystal in the North by Northwest part of the house.

Horse Compatibility

Horse with Rat: Poor match, because neither wants to compromise. Things may start out fun, but they will, for the most part, end badly as you exert your desire for freedom, and Rat extends his desire for control. Your Rat partner may be a big help to you at home, but often you will find you're not on the same level. Balance the energy by hanging a Feng Shui Crystal in the North part of the house.

Horse with Ox: Difficult to balance this relationship. You are impressed with Ox's stability, yet also bored by it. You wish Ox would not be so demanding, and pretty soon, you break out of the paddock to run free. If you're trying to get your Ox partner to drop the workload and live a little, you can try hanging a Feng Shui Crystal in the North by Northwest part of the house.

Horse with Tiger: Both enjoy good times! You and Tiger are the life of the party; you are always where the action is. As long as neither of you thinks the other should sit at home, you will have a great time. Instead of fighting about who does the housework, attract more money to pay for the help by hanging a Feng Shui Crystal in the East by Northeast part of the house.

Horse with Rabbit: Given time, this can be a good relationship. At first, you will enjoy a lot of passionate fun with Rabbit; this can easily grow into trust and companionship. But keeping up the romance will take some planning. If Rabbit feels lonely at your wanderings and starts to kick up a fuss, you can balance the energy by hanging a Feng Shui Crystal in the East part of the house.

Horse with Dragon: Lively discussions and dates for these two. You are likely to be involved in the best fun together, or the biggest fights. Both of you are powerful and energetic beings, and together you are unstoppable. Try to base your relationship on what you have in common. Look for the partnership to extend to business as well as personal, and you can attract much success. Hang a Feng Shui Crystal in the East by Southeast part of the house to attract opportunities.

Horse with Snake: This is a tough match. There's a lot of finger-pointing (at each other), yet both are guilty of something. Too much complaining leads to more fights. You might win, but that just results in a squished Snake. If you're Snake partner just seems like a stick in the mud, you can loosen up the energy by hanging a Feng Shui Crystal in the South by Southeast part of the house.

Horse with Horse: Caring and sharing and having a great time, frolicking through the pastures without a care in the world. You are beautiful together, and the world is your happy playground. Sometimes you're so alike it's uncanny... and a little boring. Spice things up by hanging a Feng Shui Crystal in the South part of the house.

Horse with Sheep: If you get past the first couple of months, this can work out just fine, but Sheep's sensitive nature may take offense when you try to be honest and straightforward. Give him time to cool off, then try again. If you find your Sheep partner glum and lifeless at times, you can stimulate the positive energy by hanging a Feng Shui Crystal in the South by Southwest part of the house.

Horse with Monkey: Quite a painful duel can result from your mixing with the tricky Monkey. But if the Monkey cares about you, he will make an effort, and things may work out over the long run. You're both smart enough to understand each other. Sometimes that makes things better, but sometimes it breeds contempt. Bring in the positive energy by hanging a Feng Shui Crystal in the West by Southwest part of the house.

Horse with Rooster: There are some pluses and minuses to this pair. You may feel that Rooster is leading you around by the nose, then dropping you without a moment's notice. Guard your heart if you're interested in this chicken. If you're feeling a little hen-pecked, hang a Feng Shui Crystal in the West part of the house.

Horse with Dog: Running and playing, two hearts beating fast, this is a great match. Dog is faithful and forgiving and looks up to your power and grace. You feel gratitude and dedication in this positive puppy. But if you feel your Dog partner snapping critically at your heels, you can hang a Feng Shui Crystal in the West by Northwest part of the house.

Horse with Pig: You can't help kicking up a fuss with the fussy Pig. Pig doesn't want to do battle, but an argument usually ensues. This can be a long term relationship if you don't mind a knock-down-drag-out every few months. If your Pig partner's clingy-ness is starting to bore you, spice things up by hanging a Feng Shui Crystal in the North by Northwest part of the house.

Sheep/Goat Compatibility

Sheep with Rat: Always starts well and ends badly, as both are under the impression they have a lot in common. But it doesn't take long to figure out that Rat is not a Sheep, and you just don't see eye to eye. If Rat seems nicer over time, you might take a chance—but don't put too much money on the bet. If you are determined to make a go at this, hang a Feng Shui Crystal in the North part of the house.

Sheep with Ox: Steer clear of this steer. You're both too stubborn to compromise, and butting heads with this giant will only give you a headache. Ox is too clingy, and you want balance; this just won't work. On the other hand, Ox will get a lot of the work done before you have even stirred, so if you want to smooth out the bumps in this relationship, hang a Feng Shui Crystal in the North by Northeast part of the house.

Sheep with Tiger: Can work it out—if you can house-train this kitty. Tiger wants worship, and you usually have more sense than that. But if you can stomach giving out all that flattery, this relationship will work just fine. If you need a little something to balance out the Tiger temper, hang a Feng Shui Crystal in the East by Northeast part of the house.

Sheep with Rabbit: Hot romance is possible with this pair. Rabbit wants to go have fun, and you are more than willing. It may be a hot date night after night. If you're a Sheep who likes to stay home, you may have a little trouble convincing this bunny, but everything will work out if you exercise some patience. To ensure this positive energy, hang a Feng Shui Crystal in the East part of the house.

Sheep with Dragon: Be prepared to be completely overwhelmed by Dragon's power and enthusiasm. Later, you may feel claustrophobic in this relationship. You will have to reach a compromise to make this work, and it will have to start with you. If you want to have Dragon share in some of the relationship responsibilities, hang a Feng Shui Crystal in the East by Southeast part of the house.

Sheep with Snake: Requires a good grip to hold onto slippery Snake. You might be a little shocked at the verbal matches you are drawn into with this forked-tongued lover. If Snake cares about you, he will tone it down, and you'll work it out in the end. The solution here will be a joint effort and a real understanding of the other's position. To facilitate compromise, hang a Feng Shui Crystal in the South by Southeast part of the house.

Sheep with Horse: A fabulous time filled with banter and playful kicks at each other. This can be a wild ride if you don't take things said too personally. You both want to run; try not to run in different directions. To have the thrill of running off into the sunset together, hang a Feng Shui Crystal in the South part of the house.

Sheep with Sheep: Your friends might think this is the dullest match ever, but you feel delight as both of you do kind and thoughtful things for the other. You're happy, dancing on cloud nine. Combine your strengths and learn you can rely on each other by hanging a Feng Shui Crystal in the South by Southwest part of the house.

Sheep with Monkey: You can work anything out if you can forgive some of Monkey's antics in the beginning. Let the past be the past, and you will find that you have a lot in common. Love will bloom after a time. To encourage the love and romance, hang a Feng Shui Crystal in the West by Southwest part of the house.

Sheep with Rooster: No one is as confusing as a Rooster. You seem to have similar beliefs, and yet you go about doing things so differently. You can become a depressed little lamb if you think that Rooster will ever see your point of view. If you find the energy of your Rooster mate a bit too dizzying, hang a Feng Shui Crystal in the West part of the house.

Sheep with Dog: It's a tough life with a Dog nipping at your heels. You're not sure you want to be herded. Dog is trying to show you loyalty and love, but sometimes it feels like you are penned in at the farm just when you want to climb mountains and be free. Soon you'll be looking to unlatch the gate. If you want to stay in this energetic match, hang a Feng Shui Crystal in the West by Southwest part of the house.

Sheep with Pig: What a pretty couple you make, and you're both so nice. Sometimes Pig is too casual, and you have to do all the heavy lifting in the relationship. But if you can let it slide, this could be a very nice romance. However, if you're finding that Pig has overbooked your social calendar and you just want a break, then hang a Feng Shui Crystal in the North by Northwest part of the house.

Monkey Compatibility

Monkey with Rat: If you've got your eye on a Rat it's because you're intrigued by his clever, money-making skills. Rat is easily flattered and impressed by your ability to take chances and fly through the trees. You can find yourself in a happy relationship with no effort at all. Boost your financial prospects by hanging a Feng Shui Crystal in the North part of the house.

Monkey with Ox: This can be a great match as long as you understand that an Ox can't climb trees. Come down to share Ox's domain every once in a while, and things will be just fine between you. Ox will give you the stability you crave while not curtailing any of the fun. But if this ends up being a contest of wills, you can balance the energy by hanging a Feng Shui Crystal in the North by Northeast part of the house.

Monkey with Tiger: Very rocky, so stay out of Tiger's reach. Tiger's impulsive nature and desire to be respected above all else rubs your fur the wrong way. Consider swinging past this potential disaster. If you've already been snared by this fellow jungle creature, you can bring more love to the relationship by hanging a Feng Shui Crystal in the East by Northeast part of the house.

Monkey with Rabbit: You can have a good time if you hold back on the tricks and teasing until Rabbit is in a happy mood. An unhappy bunny will take out their pain on you, so don't push. This can be a good combination, so save your witty remarks for someone else. If you're trying to coax this Rabbit out of the house for social occasions, you can hang a Feng Shui Crystal in the East part of the house to increase the energy of fun.

Monkey with Dragon: The perfect balance between power and intelligence, even your fights are fun. Dragon will show you the big ideas, and you will show him how it can all be done. There is so much potential for this relationship. There is also the potential to extend this partnership into money-making activities. Attract wealth energy by hanging a Feng Shui Crystal in the East by Southeast part of the house.

Monkey with Snake: A long-lasting match filled with intimacy and strong feelings. Emotionally, as time goes on, you bond more and more with the wise Snake. Anytime you want, he will wrap himself around you and gently squeeze. But although there are tumultuous times due to jealousy on either side, you can temper this energy by hanging a Feng Shui Crystal in the South by Southeast part of the house.

Monkey with Horse: Is this a relationship or a competition? Sometimes you're supportive of each other, but the inflexibility of Horse means that you have to do all the compromising and understanding. After a while, this rodeo is less and less fun. If you feel like you're always coming in second place, you can hang a Feng Shui Crystal in the South part of the house to brighten up the energy.

Monkey with Sheep: This may be fun in the beginning, but Sheep has a whole bunch of rules and regulations for you to follow to stay in this relationship—rules that are sure to drain the fun right out of it. But if you can stay, it could become a happy, loving, long-lasting relationship. Balance this uncertain energy by hanging a Feng Shui Crystal in the South by Southwest part of the house.

Monkey with Monkey: Full of fun and play; this is an easy, happy relationship. There may be times when you don't see eye to eye, but keep those times brief, or one of you may find someone else to chase. Work out some boundaries, and you will be laughing together for a long time. To bond you two into a strong partnership, hang a Feng Shui Crystal in the West by Southwest part of the house.

Monkey with Rooster: Like magnets, you feel pulled magically together, but at any moment, the poles can shift, and you will find yourself repelled by each other. This is a pair born to fight, and yet should the two of you have a long relationship, it will at least be interesting. More prosperity would help you both be happy in this match, so hang a Feng Shui Crystal in the West part of the house to attract more money.

Monkey with Dog: At first, it just doesn't seem to work. You swinging in the trees, and the Dog barking and dancing around on the ground—but if you both persist, suddenly, one day everything falls into place. If you get to that point, this can be an excellent match. Remember, it's a partnership, not a competition. To blend the skills of you both, hang a Feng Shui Crystal in the West by Northwest part of the house.

Monkey with Pig: This may be the easiest relationship you'll ever find: no hassles, no commitments, just comfort, and joy. Pig would love a commitment, but he's too much in love to ask, afraid you'll run for the hills. Consider settling down with this one; this could be one you cherish. To balance and harmonize this energy, hang a Feng Shui Crystal in the North by Northwest part of the house.

Rooster Compatibility

Rooster with Rat: You might work well together with Rat, but avoid getting into a relationship with this little mouse. He discovers all your weak spots, and he'll take you down a peg or three. If you're serious about your future happiness, kiss the Rat goodbye. But if you're committed to staying, temper the little mouse's petty complaints by hanging a Feng Shui Crystal in the North part of the house.

Rooster with Ox: Potentially a very good match, because even though you're both stubborn by nature, you are stubborn about different things. There's strength in unity, and as a united front, you can have a very happy relationship. Even your fights turn out okay. Strengthen this relationship further by hanging a Feng Shui Crystal in the North by Northeast part of the house.

Rooster with Tiger: This relationship will take a lot of effort because you both have different values. You have strength, but so does Tiger—and there will be communication issues. Your friends will try to help you stay together until they get tired of trying, and then they'll suggest you part. If you want to stay together and have fun instead of fights, hang a Feng Shui Crystal in the East by Northeast part of the house.

Rooster with Rabbit: A relationship between you and Rabbit just makes for one angry bunny. You try to use logic and reason, but you just make him madder. Even though initially you felt a kinship, you're just too different to have any harmony. To get your Rabbit partner to pitch in and pull half the weight of this relationship, hang a Feng Shui Crystal in the East part of the house.

Rooster with Dragon: The perfect pair, representing the Dragon and the Phoenix, this relationship is liberating and strengthening for both. With this winged creature, you revel in feeling on top of the world. Dragon feels like he's finally got his feet on the ground. Great times ahead. Hang a Feng Shui Crystal in the East by Southeast part of the house to capitalize on this successful union.

Rooster with Snake: You may have some differences in your daily routines, but that can be to your benefit as you will enjoy the times you are together all the more. Snake may like to argue with you, but you can hold your own. In the long run, this could work. Balance the extremes in this relationship, and you can make some serious money. Hang a Feng Shui Crystal in the South by Southeast part of the house to help.

Rooster with Horse: You are probably more interested in making this work than Horse is. When you fight, it will be you who has to say, "Sorry," first. This may be fine in the beginning, but after a while of eating crow, you may just give this one up. If you insist that this is the one for you, hang a Feng Shui Crystal in the South part of the house to soothe your differences and create harmony.

Rooster with Sheep: You are probably the more impatient one, so Sheep can outlast you anytime. This will cause conflicts at home and with raising children. Sometimes you're both playing a game to see if you can get what you want, but neither of you shares your rules with the other. If you find that Goat/Sheep has a hard head and way too soft feelings, you can hang a Feng Shui Crystal in the South by Southwest part of the house to balance the energies.

Rooster with Monkey: Hard going at first, but things can be smoothed over. You may be fascinated with Monkey's clever antics, and so you keep working on it. Over time there can be progress; it depends on how much you want to sacrifice to get this to work. If you start to think that Monkey is just in it for what he or she can get, you can hang a Feng Shui Crystal in the West by Southwest part of the house to bring the scales into balance.

Rooster with Rooster: Intense passion and intense fights will typify this relationship. Feathers will fly, and lots of words will be exchanged—but what you dish out you can receive. In the end, you will stick it out because you have put so much effort into it. If you both are too focused on being right rather than being happy, hang a Feng Shui Crystal in the West area of the house to remedy this.

Rooster with Dog: A Dog around the barnyard chases the chickens rather than being guided by one, so this relationship may be about who gets to be in charge. This power struggle will continue, and getting out may be your best bet. This is not an easy time for either of you. If all this relationship has become is two people snapping at each other, hang a Feng Shui

Crystal in the West by Northwest part of the house to bring in loving, harmonious energy.

Rooster with Pig: You have a true admirer in this relationship, yet you doubt, thinking this is too easy. Pig wants to make you feel comfortable and happy, and yet your eye is ever wandering. Learn to respect the Pig, and this could be a dream match. Or, toss it all away and get chicken-scratch in return. Things can be good here if you can welcome in the positive energy. Hang a Feng Shui Crystal in the North by Northwest part of the house and be prepared to be happy.

Dog Compatibility

Dog with Rat: It will take cool nerves to make this match work. There's a lot of nervous energy between the two of you, and you may find Rat running for the door. Keep the lines of communication open to make progress long term. You may find you only fight over little things. Ease the disruptive energy by hanging a Feng Shui Crystal in the North part of the house.

Dog with Ox: You two can be great together because you're both stable and want to protect your partner. But power struggles can ensue. Your best bet is to lean back and allow Ox to drag the relationship forward. Ox can hold on to hurts from past fights for a long time. Heal the energy by hanging a Feng Shui Crystal in the North by Northeast part of the house.

Dog with Tiger: After a rough beginning, a relationship of mutual respect and admiration blossoms. The attraction to each other runs deep, and both can feel great happiness here. There are good times ahead for this cat and Dog. Together you can do a lot a good out in the world. Hang a Feng Shui Crystal in the East by Northeast part of the house and bring in the opportunities you desire.

Dog with Rabbit: After an exhilarating chase, you could end up with a perfect match between you and the happy Rabbit. You both bring something to the relationship that the other lacks, and together you make a good team. It's the tiny things, like how he or she squeezes the toothpaste, that irritates you about your partner. Hang a Feng Shui Crystal in the East part of the house and find some peace.

Dog with Dragon: This is a star-crossed pair, intense love followed by severe pain. Dragon's power may tempt you, but he'll just fly away at some point. At some level, you know this, and so you may try to leave first. Save yourself the pain and avoid this match. If you insist on staying together, you must alternate with each other on who will lead. Hang a Feng Shui Crystal in the East by Southeast part of the house to find a truce.

Dog with Snake: If you do get together—which is not easy—you will need to work on your communication with each other. You are both smart but in different ways. You are much more loyal than Snake; don't give all your loyalty until you know it will be returned. If you stay realistic, this can work, so hang a Feng Shui Crystal in the South by Southeast to improve communication.

Dog with Horse: Dating will be an exciting chase, and if you do rope this Horse, you may end up with a very happy relationship. But Horse won't be caught easily. Be prepared for some work. Once you break this Horse of running, the romance will blossom. Hang a Feng Shui Crystal in the South part of the house to encourage cooperation.

Dog with Sheep: There is such strong attraction at first, but Sheep doesn't like being herded, and you are having trouble putting up with his not agreeing with anything you say. After quarreling constantly, you may not find anything to save in this relationship. If you find you're more irritated than in love, hang a Feng Shui Crystal in the South by Southwest part of the house and smooth over the differences.

Dog with Monkey: At first sight, you didn't think this was going to be a match... and you were right! Monkey's antics and different ideas can hurt your feelings deeply. Even when it seems to be working, the timing will be off, and the gestures you offer each other are misunderstood. But if you want to make a go of it, hang a Feng Shui Crystal in the West by Southwest part of the house to attract money, which will, in turn, attract a Monkey.

Dog with Rooster: Lots of chasing can make the beginning of this relationship a little rocky. Be patient, because there is more to this than meets the eye. There is a genuine compatibility here if you can get past some of the surface irritants. If you want to do more than just coexist, hang a Feng Shui Crystal in the West part of the house to bring out the best qualities in both of you.

Dog with Dog: You can run and play together, and you'll always be competing. You may even compete to show how much you'll sacrifice for the other. If you don't mind the constant quarreling, bickering, and barking, this will work out just fine. Hang a Feng Shui Crystal in the West by Northwest part of the house to promote mutual respect and material success.

Dog with Pig: You find that Pig is a blissful partner, and have never felt so happy. This makes you nervous, which in turn makes Pig nervous—and that could bring a breaking point. But in general this is a great match, just lie down and enjoy it. Celebrate and hang a Feng Shui Crystal in the North by Northwest part of the house to attract the resources for a comfortable and happy home.

Pig/Boar Compatibility

Pig with Rat: This is an interesting match, you share many interests. You see the world in a similar way and value similar things. The little mouse may need some puffing up sometimes, but flatter him, and together you will build a comfortable house, with lots of money in the cookie jar. Hang a Feng Shui Crystal in the North part of the house to bring abundance and happiness to the relationship.

Pig with Ox: This works at first, but if you think you will get your way, you're wrong here. You may be obstinate, but nothing beats an Ox for sheer stubbornness. The more you push, the more he will not budge. Save yourself the effort and pass on this match. If you plan to stay in this relationship, hang a Feng Shui Crystal in the North by Northeast part of the house to relieve some of the friction.

Pig with Tiger: You may think the hungry Tiger will have you for dinner on your first date, but after the initial nerves of a new relationship, you two can settle down and make a good match. Tiger's possessiveness will feel comforting and protective. Hang a Feng Shui Crystal in the East by Northeast part of the house to bring joy, laughter, and good times.

Pig with Rabbit: Once you get past the well-meaning criticism by this little bunny, you have a thoughtful, interested partner with whom you can share much. Rabbit may be slower to realize how good a match this is, so be patient. Rabbit will happily receive the outpouring of your affection, so to get some in return, hang a Feng Shui Crystal in the East part of the house.

Pig with Dragon: You are dazzled by the power and vision of your Dragon partner. He loves coming down to earth to be with you. While your friends may not understand this match, you are in heaven. You are sailing on the back of a Dragon. At times one or both of you will get carried away; balance out the energy by hanging a Feng Shui Crystal in the East by Southeast part of the house.

Pig with Snake: You have so many differences that you can't even begin to communicate. You are naturally nervous around the clever Snake, and so you become rigid and critical. It's not you; it's just a bad match. If you're staying in the partnership but can't stand all the secrets, hang a Feng Shui Crystal in the South by Southeast part of the house and let what's been hidden come out.

Pig with Horse: Horse feels this is a great relationship and that nothing needs to change. You, on the other hand, have a list of what needs to happen to start making this a happy relationship. But none of your subtle signals or overt signs will be a clue to over-confident Horse. To get your pony partner to pay attention, hang a Feng Shui Crystal in the South part of the house.

Pig with Sheep: Can work, but certainly not the most exciting relationship you'll ever have. This feels like the backup date for New Year's—maybe someone who might be a friend, but the passion's not there. If you want commitment, demand it; otherwise, let this one go. Stir up the romance here by hanging a Feng Shui Crystal in the South by Southwest part of the house and watch the magic happen.

Pig with Monkey: You and Monkey are so different, but somehow it works. This relationship is like a fine wine; it needs to age—and you both will occasionally need some time to breathe. Some irritations on both sides can make this relationship feel sour. Hang a Feng Shui Crystal in the West by Southwest part of the house to sweeten up your love life.

Pig with Rooster: As barnyard buddies, this is tough in the beginning as Rooster wants to be in charge. You will find it hard to get respect from this bossy boss as he is sure he rules the roost. But deep down, there is more love here than you may think. Give this a try before saying goodbye. Between the two of you, there is a solution to every problem. Hang a Feng Shui Crystal in the West part of the house to attract the solutions easily.

Pig with Dog: You feel secure and safe with Dog (and nipped at, and barked at, too). There are some strong positives in this relationship and a big helping of irritants. Give nervous Dog some time to settle into the relationship, and you will feel safe and loved in no time. If you find your lively pup too quick with the criticism, hang a Feng Shui Crystal in the West by Northwest part of the house to soften his or her words.

Pig with Pig: Hand in hand, here's a perfect match. You both share great depth of feeling and compassion for the other. Communication is fun and easy, and you spend many nights just staying up and talking. This may get to be a little routine after a while, but the deep feeling of happiness will last.

Together you both give too much and may find others taking advantage of your kindness. Hang a Feng Shui Crystal in the North by Northwest part of the house to protect your finances.

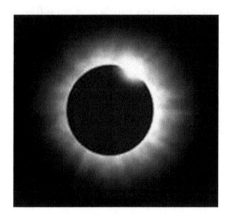

Eclipses

Eclipses, both Solar and Lunar, happen four times between January 2021 and the end of January 2022. Eclipses signal times of change. Eclipse energy can throw a wrench into your plans (fortunately, change can often be helpful). We feel the energy of an eclipse up to a couple of weeks before the actual event.

It's always a good idea to find an Astrologer to offer you some personal advice around the time of an upcoming series of eclipses. If you can find a reliable resource for information about the potential effects of a specific eclipse, you may be able to use the eclipse's energy to bring in powerful, life-changing opportunities. This gives you an opportunity to take positive action towards your goals, to compound this energy.

It makes a difference! It's as if you can choose between being hit by a wave versus being on your surfboard, ready to catch the wave and ride it all the way to the beach.

Eclipses are listed on most daily news websites and in the weather section of a newspaper, so you can see when one is about to happen. However, it takes an Astrologer to tell you exactly where the eclipses hit in your chart. You then can be aware of the approaching energy and keep an eye out for potential surfboards to grab hold of as you get ready to ride.

There will be a total Lunar eclipse on May 26, 2021. This eclipse will be at 5-degrees of Sagittarius. If you were born between **November 23 and December 2**, this eclipse will have a powerful effect on your life.

There will be an annular Solar eclipse on June 10, 2021. This eclipse will be at 19-degrees of Gemini. If you were born between **June 5 and June 15**, this eclipse will have a strong effect on your life.

There will be a partial Lunar eclipse on November 19, 2021. This eclipse will be at 27-degrees of Taurus. If you were born between **May 13 and May 23**, this eclipse will have a strong effect on your life.

There will be a total Solar eclipse on December 4, 2021. This eclipse will be at 12-degrees of Sagittarius. If you were born between **November 30 and December 9**, this eclipse will have a substantial effect on your life.

If the eclipse degrees hit close to your own personal planets (a.k.a. "hitting you"), consider the challenging areas of your life, and choose the changes to make. For instance, if you have been thinking about changing jobs for a time, it would be an excellent idea to get your resume ready at or near the time of the eclipse. If you've felt unhappy with your home, it's probably a good idea to look around for a new place. If your relationship is unsatisfying, this is the right time to sit down and have a chat with your partner (or consider packing your bags).

While eclipses may sound scary, you've been through many of them in your lifetime until now; You've experienced at least four eclipses each year since you were born. Every 8-9 years, the eclipse hits your chart with a bang—like the ringing of a loud bell—a signal that something in your life needs to change. The best course of action is to challenge yourself in whatever area of life you may feel "stuck." For more information on Eclipses, check out Diane Ronngren's booklet, *Eclipse!*

Mercury Retrograde

Each element of the five Chinese elements is ruled by a planet. The Chinese elements associated with the planets translate into the Western tradition as follows:

Wood is ruled by Jupiter, the largest planet in the solar system (named for the Roman king of the gods).

Fire is ruled by Mars, the red planet (named for the Roman god of war).

Earth is ruled by Saturn (named after the Roman god of agriculture).

Metal is ruled by Venus (named after the Roman goddess of prosperity).

Water is ruled by Mercury (named after the Roman winged messenger god).

2021 is a Metal year, so the energy of the planet Venus will figure prominently. Earth is necessary to create Metal, so Saturn is also an important planet this year. Mercury is not directly involved with the main elements this year, so it will be somewhat easier to navigate through Mercury Retrograde periods.

Mercury Retrograde is an astronomical phenomenon that happens three or four times a year. It has a very disruptive effect on those of us living on planet Earth. Things we rely on in our daily lives and work (such as our computers, cell phones, vehicles, email, snail mail, etc.) all seem to go a little haywire during Mercury Retrograde. Specifically, Mercury Retrograde can cause you to need to repeat something.

During this year, the Mercury Retrograde periods will be:

January 30, 2021, to February 20, 2021

May 29, 2021, to June 22, 2021

September 26, 2021, to October 18, 2021

A few weeks before Mercury goes retrograde each time, it's a good idea to back up your computer. While you're at it, back up your cell phone contacts. If you're planning to have some work done on the car, try to finish it before Mercury goes retrograde.

Anything you don't want to repeat—such as moving, lawsuits, root canals, surgery, expensive repairs, custody battles, break-ups—you will be better off if you can avoid doing them during Mercury retrograde.

If at all possible, avoid purchasing electronics during the retrograde, especially ones you can't return. Make copies of important documents before you send them, as they may not reach their destination. If you are issued one traffic ticket, you're likely to get a second ticket during this period, so drive safely.

If you have to return your cable box, renew your driver's license, or make a doctor's appointment, take a book with you (something long, like one by Tolstoy). It's going to take a while.

During the retrograde, plan and do things you don't mind repeating. Take a vacation—but beware, sometimes Mercury Retrograde can send your luggage to Baltimore (even if you're going somewhere else). However, if you do carry-on, you'll probably be fine.

Visit a spa, have a massage, enjoy a romantic dinner with someone you love, or have a party with good friends. These are all things you might enjoy doing multiple times.

Start exercising. If you drop the program, you will be inspired to pick it up again at the next retrograde. Or, buy yourself some jewelry or a new pair of shoes, that's something most of us don't mind repeating!

For more information on Mercury Retrograde, check out the booklet *Mercury Retrograde* by Diane Ronngren.

What Is Feng Shui and How to Use Cures

This book is different than most Chinese Astrology books. It contains information on usable Feng Shui cures to turn bad luck into good and make stuck, negative energy flow and be positive.

Feng Shui is the ancient Chinese art of placement. Feng Shui is based on the concept that everything present in our environment affects us: the colors, shapes, symbols, building layout, furniture, and décor affect our energy, mood, and decision-making process.

Consider for a moment two buildings which both represent how we connect with money: a casino, and a bank. When you walk into a casino, your head spins with all there is to see. There are flashing lights in every direction, ringing bells signaling a win, the sounds of coins falling. You can feel the abundance of good fortune and money, money, money.

Looking down at your feet, you'll see the floor carpeted in a busy, colorful pattern. Look up, and you will see moving lights, curved ceiling soffits guiding us in different directions, and huge rooms filled with aisles of machines, tables, and open chairs inviting us to be seated. There is an overwhelming feeling originating from this décor; it tantalizes: "You'd be a fool not to sit down and try your luck," it tempts us.

Contrast this feeling with the one you have in a bank. The environment here is also a large room, but this room is nearly silent. People speak in lowered voices. A velvet rope guides us to a waiting teller who sits (or stands) behind a marble counter (perhaps even behind a plexiglass shield).

Behind her is a large round door made of shiny metal, a foot and half thick, standing open to reveal a few safe deposit boxes. Even though we know there are no stacks of money in the vault and it's mostly a prop, the image created by all of it still gives us the impression that our money is safe.

We're all affected by the décor of a place. We may not think so per se, but run-down areas in need of repairs cause us to feel less hopeful. We are more apt to believe it's not worth the effort to try something new.

When we see a neighborhood with flowers and manicured yards, we become more optimistic. We feel a sense of possibility, the desire and willingness to take on new things. When we face a desk topped with disorganized clutter, we'll likely avoid working on our finances, and instead, check out what's on the television (or on Facebook).

Thousands of years ago, it was found that if you set up a temple or a palace in a certain way, the people in these environments would make better decisions. They would become more prosperous and happy. Scholars of the time collected this information and created a system they called Feng Shui. In the West, we know this system as Environmental Psychology.

Feng Shui is much more complex than merely cleaning up the clutter in your home or office—this is what many Westerners think about when they hear the term. Clearing away clutter is almost always a beneficial activity to carry out when we want to improve our environment. But it's important to understand that to achieve the best effect from our Feng Shui efforts, we must learn to place certain objects in specific places with the intention of creating harmonious change in our lives.

There are many schools of Feng Shui. Different schools emerged at different times and in different areas of China and the Far East. Some schools were formed in mountainous regions and were based on the topography of mountains, rivers, and lakes. Some schools were more focused on Astrology and timing, and these practitioners would predict the future and change things around as the seasons changed. Some schools used a compass to measure the quality and quantity of energy from each direction.

All of the schools of Feng Shui are valid. They all work. For our purposes, we're going to focus on a school called Form

School, which has straightforward principles we can readily apply to a western way of thinking about traditional and environmental practices.

Your Front Door: The front door is where all new energy will enter the home, and therefore your life. Even if you never use your front door, this is the traditional area of a home where all new energy is welcomed into the lives of the people who reside in the home. (If you found stranger coming through your back door you'd call the police). If you invited the CEO of your company to dinner, you wouldn't say, "Just go through the garage, squeeze past my car, past my boxes of Christmas decorations, and old ski equipment, until you find the door into the kitchen."

Important people are greeted at the front door and invited to enter a home or place of business. Many deliveries are made to the front door of a home or apartment residence. Using this principle, when we want something new, such as a new job, new love, money from a new source, etc., we will concentrate on the area around the front door (inside and out).

Your Bedroom: Your bedroom is where love happens. If you want to attract a new relationship or you want to improve your existing relationship, your bedroom is the area of the home we are going to focus on. We also look at the bedroom when you want to conceive a child, to rest, or to recover from illness. So, if you have trouble sleeping, or if you are recovering from something, we want to focus our attention on your bedroom.

The Kitchen: Your kitchen is your source of health and weight loss. Kitchens tend to be the most powerful rooms in the house. You can confirm this by observing that when you have a party. Often your guests want to gather together in the kitchen. Kitchens are where we cook and prepare our food; food is the key to our health and well-being.

The Living Room: If you want to attract new friends, but not necessarily an intimate partner, focus on your living room. The living room represents a public area of the home where we can welcome and entertain people without revealing the private areas of the home (like a bedroom). Thus, when we entertain people in our living room, we can enjoy people, yet safeguard the private things in our lives.

The Family Room: If you have a separate Family Room, focus on this area to enhance family relations overall—both between members of the family who live with you and those who live elsewhere. So if your family fights (or is dysfunctional in some other way), or the teenagers are sullen and uncooperative, this is the area your Feng Shui practitioner will focus on. (If you only have a Living Room, then we would focus on that area for family relations.)

The Home Office: If you have a separate room where you take care of bills and investments, or a room from which you run your home business, focus on this room when we seek to increase prosperity. If you don't have a separate office, consider the area where you do pay your bills—whether at the kitchen table, in your bedroom, or in the dining room. (Or, we can focus on enhancing the area around your front door for bringing in money.)

The Dining Room: If you have a separate dining room, it affects not only family relations but also your weight and the weight of all who live in the home. If you are trying to lose (or to gain) weight, we will consider this area, even if meals are seldom served in this room.

The Bathroom: There are a lot of Feng Shui rules and misinterpretations around the bathroom. The bathroom is an area for health, but it can also be an area that affects the prosperity of everyone in the home. When things are not going well in your life, this is the first area we consider.

Other rooms like garages, media rooms, craft rooms, guest bedrooms, and more, all have energy linked to their use. In general, they are not as significant as the rooms previously mentioned.

There are, however, some exceptions. If you run a classic car business out of your garage, then the state of your garage will affect your success in your business. If you have a guest who is driving you crazy and won't leave your home, the state of your guest room will affect how your guest is treating you—even how long they'll stay. For tips on these and other more specific situations, contact me for a personal consultation, or see my book, Feng Shui Form.

Now that we have examined the energy of the various spaces in a home, let's define the concept of a Feng Shui cure. If you've ever experienced acupuncture, you know the doctor uses tiny needles, placed in specific areas of the body to stimulate your body's energy and natural healing ability.

Feng Shui cures are similar to these acupuncture needles—they are intended to stimulate your home's energy and help create benefit, good fortune, and natural harmony by working within the environment of your home, instead of your physical body. Cures are objects which represent a specific energy: such as love or money. For example, a heart-shaped pillow would be a representation, a cure, of love energy. (The heart shape is a universal symbol of love.)

Universal and cultural symbols make the most powerful cures in Feng Shui. This may all sound a little strange, But Feng Shui cures do work, just as the acupuncture needles stimulate specific body energy and facilitate our natural healing ability. If you want to know more about the science behind Feng Shui energy, keep reading; otherwise, you can skip to the next section.

Why Feng Shui Works

It may sound strange to you that placing a gold cat bank in the far left corner of your home would attract money, but it does. The Feng Shui cure is based on two principles. The first is the idea of collective consciousness.

Collective consciousness is a shared idea which creates a unifying force in the world.

One example might be the number of people who are afraid of spiders. Spiders shouldn't be scary; they're tiny, and they tend to mind their own business. But some people are so afraid of them that they are classified arachnophobic, even when they have not had personal, life-threatening encounters with spiders. In humankind's past, spiders have been perceived to be dangerous in many cultures. So today, many, many people have this innate fear.

Likewise, most people in the world for centuries have considered round metal discs to be money. Even currency from a foreign country is still seen as valuable, even when it cannot be spent at the neighborhood store. Many objects not only have a universal meaning but also evoke an emotion. They are potent symbols in our collective consciousness.

Besides universal symbols, there are also cultural symbols—particular to one culture, but not another. They also can be used very effectively (in fact, I have found using symbols from a different culture is particularly effective).

A symbol, such as a gold cat bank (a.k.a. Lucky Money Cat), is a popular symbol in Asia and works very well here in the U.S. If you have enjoyed a meal at a Chinese restaurant recently, you have probably seen one of these symbols next to the cash register, Lucky Money Cat waving his little golden arm, calling in money.

The reason cultural symbols work is there are enough people in the world who understand the symbol and connect to it emotionally; a mini "collective consciousness" is formed.

Our Reticular Activating System

The second reason Feng Shui cures work is our Reticular Activating System. This is a system within each of us, which allows us to filter the information reaching us through our five senses. If we were actually aware of all of the information bombarding us all the time, we would go mad.

For instance, just sitting here at my computer, if I were also listening to the computer hum, and the traffic outside, and the ticking clock, while watching the sun go down, observing the computer screen, not to mention all the things I'm touching, smelling, and tasting simultaneously, I would be completely overwhelmed. But fortunately, my Reticular Activating System allows me to focus only on the task at hand.

Your own Reticular Activating System activates when you place a Lucky Money Cat somewhere in your space. When you place your Lucky Money Cat in the far left corner of your home, also known as "the wealth corner," your subconscious awakens and begins to look for money opportunities.

When the money opportunity is detected, your ERAS-system alerts your brain. These opportunities were around you already, but you were unable to identify them specifically. Therefore, it was impossible for you to grasp them or focus on taking necessary action. But when your Reticular Activating System uncovered the opportunities around you, they became clear to your conscious mind, and now it is easy to welcome in the new money.

Because of these two reasons, Feng Shui cures work. It is essential to understand why we use universal or cultural symbols, rather than just any old item/personal symbol. For example, you might tell me that for you, the vulture is a symbol of love because your beloved had a vulture tattoo on his right shoulder.

But this symbol is only a love symbol for you (and this particular relationship). So all the energy behind this symbol must be generated by you alone. If you're interested in focusing on vulture-tattoo-guy, you can fill your house with vultures, and it will possibly attract his energy to your door.

But let's say you want to attract a new man—maybe one who is vulture-free. In that case, it will be much easier to attract the new love energy if you choose to use a universal or cultural symbol of love. Many other people recognize these symbols. When you choose to use one of them, the combined energy of all of these others who acknowledge this symbol as a sign of love combines with your energy to attract what you want.

The peony flower is a cultural symbol of love. In Chinese art, this symbol is used to represent love and beauty. So if you choose to use this symbol, your energy combines with a couple of billion other people who also use this symbol to attract love. By using the collective consciousness, and your Reticular Activating System, you can use specific objects to attract wealth, love, and other things you want into your life.

As we talk about the individual predictions for each sign, I will be suggesting specific Feng Shui cures for creating the most positive energy for your year. You can substitute these cultural symbols for universal symbols if you choose. If you have questions about these concepts or substituting cures, you can write to me at DONNASTELLHORN@GMAIL.COM

2021 Flying Star

7—Northwest	2—North	9—Northeast
Violent Star: unlucky	Illness Star: unlucky	Future Prosperity Star: lucky
To decrease bad luck, add water. To protect from robbery, legal problems, injury, and health issues, burn off negative energy by burning black or dark blue candles. Add exterior lighting or keep porch light on.	To protect from illness and loneliness, reduce the negative energy by adding plants, dried medicinal herbs, or pictures of flowers. To balance health, pregnancy, or communication, add a six-rod metal windchime.	To increase achievement and growth, add wood—like a green, healthy plant. To have good luck, add fire by burning purple or gold candles.
8—West	6—Center	4—East
Prosperity Star: very lucky	Luck Star: lucky	Romance Star: lucky
To increase happiness, wealth, and family unity, add fire by burning white or gold candles. To balance career energy and have good relations with kids, add earth by placing a clear quartz crystal.	To increase success in career, military, science, or technology, add large crystals like citrine, amethyst, or smoky quartz. To balance energy of health and wealth, add brass vases or bowls.	To have romance and better education and career choices, add the color red and pairs of ducks. To protect against bad investments, divorce, or family pressure, add silver or Chinese coins.
3—Southwest	1—South	5—Southeast
Conflict Star: unlucky	White Star: very lucky	Misfortune Star: very unlucky
If problems with career, lawsuits, or arguments, burn off the excess energy by burning a blue or yellow candle.	To increase wealth and fame and improve career add earth by adding granite, marble, or citrine. To balance spirituality and thinking, add metal in the form of a music box or iPod dock.	To protect from accidents, illness, and lawsuits, remove stone and heavy objects. To balance mental energy and have happier children, place coins.

2021 Flying Star

Each year the energy changes and "stars" fly into new locations. Some directions, which may have indicated positive, lucky energy last year, become weaker and unlucky this year. Some, which vibrated with weak, unlucky energy in the past, have found strength and become more favorable for us now.

In other forms of Feng Shui, we are concerned with the directions of our home, based on the position of the front door, but not with Flying Star. With Flying Star, we are concerned with compass directions.

The general principle of Flying Star is to increase energy in the directions of good stars and reduce energy in the direction of bad stars. If you live in a giant mansion and your bedroom is now on a negative star, you can choose a new bedroom to sleep in. But for the rest of us, we use "cures" to mitigate the negative energy and increase the positive energy. Here's the forecast for 2021:

Flying Star 1—The White Star: Luck finds its way to the South of the house with the 1-Star. This is a star whose energy has changed over the last few thousand years. It has become luckier, although it's a good idea to keep its history in mind as you increase the energy of this star.

If, after placing the cures, you find things are not going as well as you hoped, switch from increasing the energy (by adding water or metal cures) to reducing the energy (by adding wood cures).

That being said, to increase wealth and fame and improve career, increase the earth energy by adding granite, marble, or citrine (a gemstone) to your space. To balance spirituality and clear thinking, add metal in the form of a music box, or an iPod/radio.

Flying Star 2—The Illness Star: A somewhat unlucky star, the 2-Star, flies to the North. I say this star is somewhat unlucky because years ago in China, this was a lucky star for those people working in government. Therefore, if you have a government job, you can receive some benefit from this star.

For the rest of us, this Star can cause health problems, especially digestive and intestinal problems. To protect from illness and loneliness, reduce the effects of the negative energy by adding live plants, bundles of dried medicinal herbs, or pictures of flowers to the North part of your home.

If you are or become pregnant, you can support and protect pregnancy energy by adding a six-rod metal wind chime outside of the North part of the house.

Flying Star 3—The Conflict Star: The somewhat unlucky 3-Star flies to the Southwest this year. This is the star of quarreling and disputes, but its energy can be directed positively to help you keep a job and pay your bills. Balancing the energy of the 3-Star is important.

If you are having problems with career, lawsuits, or arguments, burn off the excess negative energy by burning a blue or yellow candle in this area once a month on the full moon. If you are searching for a job, need more work, or wish to preserve a source of income, set some coins on a windowsill facing the Southwest of the space.

Flying Star 4—The Romance Star: The 4-Star lands in the East this year and brings mixed luck. This star is both associated with positive romance and career opportunities, but it is also known as "The Six Curses." Like the 1-Star in the South, as you enhance the energy in the East, notice how your luck changes.

If you find that your experiences in romance are not as positive as you would like, add fire (by burning candles or wood in a fireplace) to reduce the 4-Star energy. Also, be cautious about participating in games of speculation, or signing off on risky investments.

To enjoy more romance, add the color red, and pairs of Mandarin ducks as cures. To protect against bad investments, add silver or Chinese coins. For better education and career choices, add green plants with round-shaped leaves.

Flying Star 5—The Misfortune Star: Trouble comes as the 5-Star flies to the Southeast this year. This star represents illness, potential disaster, and lack of knowledge. To protect from accidents, illness, and lawsuits, remove stone and heavy objects from the house's Southeast area.

If heavy objects are attached to the house (such as a stone fireplace), channel some of that energy away from the Southeast of the house by adding objects made of wood, like a wood bowl, wood furniture, or a picture of trees. To balance stressful energy and to have happier children, place photos of them in metal frames in this area.

Flying Star 6—The Heaven Luck Star: The 6-Star flies to the Center this year, and luck comes with it. To increase success in career, military service, science, or technology, add large crystals (over 2 inches in size) such as citrine, amethyst, and smoky quartz to the Center part of the home.

To balance the energy of health and wealth, add brass vases or bowls. You can place messages and wishes for your family's health and prosperity in the bowls each New Moon.

Flying Star 7—The Violent Star: The unlucky 7-Star flies to the Northwest this year, and brings the very unlucky energy of robbery, legal troubles, fire, injury, and arguments. To decrease bad luck, add the Water element. Good Water element representations are fountains, fish tanks, pictures of moving water, or decorative objects made of glass.

To protect yourself from robbery, legal problems, injury, and health issues, it is best to 'burn off' excess negative energy by burning black or dark blue candles once a month. Because this is the Violent Star, adding protective symbols to the Northwest of your home is wise. These can be things from your ancestors, your religion, or your country.

Flying Star 8—The Prosperity Star: Luck moves to the West as the 8-Star finds its home there for the year. This is your home or space area to enhance and experience increased happiness, wealth, and family unity. Do so by adding representations of fire. For instance, you can place red pillows or art that depicts a distinct triangular shape; or burn white or gold candles in this part of the home.

To balance career energy and enhance good relations with children and young people, add earth to the 8-Star area by placing clear quartz crystals on a table at the West of the house.

Flying Star 9—The Future Prosperity Star: This star brings us more lucky energy. The very lucky 9-Star flies to the Northeast this year. This is your success area for the year. Try to do things like goal setting, meditating, beginning new projects, or making essential contacts by phone from this area of your home or office.

To increase achievement and growth, add wood energy to the space with things like green, healthy plants, pictures of forests and greenery, or a new wood floor. To increase good luck and good fortune, add fire cures by burning purple or gold candles once a month.

For more information on the cures mentioned in this book, refer to the Feng Shui cure guide at the back of my book, "Feng Shui Form." In it, you will find an 80-page guide to how to use Feng Shui cures.

The Grand Duke (or Tai Sui) lives in the Northeast area this year between 22.6 degrees and 37.5 degrees. You can use a compass to locate these exact degrees.

The Grand Duke doesn't like being disturbed. The Grand Duke is like the King of all the Kings. It's said that you cannot confront him, only show him deference and respect. This year, those born in the Year of the Sheep (or Goat or Ram) should keep a protective Feng Shui cure by their bed. This could be a Pi Yao (winged lion) statue or a Tai Sui plaque.

This year you can plant a tree in the Grand Duke's section of your property to show your respect. But beware, you cannot cut down a tree in this direction, or there will be misfortune. Also, be cautious about construction or renovation in this area of your home or your property this year, as the process can be plagued with problems, and bring trouble to the household.

The Five Elements

The natural element of Ox is Yin Water. With the steady, determined Ox energy this year, we feel the methodical and self-reliant nature of this element. In 2021 we are in a Yin Metal year. With this combination, the desire to simplify and rebuild will be strong. Measured, well thought out actions bring success. Prosperity comes through hard work this year. At the same time, we need to be aware that others may try to rush through this process and look for shortcuts. You don't need to follow them, but to allow them their journey at the speed they choose. This year, don't rush, but take the time you need to do things well.

Earth and Water are just two of the elements. The ancient Chinese philosophers looked at the world and categorized all they could see into five elements, five building blocks, which are the basis of all things. The five elements and their representations are:

Wood—represents growth and all things that grow.

Fire—represents energy itself and all the things energy creates or produces.

Earth—represents stability and things in a state of rest.

Metal—represents resources and things that make up the material of tools.

Water—symbolizes connectivity, things that help connect one thing to another.

As mentioned, each of the five elements can be Yin or Yang. Yin represents the more subtle and flowing energy, and Yang represents the more "in-your-face," direct energy. The Yin/Yang symbol is probably familiar to you. The black part represents Yin, and the white part is Yang.

The dot in the opposing color in the Yin/Yang symbol represents the concept: "One cannot exist without the other." To understand the concept of larger, we must be familiar with smaller. For us to understand the essence of weaker, we must know stronger.

Each of the five elements exists in a state of Yin or Yang.

Yang Wood is like a forest of the tallest trees, growing in the wild. Or, energetically, it is expressed in the life of the student who studies all the time. It is like the feeling of being on a new job where you have to learn everything as quickly as possible (and you love every moment of it.)

Yin Wood is like a seedling, just popping out of the dirt to see the sun for the first time. It's the realization that you've grown as a person and don't need as much help as you did when you were younger. It's the act of tweaking a favorite recipe with just one new ingredient to see how it will taste.

Yang Fire is a forest fire burning out of control. It's like celebrating a college spring break at a beachside resort, daddy's credit card in hand. Or, it's like driving in a NASCAR race, exhilarating, demanding your entire focus and all your attention, purely to keep from crashing.

Yin Fire is represented by the image of a match or a single candle. Imagine the energy of taking a stroll down a beautiful path and having the time to enjoy nature. Or, think of the amount of energy our body uses to digest food: it happens automatically, without effort or thought.

Yang Earth is a tall mountain, majestic and still. It's like a lazy retirement, one where you enjoy your time sitting on the porch, day after day, in a comfortable chair. There are no worries about finances. There are no obligations to create stress in your life.

Yin Earth is like a sandy beach, flat and smooth. It's like a Sunday afternoon in summer, nothing pulling at you, your list of chores complete. You take a restful, peaceful nap.

Yang Metal is similar to the power of collecting gold bars, having them stacked, and representing greater abundance than you will ever need. It's a world filled with unlimited resources. You can present a Black Visa card and purchase anything you wish. Or, it's like becoming CEO and receiving or having access to all the perks.

Yin Metal is like possessing a stack of coins or receiving a regular paycheck. You have just enough to feel secure; you can count on support to arrive as expected, week after week. It's like having just the right amount of cash in your pocket to buy what you need.

Yang Water is a springtime waterfall, rushing downhill and churning up the body of water below. It's water bursting from a dam and rushing towards the town. Or, it's like melted snow pouring down the mountainside to flood the fields below.

Yin Water is like a still pond on a summer's day, no movement on the surface, it appears to be as still as a sheet of glass in the sunlight. Or, it's like a peaceful lake in the quiet of a moonlit night, the moon's reflection glimmering on the surface. It's a glass of water, the exact perfect amount you need to drink to quench your thirst.

When the ancient people who brought us Feng Shui looked at the world, they divided every existing thing into these Five Elements. They also observed how one element could interact with another. This interaction can be seen in a *Creative Cycle* or a *Destructive Cycle.*

The Creative Cycle is: Wood creates Fire, Fire creates Earth (by producing ash), Earth produces Metal (because when we dig into the earth, we find metal), Metal produces Water (when metal becomes cold it pulls water from the air in the form of condensation) and Water produces Wood (when water is poured on the ground, things grow).

The Destructive Cycle is: Wood depletes Earth (Trees and plants take nutrients from the earth), Earth blocks Water (dams can be made of earth), Water puts out Fire, Fire melts Metal, and Metal chops Wood (when metal is formed into an ax or other sharp tool, it can cut wood).

In Feng Shui, we are always looking for the *larger* to support the *smaller.* For example, if you, as a single individual, need to feed and clothe your entire community, you would soon become depleted of energy and resources. But if the community helps feed and clothe you, food and clothing would be abundant for you.

This year is a Metal Year. Your individual element may be in harmony with this year's element being part of the Creative Cycle. Your individual element may be in disharmony with this year's element by being part of the Destructive Cycle. Check the list at the beginning of the book and find your element.

If your element is Wood: Your element is Wood, and the element this year is Metal. You are on the destructive cycle as Metal chops Wood. The opportunities coming your way may not be in a form you initially recognize. You might think you're not qualified for the job, or this is not the type of person you normally date. But in the destructive cycle, if you allow it, the opportunities can remake you into something stronger and better. You may feel some fear, but fortunately, Wood element people are nearly fearless when they have the opportunity for growth.

At the same time, in this destructive cycle, there will be many who tell you who you should be. These might be teachers or advertisers, or it might be your parents or your partner. Some will mean well, and some just want your money. Stay focused on your goals. This year the path to success will feel like a slow, steady march, where you make incremental progress day after day. It's helpful to look at your processes and systems and make minor improvements. Over time, these improvements will compound and you will reach your goals.

If your element is Fire: Your element is Fire, and the element of this year is Metal; Fire melts Metal. You, the individual, are trying to melt the world, form it into what you want, and hammer out the opportunities you've been looking for. This means you have an endless supply of materials (opportunities for career, for love, for creativity), but since you are only one person, your flame is much smaller than the world. You must work at building your flame through the practice of your craft and the understanding of what you want to create.

Many people will be coming to you with offers and opportunities, but you have limited resources, and so, in the words of the old saying, "How do you eat an elephant? One bite at a time." It will be necessary for you to have patience in an impatient world. You will need to do homework ahead of time, not on the bus on your way to the test. But if you can get a clear picture of what you want to achieve and the people you want to connect with, this will be an exceptional year because an abundance of choices is available to you.

If your element is Metal: Your element is Metal, and this year's element is Metal, so you are in harmony with the energy. You have an innate understanding of the energy of Metal and its desire to collect and organize resources. You are admired for your skill and efficiency this year. Cultivate your ability to see situations clearly, make the list of steps, outline the action plan, and find the support and resources to begin. Beginning will be the most important action this year. Without beginning, it's just a plan on paper.

Your challenge this year is to avoid getting bogged down, doing so much planning and organizing that the real work doesn't begin. You can gain much insight by brainstorming with friends and organizing your ideas on paper (or an app will work too). Early in the planning stages, implement parts of the plan to test viability. Make small micro-adjustments along the way. Create systems to streamline your process.

If your element is Water: Your element is Water, and this is a Metal year. You are on the creative cycle as Metal creates Water. This year the whole world is available to offer support and help with your ventures. This doesn't mean everyone will line up in perfect order. There will be many who come to you with an agenda. But in the context of what they are offering, it's possible to find some benefit for both of you.

Water takes no particular shape. It wants to flow from one place to another. The Metal element represents a container. This means many opportunities coming to you may seem limiting, even constricting. We all see how Metal creates Water as water drops gather outside of a cool metal container. Water is not contained. So when the opportunities come, it would be good for you to remake the job into what you want it to be; or shift the friendship in the direction that suits you. You are in a powerful position this year. Any limitations you perceive are based on your fears. Release them, and you will find success.

If your element is Earth: Your element is Earth, and this year the element is Metal. You are on the creative cycle as Earth creates Metal, however you, the smaller, are trying to create the larger: the whole Earth. This means that nearly everyone you meet will believe you are vital to their success. You are pulled in every direction. Many projects and opportunities will come to you, but many of these will be more work than you are looking for, and certainly not all of them will be along the path you want to take.

This year you must consider what you want to accomplish and be choosy about where and when you get involved in other people's plans. As you begin to gather a team for yourself, others may say their projects are more important, and move yours to the bottom of the list. You are experiencing positive energy this year, so you can make sure this doesn't happen. But if you are not paying attention, you may end up doing the lion's share for little credit. Take the time to find the right fit, and you will achieve what you want.

Using and Clearing Feng Shui Cures

"Okay, I did what you said, and it worked for a little while, but now it's not working."

When we place an object to attract new energy—and we place it correctly—we will get results within the first week. But after that, the energy will start to dissipate. There are several reasons for this.

Mainly, we are very quick to adapt to the new energy, and so even though new energy is flowing in; we cease to notice it. Also, when we first place the Feng Shui cure, we see it every day, but after a time it becomes part of the background and therefore is no longer activating our subconscious.

Often, the solution is to move the cure, or if that's not possible, to take the cure down and dust it off and then replace it where it was. I had a client who was using my "double lucky money fish" cure to attract money. She placed a pair of fish by her front door, and business started to flow in effortlessly. However, after a week or two, she would become overwhelmed by so many new clients.

So she would take the "double lucky money fish" cure away from her front door, and place the cure in her home office instead. The result of this was she would receive quick and easy payment from her clients.

Then, after a couple of weeks, she would find she needed new clients again. So she would take the "double lucky money fish" cure and once again hang them by her front door. By moving the fish over and over, she was always attracting positive money energy.

How to Clear Gemstones and Crystals

After a few weeks, gemstones and crystals have been absorbing energy, and it can seem they are not as effective as they were when you first placed them. Here is an easy solution. The gemstone or crystal needs clearing. There are several methods you can use. Each is very effective, choose the method that is most convenient for you.

Clearing with Sage: you can smudge the gemstone or crystal using Sage. Take your smudge stick and light it, then pass the crystal through the smoke several times. Turn the crystal so the smoke touches all sides. The crystal is now clear, and you can hang it back up where it was. You should see a bump up in the energy levels during the next few days.

Clearing with Salt: you can clear gemstones and crystals using salt. Some gemstones and crystals are sensitive to salt, When clearing these with salt, place the crystal on a dish and draw a ring of salt around the crystal. (The salt should not touch the crystal.) Then place the dish where it will not be disturbed for 24 hours.

Once the 24-hour period is completed, remove the crystal from the plate and dispose of the salt in a trash can outside of your home. (Tossing the salt in the kitchen garbage will just release the energy back into the house.) Replace the crystal where it was. You'll see an increase in energy within the next few days.

Clearing with Sunlight: you can also clear gemstones and crystals in sunlight. Take the crystal down and wash it thoroughly in clear water and a gentle soap. Dry the crystal with a soft cloth. Place the crystal on a dish outside in the sunlight for a full day. In the evening bring the crystal back into the house and allow it to cool. Then re-hang the crystal where it was. If you don't see an increase in energy in the first week, use one of the other two methods to clear the crystal.

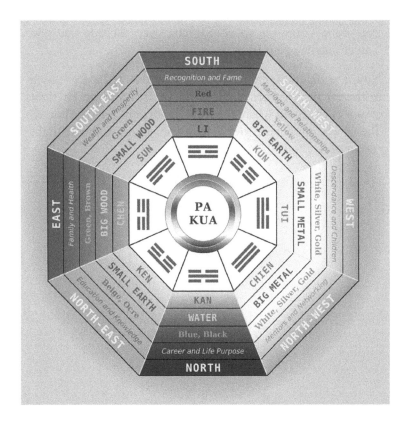

How to Identify the Wealth and Love Areas of Your House

To identify the Wealth areas of your home, stand inside the front door entrance to the house, take the above diagram, and place the side that says "career" up against your closed front door. The diagram will show you the location of the Wealth area.

In fact, you will quickly identify two Wealth areas: one is the far left corner of the entrance area (or, the far left corner of the room where the front door opens into the home). The other important Wealth area in your home is the far left corner of the whole house.

To identify your "love" areas, stand inside your home by your front door. Using the above diagram, place the side that says "career" against your front door.

Now the diagram shows you the location of the Love area in the far right corner of the entrance area (or, the far right corner of the room where the front door opens into the home). The other significant Love area in your home is the far right corner of the house.

Bibliography and Recommended Reading

Bartholomew, Sarah, "Feng Shui: It's Good for Business," ETC Publishing, Carlsbad, CA, 2005

Brown, Simon, "Practical Feng Shui," Wardlock, London, 1997

Carus, Paul, "Chinese Astrology," Open Court, LaSalle, IL, 1974

Chuen, Master Lam Kam, "Personal Feng Shui Manual: How to Develop a Healthy and Harmonious Lifestyle," Henry Holt & Co, New York, 1998

Craze, Richard, "Teach Yourself Chinese Astrology," Arbingdon, England, Bookpoint, 1997

Cunningham, Scott, "Cunningham's Encyclopedia of Crystal, Gem and Metal Magic,."Llewellyn Publications, St. Paul, MN 1988

Cunningham, Scott, "Cunningham's Encyclopedia of Magical Herbs,." Llewellyn Publications, St. Paul, MN 1997

Cunningham, Scott, "The Magic of Food," Llewellyn Publications, St. Paul, MN 1996

Eberhard, Wolfram, "A Dictionary of Chinese Symbols," Routledge, London, 1983

Gong, Rosemary, "Good Luck Life," New York, Harper Collins, 2005

Kwok, Man-Ho, "The Elements of Feng Shui," Elements Books Limited, Dorset, England, 1991

Lau, Kwan, ."Secrets of Chinese Astrology: Handbook for Self-Discovery,." Tengu Books, Trumbull, CT, 1994

Lau, Theodora, "The Handbook of Chinese Horoscopes," New York, Harper & Row, 1979

Lip, Evelyn, "Chinese Numbers," Heian International, Union City, California 1992

Lip, Evelyn, "Chinese Practices and Beliefs," Torrance, Heian International, 2000

Ronngren, Diane, "Color: A Secret Language Revealed," ETC Publishing, Carlsbad, CA, 1997

Ronngren, Diane, "Eclipses," ETC Publishing, Carlsbad, CA, 2001

Ronngren, Diane, "Mercury Retrograde," ETC Publishing, Carlsbad, CA, 2000

Ronngren, Diane, "Sage & Smudge: The Ultimate Guide," ETC Publishing, Carlsbad, CA, 2003

Ronngren, Diane, "Simple Feng Shui Secrets," ETC Publishing, Carlsbad, CA, 2005

Ronngren, Diane and Stellhorn, Donna, "Money and Prosperity Workbook," ETC Publishing, Carlsbad, CA, 1999

Rossbach, Sarah, "Interior Design with Feng Shui," Arkana, London, 1987

Skinner, Stephen, "Flying Star Feng Shui," Tuttle, Boston, MA, 2003

Stellhorn, Donna, "Feng Shui Form," ETC Publishing, Carlsbad, CA, 2006

Stellhorn, Donna, "How to Use Magical Oils," ETC Publishing, Carlsbad, CA, 2002

Stellhorn, Donna, "Sage & Smudge: Secrets to Clearing Your Personal Space," ETC Publishing, Carlsbad, CA, 1999

Sun, Ruth Q, "The Asian Animal Zodiac," Castle Books, Boston, MA, 1974

Tai, Sherman, "Principles of Feng Shui: An Illustrated Guide to Chinese Geomancy," Asiapac Books, Singapore, 1998

Too, Lillian, "Easy-To-Use Feng Shui: 168 Ways to Success," Collins & Brown, London, 1999

Too, Lillian, "Unlocking the Secrets of Chinese Fortune Telling," Metro Books, New York, 2006

Twicken, David, "Classical Five Element Chinese Astrology Made Easy," Writers Club Press, New York, 2000

Twicken, David, "Flying Star Feng Shui Made Easy," Writers Club Press, New York, 2002

Walters, Derek, "Chinese Astrology," Watkins Publishing London, 2002

Walters, Derek, "The Feng Shui Handbook," Aquarian Press, San Francisco, CA 1991

Williams, C.A.S., "Outlines of Chinese Symbolism & Art Motifs," Dover Publications, New York, 1976

Wydra, Nancilee, "Feng Shui: The Book of Cures," Contemporary Books, Lincolnwood, IL 1993

Acknowledgments

I want to thank Diane, Gary and Kelly at ETC Publishing for their support, patience and hard work on these books each year. I couldn't have done it without their help. All their names should be on the cover too.

About Donna Stellhorn

Author, Astrology and Feng Shui expert, Donna Stellhorn, is a speaker, a supportive personal coach, and a practical business consultant with over 25 years of experience. In addition to building three successful businesses of her own and logging more than 20,000 hours of consultations with clients, she teaches a variety of classes, offers apprenticeship programs, leads workshops, and continues to write on various topics. She believes in encouraging others to achieve success in their careers and their personal lives.

Donna has written 16 books. Her Chinese Astrology series, of which this book is the latest one, *2021 Chinese Astrology Year of the Metal Ox*, is the most popular Chinese Astrology book series according to Amazon.

One of her earliest books is *Feng Shui Form*. First published in Germany, it is a collection of the best and most popular concepts to help her readers create a supportive and comfortable living and working environment.

Her best-selling booklet for more than 20 years, *Sage and Smudge: Secrets of Clearing Your Personal Space*, shares the concept of how to cleanse and clear space, objects, or environments.

A recent book is a Feng Shui expert's look at the fertility puzzle, entitled *A Path to Pregnancy: Ancient Secrets for the Modern Woman*.

Donna has video courses on Udemy.com, including *Plate Size Matters*, a Feng Shui expert's guide to losing weight by changing how you eat, where you eat, and how best to store your food in the home.

Donna lectures on both Chinese Astrology and Western Astrology, as well as Feng Shui. Recently, Donna has lectured at Western Digital, Warner Records, Room & Board, the Rancho Santa Fe Water District, Brion Jeannette Architecture, and the San Diego Airport Authority. She's been on Coast to Coast AM with George Noory. She spoke at the 2018 United Astrology Conference in Chicago and the 2019 NCGR conference in Baltimore. Donna writes for Horoscope.com, Astrology. com, SunSigns.com, and Conscious Community magazine. She is on the Boards of the International Feng Shui Guild and the National Council for Geocosmic Research—San Diego.

For fun, Donna does improv comedy with ImprovCity. She lives in Orange County, California, with the magical cat, LaRue.

YouTube Channel: HTTPS://WWW.YOUTUBE. COM/C/DONNASTELLHORN

Website: HTTP://WWW.FENGSHUIFORM.COM/

or email her at DONNASTELLHORN@GMAIL.COM

One last thing...

Thank you so much for purchasing this book. I hope you found the information helpful, and if you did, please let your friends know about it. If you can take a moment and give it a review at your favorite retailer, I would be very grateful.

CPSIA information can be obtained
at www.ICGtesting.com
Printed in the USA
LVHW052314291221
707466LV00013B/877

9 781944 622435